*Everyman, I will go with thee
and be thy guide*

THE EVERYMAN
LIBRARY

*The Everyman Library was founded by J. M. Dent
in 1906. He chose the name Everyman because he wanted
to make available the best books ever written in every
field to the greatest number of people at the cheapest possible
price. He began with Boswell's 'Life of Johnson';
his one-thousandth title was Aristotle's 'Metaphysics',
by which time sales exceeded forty million.*

*Today Everyman paperbacks remain true to
J. M. Dent's aims and high standards, with a wide range
of titles at affordable prices in editions which address
the needs of today's readers. Each new text is reset to give
a clear, elegant page and to incorporate the latest thinking
and scholarship. Each book carries the pilgrim logo,
the character in 'Everyman', a medieval mystery play,
a proud link between Everyman
past and present.*

William Shakespeare

MEASURE FOR MEASURE

Edited by
JOHN F. ANDREWS

Foreword by
TIM PIGOTT-SMITH

EVERYMAN
J. M. DENT · LONDON
CHARLES E. TUTTLE
VERMONT

Photoset by Deltatype Ltd, Ellesmere Port, Cheshire
Printed in Great Britain by
The Guernsey Press Co. Ltd, Guernsey, C.I.
for
J. M. Dent
Orion Publishing Group
Orion House, 5 Upper St Martin's Lane
London WC2H 9EA
and
Charles E. Tuttle Co., Inc.
28 South Main Street
Rutland, Vermont, 05701 – USA

British Library Cataloguing-in-Publication Data is available
upon request

ISBN 0 460 87454 3

CONTENTS

NOTE ON THE AUTHOR AND EDITOR

WILLIAM SHAKESPEARE is held to have been born on St George's Day, 23 April 1564. The eldest son of a prosperous glove-maker in Stratford-upon-Avon, he was probably educated at the town's grammar school.

Tradition holds that between 1585 and 1592, Shakespeare first became a schoolteacher and then set off for London. By 1594 he was a leading member of the Lord Chamberlain's Men, helping to direct their business affairs, as well as being a playwright and actor. In 1598 he became a part-owner of the company, which was the most distinguished of its age. However, he maintained his contacts with Stratford, and his family seem to have remained there.

From about 1610 he appears to have grown increasingly involved in the town's affairs, suggesting a withdrawal from London. He died on 23 April 1616, in his 53rd year, and was buried at Holy Trinity Church on the 25th.

JOHN F. ANDREWS has recently completed a 19-volume edition, *The Guild Shakespeare*, for the Doubleday Book and Music Clubs. He is also the editor of a 3-volume reference set, *William Shakespeare: His World, His Work, His Influence*, and the former editor (1974–85) of the journal *Shakespeare Quarterly*. From 1974 to 1984 he was director of Academic Programs at the Folger Shakespeare Library in Washington and Chairman of the Folger Institute.

CHRONOLOGY OF SHAKESPEARE'S LIFE

Year[1]	Age	Life
1564		Shakespeare baptized 26 April at Stratford-upon-Avon
1582	18	Marries Anne Hathaway
1583	19	Daughter, Susanna, born
1585	21	Twin son and daughter, Hamnet and Judith, born
1590–1	26	*The Two Gentlemen of Verona* & *The Taming of the Shrew*
1591	27	*2 & 3 Henry VI*
1592	28	*Titus Andronicus* & *1 Henry VI*
1592–3		*Richard III*
1593	29	*Venus and Adonis* published
1594	30	*The Comedy of Errors. The Rape of Lucrece* published
1594–5		*Love's Labour's Lost.* An established member of Lord Chamberlain's Men
1595	31	*A Midsummer Night's Dream, Romeo and Juliet,* & *Richard II.*
1596	32	*King John.* Hamnet dies
1596–7		*The Merchant of Venice* & *1 Henry IV*

[1] It is rarely possible to be certain about the dates at which plays of this period were written. For Shakespeare's plays, this chronology follows the dates preferred by Stanley Wells and Gary Taylor, the editors of The Oxford Shakespeare. Publication dates are given for poetry and books.

CHRONOLOGY OF HIS TIMES

Year	Literary Context	Historical Events
1565–7	Golding, Ovid's *Metamorphoses*, tr.	Elizabeth I reigning
1574	*A Mirror for Magistrates* (3rd ed.)	
1576	London's first playhouse built	
1578	John Lyly, *Euphues*	
1579	North, Plutarch's *Lives*, tr.	
	Spenser, *Shepherd's Calender*	
1587	Marlowe, *I Tamburlaine*	Mary Queen of Scots executed
1588	Holinshed's *Chronicles* (2nd ed.)	Defeat of Spanish Armada
1589	Kyd, *Spanish Tragedy*	Civil war in France
	Marlowe, *Jew of Malta*	
1590	Spenser, *Faerie Queene*, Bks I–III	
1591	Sidney, *Astrophel and Stella*	Proclamation against Jesuits
1592	Marlowe, *Dr Faustus* & *Edward II*	Scottish witchcraft trials
		Plague closes theatres from June
1593	Marlowe killed	
1594	Nashe, *Unfortunate Traveller*	Theatres reopen in summer
1594–6		Extreme food shortages
1595	Sidney, *An Apologie for Poetry*	Riots in London
1596		Calais captured by Spanish
		Cadiz expedition

Year	Age	Life
1597	33	Buys New Place in Stratford
		The Lord Chamberlain's Men's lease to play at the Theatre expires; until 1599 they play mainly at the Curtain
1597–8		*The Merry Wives of Windsor* & *2 Henry IV*
1598	34	*Much Ado About Nothing*
1598–9		*Henry V*
1599	35	*Julius Caesar.* One of syndicate responsible for building the Globe in Southwark, where the Lord Chamberlain's Men now play
1599–1600		*As You Like It*
1600–1		*Hamlet*
1601	37	*Twelfth Night.* His father is buried in Stratford
1602	38	*Troilus and Cressida.* Invests £320 in land near Stratford[2]
1603	39	*Measure for Measure.* The Lord Chamberlain's Men become the King's Men. They play at court more than all the other companies combined
1603–4		*Othello*
c.1604	40	Shakespeare sues Philip Rogers of Stratford for debt
1604–5		*All's Well That Ends Well*
1605	41	*Timon of Athens.* Invests £440 in Stratford tithes
1605–6		*King Lear*
1606	42	*Macbeth* & *Antony and Cleopatra*
1607	43	*Pericles.* Susanna marries the physician John Hall in Stratford
1608	44	*Coriolanus.* The King's Men lease Blackfriars, an indoor theatre. His only grandchild is born. His mother dies
1609	45	*The Winter's Tale.* 'Sonnets' and 'A Lover's Complaint' published
1610	46	*Cymbeline*
1611	47	*The Tempest*
1613	49	*Henry VIII.* Buys house in London for £140
1613–14		*The Two Noble Kinsmen*
1616	52	Judith marries Thomas Quiney, a vintner, in Stratford. On 23 April Shakespeare dies; is buried two days later
1623		Publication of the First Folio. His widow dies in August

[2] A schoolmaster would earn around £20 a year at this time.

Year	Literary Context	Historical Events
1597	Bacon, *Essays*	
1598	Marlowe and Chapman, *Hero and Leander* Jonson, *Every Man in his Humour*	Rebellion in Ireland
1599	Children's companies begin playing Thomas Dekker's *Shoemaker's Holiday*	Essex fails in Ireland
1601	'War of the Theatres' Jonson, *Poetaster*	Essex rebels and is executed
1602		Tyrone defeated in Ireland
1603	Florio, Montaigne's *Essays*, tr.	Elizabeth I dies, James I accedes Raleigh found guilty of treason
1604	Marston, *The Malcontent*	Peace with Spain
1605	Bacon, *Advancement of Learning*	Gunpowder plot
1606	Jonson, *Volpone*	
1607	Tourneur, *The Revenger's Tragedy*, published	Virginia colonized Enclosure riots
1609		Oath of allegiance Truce in Netherlands
1610	Jonson, *Alchemist*	
1611	Authorised Version of the Bible Donne, *Anatomy of the World*	
1612	Webster, *White Devil*	Prince Henry dies
1613	Webster, *Duchess of Malfi*	Princess Elizabeth marries
1614	Jonson, *Bartholomew Fair*	
1616	Folio edition of Jonson's plays	

Biographical note, chronology and plot summary compiled by John Lee, University of Bristol, 1993.

FOREWORD *by Tim Pigott-Smith*

In Act III Isabella asks her brother to sacrifice his life to save her virginity. In Act IV Angelo makes love to Mariana instead of Isabella and does not notice he has the wrong woman in his bed. These are two of the events in this unusual play which have created difficulties of understanding, and for many years it has been routinely catalogued as a problem play. It is not!

It seems to me quite logical for a young nun, beginning her life of exclusive devotion as a bride of Christ, to regard her own hymen as more important than the life of her brother. Indeed, if you do not take on board the extremism of this stance – and we live in a world of much more dangerous fanaticisms than Isabella's – you will miss an essential ingredient of the play. Isabella's unsympathetic belief is absolutely central to her character; my view is that Shakespeare goes on to suggest to her, and us, that it is 'beyond measure'.

The play *M. Butterfly* is based on the true story of a French diplomat who enjoyed a long and successful sexual relationship with a woman, not discovering for many years that 'she' was a man. Clearly, Monsieur, like Angelo, was not a man for leaving the light on! I have always imagined that, consumed by lust, and trembling with guilt, Angelo was thinking less of the lady than of himself. Shakespeare is pursuing his theme: behaviour that is uncontrolled, beyond measure.

Shakespeare is not easy to read. No great writer is; you have to work at them. I would expect to read a great play at least four or five times before I began to feel at all confident about the author's intentions. Actors spend hours debating the nuances and meanings within one line. These meanings can also shift as your perspective on the play develops, and as you yourself change. If you can see a performance of the play you are working on, it helps. That said, of the dozen or so times I have seen *Measure for Measure*, I have only ever seen the whole play work satisfactorily on one occasion. Bits of it nearly always come off, but it is a hard play to realize fully. The cheapest, and sometimes the best, seat in the theatre is in your own imagination; always imagine the play in action as you read.

When I have achieved an overview, I try to establish clearly in my mind the differing narratives, and then see how they relate to the theme. First then, the main narrative threads.

Story One – the Duke. The play begins with a man seeking refuge from responsibility, and creating a chance to observe the dispensation of power. He is obliged to return in secret when things go dangerously wrong, and falls in love – with a nun! This complicates the *dénouement* (literally 'unknotting') that follows his return as the Duke in person. He resumes control, hands out justice, and asks Isabella for her hand in marriage. Her response is the big debating point of any production.

Story Two – the Deputy. When the Duke leaves, he has knowingly established a situation which will expose the person who has to take over the reins of power: Angelo is the man. Shakespeare demonstrates him to be of cold temperament, guided by the letter and not the spirit of the law he invokes. Wonderful irony that it is the shining purity of the nun who inspires in poor Angelo unsuspecting depths of carnal lust, and leads him into a lawlessness he condemns brutally in others.

Story Three – the Nun. Torn from the sanctuary of the Convent, and the security of newly spoken vows, Isabella is thrown into a maelstrom of danger and passion: the justice who could help her (Angelo) tries to seduce her. The friar who comes to advise her (the Duke in disguise) falls in love with her. She has to choose between her virginity and her brother. The closing moments of the play offer her a profound choice of life, either as a nun or as a wife. Shakespeare does not tell us her response: hence the debate.

Story Four – Lucio. This rakish character is the link between the world of the court and the world of the brothel. He is a parasite, a fast double-talker who will say whatever is needed to survive the moment. He is a creep who tries to ingratiate himself, is found out, and receives pretty short shrift when the Duke finally doles out justice.

Story Five – the Low Life. There is a rich array of characters whose bawdy comedy and irreverence reflect the coming to terms with lust and life that are being debated through the main story.

I think Shakespeare often gives you a bald idea of his theme early on. In this play he does so in the first line: 'Of government, the properties to unfold . . .' He looks at the regulation of the state, at individual self-government, and then goes on to examine the question of how to control the darker sides of human nature. And he does so in classic Shakespearean style. Act I is expositional; Acts II, III, and IV explore the intricacies of character exposed by the story; Act V resolves.

The Duke learns that you cannot escape responsibility: he discovers that leaders must lead. His proper resumption of power at the close of the play, and the verdicts he delivers, are essential to the regulated continuance of his society.

Angelo learns that repression is no answer; demons cannot be ignored, you must come to terms with them. Angelo is let off lightly for his sins, and given the bonus of a devoted, loving wife. Love is what he needs to balance his personality out: in time the good in him will function fruitfully.

The real villain of the piece – whom Shakespeare does not like at all – is Lucio. He is entertaining, but he is deceptive. You never know where you are with a man like this, and through the Duke Shakespeare is harsh on him. There will always be people in any society who require punishment. Shakespeare does not *pursue* the debate about social discipline, but he is in no doubt as to the need for it.

There is something refreshingly honest about the pimps and bawds. They know they live at the sharp end, and they survive as best they can, providing people with what they want, and doing their best not to get caught for it. Pompey says he is a bawd, and come what may he's sticking to his vocation – people want sex, and if he doesn't provide it someone else will. Barnardine says that he will not die today because he is not ready. Fortunately, there is a real criminal conveniently on hand to enable justice by having his head chopped off.

Finally, Isabella. What a remarkable journey she travels through the play. Her early speeches about authority are dazzlingly pure; her pleading with her brother is agonizing in its blind simplicity. Her denunciation of Angelo is powerful and passionate, and her calm plea for his life is a deeply moving moment, which shows how massively she has developed from the pure but limited innocent of Act I.

I am sure that the reason Shakespeare does not mention the question of her marriage is that after we have witnessed Isabella plead for the life of the man who has so grossly wronged her it is a foregone conclusion: this woman has changed beyond recognition. She has learnt to make allowances for human frailty. For her to continue life as a nun would be a denial of all the lessons of the play, a negative conclusion to its healing momentum.

The most satisfying solution I have seen to the ending of the play left only the Duke and Isabella on stage. Their eyes met; then the Duke moved slowly, hopefully away. Isabella stood alone in the simple black nun's robes that she had worn throughout. She then removed her cowl, and beautiful long tresses of golden hair tumbled down around her shoulders. The impact of this visual change stopped my breath. After a long moment of stillness, she followed the Duke. The implication was that she *would* marry the Duke, but it was immaterial; she was renouncing her vocation and was entering, instead, the real world of human complexity, to be more than a nun, to be a woman. The staging stated eloquently Isabella's preparedness to come to terms – as we, the audience, do in our daily lives – with responsibility, power, lust, spiritual need, hypocrisy, and crime: some of the darknesses presented in the play. This positive conclusion supported a message that is common in Shakespeare – if human beings are to live in harmony with themselves, and each other, extremism of any kind is dangerous, balance is essential. An eye for an eye; measure for measure.   TIM PIGOTT-SMITH

EDITOR'S INTRODUCTION TO
Measure for Measure

> The say best Men are moulded out of Faults,
> And for the most, become much more the better
> For being a little bad. (V.i.432–34)

So pleads Mariana in a speech that penetrates to the heart of *Measure for Measure*. Her sentiments are specific to the occasion that elicits them, of course, but they apply with equal pertinence to other aspects of a drama about the kinds of 'Profanation' that 'good Christians ought to have' (II.i.54–57).

Like *All's Well That Ends Well*, its predecessor and companion-piece in the Shakespearean canon, *Measure for Measure* pivots on what the heroine of the earlier play calls a 'Sinful Fact' – an illicit assignation that enables a spurned maiden to effect a 'Repair i'th' Dark' (IV.i.42) and thereby secure as her husband a man so debased as to seem beyond reclamation. In the process, by means of a paradox that illustrates the New Testament concept of Grace, the action of the tragicomedy transfigures a 'Wicked Meaning' into a shadowy 'Deed' (*All's Well That Ends Well*, III.vii.44–48) that proves not only absolvable – if not entirely justifiable – but redemptive.

Deriving from a period (1603–4) when Shakespeare was devoting most of his efforts to tragedy, *Measure for Measure* is frequently labelled a 'black comedy' or a 'problem play'. Its tone is less festive than the holiday mood we relish in earlier titles like *A Midsummer Night's Dream* and *As You Like It*. In places, indeed, its atmosphere is so grim that we sense closer affinities with the sombre settings of *Hamlet* and *Troilus and Cressida*, *Othello* and *King Lear*, four works that appear to have bracketed *All's Well That Ends Well* and *Measure for Measure* in Shakespeare's career as a dramatist.

As we perceive what happens in the council rooms, brothels, and prison cells of the Vienna portrayed in *Measure for Measure*, we're continually reminded that human nature is so frail as to render personal transgressions and societal discords all but inevitable. At the same time, however, and in a way that anticipates the 'Wonder' so prevalent in Shakespeare's final Romances, we're given intimations of a 'Powre Divine' (V.i.362) that looks sympathetically upon our flaws and attends to even the most egregious of them with a 'Physic / That's Bitter to Sweet End' (IV.vi.7–8).

In this play the self-designated agent of Heaven's restorative therapy is a duke, Vincentio, who relinquishes his secular office for a season and appoints as his deputy the 'Prenzie, Angelo' (III.i.92). Lord Angelo, we soon learn, is 'A Man of Stricture and firm Abstinence' (I.iv.12), and the ruler who commissions him expects the young nobleman to implement policies that will address the licentiousness that has become rampant through the Duke's own 'permissive Pass' (I.iv.38). To keep abreast of what transpires as a consequence, Vincentio goes undercover and dons the habit of a 'meddling Friar' (V.i.127). From this perspective he sees things he would not have been in a position to observe under normal conditions. He also hears things that would otherwise have escaped his notice, among them the slanders of a loose-tongued libertine who refers to Vienna's absent head of state as 'the old fantastical Duke of Dark Corners' (IV.iii.161–62).

Because of the 'Craft' he eventually deploys against the 'Vice' his own leniency has helped foster (III.i.579), Vincentio has impressed many of today's critics and directors as a manipulative Machiavellian, a shady character with more than a trace of the seedy deviousness that Lucio ascribes to the truant Duke. Regardless of what present-day readers may be disposed to think about Vincentio's *modus operandi*, however, he is a figure whose role in the plot would assuredly have pleased the most influential of the tragicomedy's original audiences.

The first performance of the play that can be dated with certainty occurred at the court of King James I on 26 December

1604, and it is reasonable to infer that the monarch himself was probably on hand to see the work 'His Majesty's Servants' were presenting as royal entertainment. *Measure for Measure* echoes some of the new king's own writings on the principles of good government, among them his views on the need for a ruler to exercise measure (temperance) in the administration of justice. It is thus likely that Shakespeare's regal patron would have seen himself as the principal model for a 'Sword of Heaven' (III.i.563) who balances justice with mercy, and whose severest punishment is reserved for a scandalmonger who epitomizes the kind of 'unreverent speaker' that James is reported to have found particularly irritating.

As he divests himself of all the trappings of imperial dignity, Vincentio recalls 'the Mirror of all Christian Kings', as Shakespeare's Chorus had depicted England's 'Warlike Harry' in *Henry V*, when the army's commander in chief disguises himself as an ordinary soldier and mingles with his unsuspecting subordinates on the eve of the battle of Agincourt. Meanwhile, as he secludes himself and his purposes from those who oversee the city in his stead, the Duke resembles the *Deus absconditus*, the unfathomable hidden God, whose mysteries would later inspire the reflections of Blaise Pascal. It would be going too far, no doubt, to suggest that Vincentio's descent into 'Beggary' (III.i.383) is designed to echo the way Christ's Incarnation is described in Philippians 2:5–8. But there can be no question that in his various guises as 'Father', 'Shepherd', 'dread Lord', and 'Grace', Vienna's head of state is intended to keep us aware that in Renaissance England a monarch's subjects were enjoined to regard him or her as God's anointed surrogate.

Shakespeare's earliest audiences would not have been surprised, then, to see the Duke of *Measure for Measure* don the persona of another minister of Heaven's will. Nor would they have been shocked by his resort to a 'Deceit' (III.i.270) with biblical precedent (see Genesis 38 for a divinely assisted ruse with analogies to the bed-tricks in both *Measure for Measure* and *All's Well That Ends Well*), especially when that undertaking brings about a 'Consummation' that can be construed as both devout and 'devoutly to be wished' (*Hamlet*, III.i.60–61). If we take Vincentio at his own estimate, he functions as an exemplar of Providence who subjects other characters to a siege of testing to determine what they are made of, to teach them something about their own limitations, and in time to bring each of them to a crisis where he or she is called upon to display a spirit of charity – a manifestation of humility, penitence, forgiveness, or love – that was either lacking or deficient at the outset.

The Duke's labours commence with Angelo, a 'Substitute' (III.i.191) so straitlaced in his own life that he can be depended upon to bring the same rigour to his enforcement of the laws of Vienna. And so he does: notwithstanding the demurrals of Escalus, a more experienced, equitable, and humane justice, Angelo sentences to death a man whose only crime is to have slept with his bride before the public consecration of their marriage vows. When Angelo's colleague observes that Claudio's offence is little more than a technicality, the sort of 'Fault' that anyone with 'Affections' and 'Blood' might have succumbed to, the Deputy replies, ' 'Tis one thing to be tempted, Escalus, / Another thing to fall' (II.i.8–18). Similarly, when Claudio's sister asks the Deputy to spare a remorseful fellow sinner, Angelo assures Isabella that 'It is the Law, not I, condemn your Brother' (II.ii.81). Genuinely believing himself to be without guilt, hypocrisy, or arrogance, Angelo maintains that by executing 'strict Statutes' (I.iv.19) with unstinting exactitude he is merely assessing the behaviour of Vienna's other citizens by the same high standards he requires of, and adheres to, himself.

But suddenly Angelo feels 'Motions of the Sense' (I.v.60) that are new to him. Words meant in all innocence evoke thoughts and feelings he recognizes to be anything but innocent. Before the end of his first conversation with Isabella, he realizes something he had not previously imagined: that he is *not* 'a man whose Blood / Is very Snow-broth' (I.v.58–59). No, Angelo is hooked by the same 'Affections' that touch other mortals, and by the time Claudio's advocate arrives for her second visit the Deputy is beginning to sound like the tormented Claudius of *Hamlet*'s Prayer Scene. 'Heaven hath my empty Words,' Angelo laments, 'Whilst my Invention, hearing not my Tongue, / Anchors on Isabel' (II.iv.2–4).

Like the Apostle Paul, Angelo discovers to his dismay that sin, 'that it might appear sin', has wrought mortality in him 'by that which is good' (Romans 7:13). The zeal with which he has prosecuted his duties proves ineffectual against the stirrings of the flesh, and in due course the Deputy violates the same law that he has brought to bear upon Claudio. Upon the Duke's reappearance at the conclusion of the play, that situation precipitates an *ad hoc* court session in which stern Justice demands 'An Angelo for Claudio, Death for Death' (V.i.402).

As it happens, through the prior manoeuvrings of the 'Friar', the requirements of Vienna's legal system turn out to be less grievous than the penalty the ensnared Deputy assumes he deserves. What Angelo has earlier interpreted as a fall from Grace (IV.iv.34–35) emerges as a fall *into* Grace, a *felix culpa* ('happy fault' or fortunate fall), and one that leaves the pharisaical young lord shaken but both wiser and better than the naive puritan of the play's opening moments.

But this can be so only because of a parallel pilgrimage by Isabella. When we meet her in Act I, Claudio's sister seems remarkably similar to the icy Deputy. Like Angelo, she desires 'a more strict Restraint' (I.v.4). And in her first interview with the Deputy, she insists upon Mercy with just as much rigidity as Angelo insists upon Justice. We are surely meant to commend Isabella's admonition that 'all the Souls that were were Forfeit once; / And he that might the Vantage best have took / Found out the Remedy' (II.ii.74–76). At the same time, however, we are almost certainly to be alarmed by the steely conviction with which a novice aspiring to be a nun can later pronounce that 'More than our Brother is our Chastity' (II.iv.187).

By the climax of the drama Isabella is afforded an opportunity to be absolute for chastity in much the same way that Claudio has been instructed to 'Be absolute for Death' (III.i.4). Her final trial places her in an agonizing plight in which Mariana begs her to pray for the life of a self-confessed tyrant who has not only committed a worse crime than Isabella's brother but has reneged on his pledge to release the condemned Claudio in recompense for the lewd ransom the Deputy has extorted. Hearing Mariana's plea to Isabella, the Duke exclaims, 'Should she kneel down in Mercy of this Fact, / Her Brother's Ghost his paved Bed would break / And take her hence in Horror' (V.i.424–26).

After one of the most suspenseful pauses in all of Shakespeare, Isabella makes a choice that might appear to be a reiteration of her earlier refusal to act as her brother's keeper. The difference is that now 'the Case is alter'd' (3 Henry VI, IV.iii.31), and this time the sister who is put in 'the Top of Judgement' responds with the kind of compassion she'd earlier credited with the capacity to transform an unbending judge into a 'Man new made' (II.ii.76–80). Her reward, supposedly through 'an Accident that Heaven provides' (IV.iii.82), is to regain what she had presumed lost. By declining the course her ruler and spiritual mentor appears to be urging upon her, she metamorphoses a potential revenge tragedy into a comedy of forgiveness and reconciliation, and one that resonates with the deepest chords of rebirth and resurrection.

Shakespeare drew upon multiple sources for *Measure for Measure*. Of these perhaps the most important was a familiar passage from the Sermon on the Mount, where Jesus says, 'Judge not, that ye be not judged. For with what judgment ye judge, ye shall be judged: and with what measure ye mete, it shall be measured to you again' (Matthew 7:1–2). The playwright also alluded to several parables from the Gospels. And in his presentation of the dilemma generated by Isabella's exchanges with Angelo, he dramatized Paul's observation that 'the flesh lusteth against the Spirit, and the Spirit against the flesh: and these are contrary the one to the other: so that ye cannot do the things that ye would' (Galatians 5:17).

Behind Angelo's proposition to Isabella lay a number of narratives about corrupt magistrates, among them (a) a novella that appeared in a popular Italian collection, the *Hecatommithi* (1565), by Giraldi Cinthio, (b) a play on the theme by the same author (*Epitia*, published posthumously in 1583), and two English renderings of the tale, (c) a drama (*The Right Excellent and Famous History of Promos and Cassandra*, 1578) and (d) a prose discourse (included in the *Heptameron of Civil Discourses*, 1582), by George Whetstone. Shakespeare probably consulted all of these sources, and in each of them he would have found that the woman who corresponds to Isabella reluctantly accepts the bargain proffered by the magistrate who corresponds to Angelo. The playwright would also have noted that in every case the magistrate cheats the woman he has seduced and orders her brother's execution to proceed without delay.

In the earliest of Cinthio's treatments of the story, the character who corresponds to Claudio is actually beheaded; but in Cinthio's *Epitia* and in Whetstone's two versions of *Promos and Cassandra*, the sentenced convict is secretly spared by the prison officer who corresponds to the Provost in Shakespeare's play. In all four redactions of the fable, when the betrayed heroine appeals to a higher authority, the ruler who holds jurisdiction over the wicked magistrate orders him to marry her and then be put to death. Once the wedding has taken place, however, despite the injustice the magistrate has done her and her brother, the abused sister implores the ruler to pardon him. After much persuasion the ruler relents and does so, and the heroine joyfully claims her now repentant husband as the man with whom she will live happily ever after.

Only in Shakespeare is the Isabella character a neophyte in preparation for holy orders. And only in *Measure for Measure* is there a role of the type that Mariana discharges. Shakespeare probably adapted her part and the device of the bed-substitution from the same sources — Giovanni Boccaccio's *Decameron* (1348–58) and William Painter's *Palace of Pleasure* (1566) – that the playwright had turned to when he wrote *All's Well That Ends Well*.

THE TEXT OF THE EVERYMAN SHAKESPEARE

Background

THE EARLY PRINTINGS OF SHAKESPEARE'S WORKS

Many of us enjoy our first encounter with Shakespeare when we are introduced to *Julius Caesar* or *Macbeth* at school. It may therefore surprise us that neither of these tragedies could ever have been read, let alone studied, by most of the playwright's contemporaries. Along with seventeen other titles that never saw print during Shakespeare's lifetime, they made their inaugural appearance as 'literary' works seven years after his death, in the 1623 collection we know today as the First Folio.

The Folio contained thirty-six titles in all. Of these, half had been issued previously in the small paperbacks we now refer to as quartos.* Like several of the plays first published in the Folio, the most trustworthy of the quarto printings appear to have been set either from the dramatist's own manuscripts or from faithful copies of them. It's not impossible that the poet himself prepared some of them for the press, and it's intriguing to imagine him reviewing proof-pages as the words he'd written for actors to speak and embody were being transposed into the type that readers would filter through their eyes, minds, and imaginations. But, alas, there's no indisputable evidence that Shakespeare had any direct involvement with the publication of these early texts of his plays.

What about the plays that appeared in print for the first time in the Folio? Had the dramatist taken any steps to give them the

---

* Quartos derived their name from the four-leaf units of which these small books were comprised: large sheets of paper that had been folded twice after printing to yield four leaves, or eight pages. Folios, volumes with twice the page-size of quartos, were put together from two-leaf units: sheets that had been folded once after printing to yield four pages.

permanency of book form before he died? We don't know. All we can say is that when he became fatally ill in 1616, Shakespeare was denied any opportunities he might otherwise have taken to ensure that his 'insubstantial Pageants' survived their creator, who was now slipping into the 'dark Backward and Abysm of Time'.

Fortunately, two of the playwright's collegues felt an obligation, as they put it, 'to procure his Orphans Guardians'. Sometime after Shakespeare's death John Heminge (or Heminges) and Henry Condell made arrangements to preserve his plays in a manner that would keep them vibrant for posterity. They dedicated their endeavour to two noblemen who had helped England's foremost acting company through some of its most trying vicissitudes. They solicited several poetic tributes for the volume, among them a now-famous eulogy by fellow writer Ben Jonson. They commissioned a portrait of Shakespeare to adorn the frontispiece. And they did their utmost to display the author's dramatic works in a style that would both dignify them and and make them accessible to 'the great Variety of Readers'.

As they prepared Shakespeare's plays for the compositors who would set them in stately Folio columns, Heminge and Condell (or editors designated to carry out their wishes) revised and augmented many of the entrances, exits, and other stage directions in the manuscripts. They divided most of the plays into acts and scenes.* For a number of plays they appended 'Names of the Actors', or casts of characters. Meanwhile they made every effort to ensure that the Folio printers had reliable copy-texts for each of the titles: authoritative manuscripts for the plays that had not been published previously, and good quarto printings (annotated in some instances to insert staging details, mark script changes, and add supplementary material) for those issued prior to the Folio. For several titles they supplied texts that were substantively different from, if not always demonstrably superior to, the quarto versions that preceded them.

* The early quartos, reflecting the unbroken sequence that probably typified Elizabethan and Jacobean performances of the plays, had been printed without the structural demarcations usual in Renaissance editions of classical drama.

Like even the most accurate of the earlier printings, the Folio collection was flawed by minor blemishes. But it more than fulfilled the purpose of its generous-minded compilers: 'to keep the memory of so worthy a Friend and Fellow alive as was our Shakespeare'. In the process it provided a publishing model that remains instructive today.

MODERN EDITIONS OF THE PLAYS AND POEMS

When we compare the First Folio and its predecessors with the usual modern editions of Shakespeare's works, we're more apt to be impressed by the differences than by the similarities. Today's texts of Renaissance drama are normally produced in conformity with twentieth-century standards of punctuation and usage; as a consequence they look more neat, clean, and, to our eyes, 'right' than do the original printings. Thanks to an editorial tradition that extends back to the early eighteenth century, most of the rough spots in the early printings of Shakespeare have long since been smoothed away. Textual scholars have ferreted out redundancies and eradicated inconsistencies. They've mended what they've perceived to be errors and oversights in the author's playscripts, and they have systematically attended to what they've construed as misreadings by the copyists and compositors who transmitted those playscripts to posterity. They've added '[Within]' brackets and other theatrical notations. They've revised stage directions they've judged incomplete or inadequate in the initial printings. They've regularized disparities in the speech headings. They've returned to the playwright's sources and reinstated the proper forms for many of the character and place names a presumably hasty or inattentive author got 'wrong' as he conferred identities on his dramatis personae and stage locales. They've replaced obsolete words like *bankrout* with their modern heirs (in this case *bankrupt*). And in a multitude of other ways they've accommodated Shakespeare to the tastes, interests, and expectations of latter-day readers.

The results, on the whole, have been splendid. But interpreting the artistic designs of a complex writer is always problematical, and the task is especially challenging when that writer happens to have been a poet who felt unconstrained by many of the 'rules' that more conventional dramatists respected. The undertaking becomes further complicated when new rules, and new criteria of linguistic and social correctness, are imposed by subsequent generations of artists and critics.

To some degree in his own era, but even more in the neoclassical period (1660–1800) that came in its wake, Shakespeare's most ardent admirers thought it necessary to apologise for what Ben Jonson hinted at in his allusion to the 'small Latin, and less Greek' of an untutored prodigy. To be sure, the 'sweet Swan of Avon' sustained his popularity; in fact his esteem rose so steadily that by the end of the eighteenth century he'd eclipsed Jonson and his other coevals and become the object of near-universal Bardolatry. But in the theatre most of his plays were being adapted in ways that were deemed advisable to tame their supposed wildness and bring them into conformity with the taste of a society that took pride in its refinement. As one might expect, some of the attitudes that induced theatre proprietors to metamorphose an unpolished poet from the provinces into something closer to an urbane man of letters also influenced Shakespeare's editors. Persuaded that the dramatist's works were marred by crudities that needed expunging, they applied their ministrations to the canon with painstaking diligence.

Twentieth-century editors have moved away from many of the presuppositions that guided a succession of earlier improvers. But a glance at the textual apparatus accompanying virtually any modern edition of the plays and poems will show that emendations and editorial procedures deriving from such forebears as the sets published by Nicholas Rowe (1709), Alexander Pope (1723–25, 1728), Lewis Theobald (1733, 1740, 1757), Thomas Hanmer (1743–45, 1770–71), Samuel Johnson (1765), Edward Capell (1768), and George Steevens (1773) retain a strong hold on today's renderings of the playwright's works. The result is a 'Shakespeare' who offers the tidiness we've come to expect in our libraries of classical authors, but not necessarily the playwright a 1599 reader of the Second Quarto of *Romeo and Juliet* would recognize as a contemporary.

OLD LIGHT ON THE TOPIC

Over the last two decades we've learned from art curators that paintings by old Masters such as Michelangelo and Rembrandt look much brighter when centures of grime are removed from their surfaces – when hues dulled coated with soot and other extraneous matter are restored to something approximating their pristine luminosity. We've learned from conductors like Christopher Hogwood that there are aesthetic rewards to be gained from a return to the scorings and instruments with which Renaissance and Baroque musical compositions were first presented. We've learned from twentieth-century experiments in the performance of Shakespeare's plays that an open, multi-level stage analogous to that on which the scripts were originally enacted does more justice to their dramaturgical techniques than does a proscenium auditorium devised for works that came later in the development of Western theatre. We've learned from archaeological excavations in London's Bankside that the foundations of playhouses such as the Rose and the Globe look rather different from what many historians had expected. And we're now learning from a close scrutiny of Shakespeare's texts that they too look different, and function differently, when we accept them for what they are and resist the impulse to 'normalize' features that strike us initially as quirky, unkempt, or unsophisticated.

The Aims that Guide the Everyman Text

Like other modern editions of Shakespeare's plays and poems, The Everyman Shakespeare owes an incalculable debt to the scholarship that has led to so many excellent renderings of his works. But in an attempt to draw fresh inspiration from the spirit that animated those remarkable achievements at the outset, the

Everyman edition departs in a number of respects from the usual post-Folio approach to the presentation of Shakespeare's texts.

RESTORING SOME OF THE NUANCES OF
RENAISSANCE PUNCTUATION

In its punctuation Everyman tries to give equal emphasis to sound and sense. In places where Renaissance practice calls for heavier punctuation than we'd normally employ – to mark the caesural pause in the middle of a line of verse, for instance – Everyman sometimes retains commas that other modern editions omit. Meanwhile, in places where current practice usually calls for the inclusion of commas – after vocatives and interjections such as 'O' and 'alas', say, or before 'Madam' or 'Sir' in phrases such as 'Ay Madam' or 'Yes Sir' – Everyman follows the original printings and omits them.

Occasionally the absences of a comma has a significant bearing on what an expression means, or can mean. At one point in *Othello*, for example, Iagō tells the Moor 'Marry patience' (IV.i.90). Inserting a comma after 'Marry', as most of today's editions do, limits Iago's utterance to one that says 'Come now, have patience'. Leaving the clause as it stands in the Folio, the way the Everyman text does, permits Iago's words to have the additional, agonizingly ironic sense 'Be wed to Patience'.

The early texts generally deploy exclamation points quite sparingly, and the Everyman text follows suit. Everyman also follows the early editions, more often than not, when they use question marks in places that seem unusual by current standards: at the ends of what we'd normally treat as exclamations, for example, or at the ends of interrogative clauses in sentences that we'd ordinarily denote as questions in their entirety.

The early texts make no orthographic distinction between simple plurals and either singular or plural possessives, and there are times when the context doesn't indicate whether a word spelled *Sisters*, say, should be rendered *Sisters*, *Sisters'*, or *Sister's* in today's usage. In such situations the Everyman edition prints the words in the form modern usage prescribes for plurals.

REVIVING SOME OF THE FLEXIBILITY OF RENAISSANCE SPELLING

Spelling had not become standardized by Shakespeare's time, which meant that many words could take a variety of forms. Like James Joyce and some of the other innovative prose and verse stylists of our own century, Shakespeare revelled in the freedom a largely unanchored language provided, and with that in mind Everyman retains original spelling forms (or adaptations of those forms that preserve their key distinctions from modern spellings) whenever there is any reason to suspect that they might have a bearing on how a word was intended to be pronounced or on what it meant, or could have meant, in Shakespeare's day. When there is any likelihood that multiple forms of the same word could be significant, moreover, the Everyman text mirrors the diversity to be found in the original printings.

In many cases this practice affects the personalities of Shakespeare's characters. One of the heroine's most familiar questions in *Romeo and Juliet* is 'What's in a Name?' For two and a half centuries readers – and as a consequence actors, directors, theatre audiences, and commentators – have been led to believe that Juliet was addressing this query to a Romeo named 'Montague'. In fact 'Montague' *was* the name Shakespeare found in his principal source for the play. For reasons that will become apparent to anyone who examines the tragedy in detail, however, he changed his protagonist's surname to 'Mountague', a name that plays on both 'mount' and 'ague' (fever). The playwright was surely also aware that *Capulet*, like *Capilet* in *Twelfth Night* and in *All's Well That Ends Well*, was a name that meant 'small horse'. Setting aside an editorial practice that began with Lewis Theobald in the middle of the eighteenth century, Everyman resurrects the name Shakespeare himself gave Juliet's lover.

Readers of *The Merchant of Venice* in the Everyman edition will be amused to learn that the character modern editions usually identify as 'Lancelot' is in reality 'Launcelet', a name that calls attention to the clown's lusty 'little lance'. Like Costard in *Love's Labour's Lost*, another stage bumpkin who was probably played by the actor Will Kemp, Launcelet is an upright 'Member of the Commonwealth'; we eventually learn that he's left a pliant wench 'with Child'.

Readers of *Hamlet* will find that 'Fortinbras' (as the name of the Prince's Norwegian opposite is rendered in the First Folio and in most modern editions) appears in the earlier, authoritative 1604 Second Quarto of the play as 'Fortinbrasse'. In the opening scene of that text a surname that meant 'strong in arms' in French is introduced to the accompaniment of puns on *brazen*, in the phrase 'brazon Cannon', and on *metal*, in the phrase 'unimprooued mettle'. In the same play readers of the Everyman text will encounter 'Ostricke', the ostrich-like courtier who invites the Prince of Denmark to participate in the fateful fencing match that draws *Hamlet* to a close. Only in its final entrance direction for the obsequious fop does the Second Quarto call this character 'Osrick, the name he bears in all the Folio text's references to him and in most modern editions of Shakespeare's most popular tragedy.

Readers of the Everyman text of *Macbeth* will discover the fabled 'Weird Sisters' appear only as the 'weyward' or 'weyard' Sisters. Shakespeare and his contemporaries knew that in *Chronicles of England, Scotland, and Ireland* Raphael Holinshed had used the term 'weird sisters' to describe the witches who accost Macbeth and Banquo on the heath; but no doubt because he wished to play on *wayward*, the playwright changed their name to *weyward*. Like Samuel Johnson, who thought punning vulgar and lamented Shakespeare's proclivity to seduction by this 'fatal Cleopatra', Lewis Theobald saw no reason to retain the playwright's 'weyward' spelling of the witches' name. He thus restored the 'correct' form from Holinshed, and editors ever since have generally done likewise.

In many instances Renaissance English had a single spelling for what we now define as two separate words. For example, *humane* combined the senses of 'human' and 'humane' in modern English. In the First Folio printing of *Macbeth* the protagonist's wife expresses a concern that her husband is 'too full o'th' Milke of humane kindnesse'. As she phrases it, *humane kindnesse* can mean several things, among them 'humankind-ness', 'human kindness', and 'humane kindness'. It is thus a reminder that to be true to his or her own 'kind' a human being must be 'kind' in the sense we now attach to 'humane'. To disregard this logic, as the protagonist and his wife will soon prove, is to disregard a principle as basic to the cosmos as the laws of gravity.

In a way that parallels *humane, bad* could mean either 'bad' or 'bade', *borne* either 'born' or 'borne', *least* either 'least' or 'lest', *lye* either 'lie' or 'lye', *powre* either 'poor' or 'power', *then* either 'than' or 'then', and *tide* either 'tide' or 'tied'.

There were a number of word-forms that functioned in Renaissance English as interchangeable doublets. *Travail* could mean 'travel', for example, and *travel* could mean 'travail'. By the same token *deer* could mean *dear* and vice-versa, *dew* could mean *due*, *hart* could mean *heart*, and (as we've already noted) *mettle* could mean *metal*.

A particularly interesting instance of the equivocal or double meanings some word-forms had in Shakespeare's time is *loose*, which can often become either 'loose' or 'lose' when we render it in modern English. In *The Comedy of Errors* when Antipholus of Syracuse compares himself to 'a Drop / of Water that in the Ocean seeks another Drop' and then says he will 'loose' himself in quest of his long-lost twin, he means both (a) that he will release himself into a vast unknown, and (b) that he will lose his own identity, if necessary, to be reunited with the brother for whom he searches. On the other hand, in *Hamlet* when Polonius says he'll 'loose' his daughter to the Prince, he little suspects that by so doing he will also lose his daughter.

In some cases Shakespeare employs word-forms that can be translated into words we wouldn't think of as related today: *sowre*, for instance, which can mean 'sour', 'sower', or 'sore', depending on the context. In other cases he uses forms that do have modern counterparts, but not counterparts with the same potential for multiple connotation. For example, *onely* usually means 'only' in the modern sense; but occasionally Shakespeare gives it a figurative, adverbial twist that would require a nonce word such as 'one-ly' to replicate in current English.

In a few cases Shakespeare employs word-forms that have only seeming equivalents in modern usage. For example, *abhominable*, which meant 'inhuman' (derived however incorrectly, from *ab*, 'away from', and *homine*, 'man') to Shakespeare and his contemporaries, is not the same word as our *abominable* (ill-omened, abhorrent). In his advice to the visiting players Hamlet complains about incompetent actors who imitate 'Humanity so abhominably' as to make the characters they depict seem unrecognizable as men. Modern readers who don't realize the distinction between Shakespeare's word and our own, and who see *abominable* on the page before them, don't register the full import of the Prince's satire.

Modern English treats as single words a number of word-forms that were normally spelled as two words in Shakespeare's time. What we render as *myself*, for example, and use primarily as a reflexive or intensifying pronoun, is almost invariably spelled *my self* in Shakespeare's works; so also with *her self*, *thy self*, *your self*, and *it self* (where *it* functions in the way that *its* does today).

Often there is no discernible difference between Shakespeare's usage and our own. At other times there is, however, as we are reminded when we come across a phrase such as 'our innocent self' in *Macbeth* and think how strained it would sound in modern parlance, or when we note how naturally the self is objictified in the balanced clauses of the Balcony Scene in *Romeo and Juliet*:

> Romeo, doffe thy name,
> And for thy name, which is no part of thee,
> Take all my selfe.

Yet another manifestation of the differences between Renaissance orthography and our own can be exemplified with words such as *today*, *tonight* and *tomorrow*, which (unlike *yesterday*) were treated as two words in Shakespeare's time. In *Macbeth* when the Folio prints 'Duncan comes here to Night', the unattached *to* can function either as a preposition (with *Night* as its object, or in this case its destination) or as the first part of an infinitive (with *Night* operating figuratively as a verb). Consider the ambiguity a Renaissance reader would have detected in the original publication of one of the most celebrated soliloquies in all of Shakespeare:

> To morrow, and to morrow, and to morrow,
> Creeps in this petty pace from day to day,
> To the last syllable of Recorded time:
> And to all our yesterdayes, have lighted Fooles
> The way to dusty death.

Here, by implication, the route 'to morrow' is identical with 'the way to dusty death', a relationship we miss if we don't know that for Macbeth, and for the audiences who first heard these lines spoken, *to morrow* was not a single word but a potentially equivocal two-word phrase.

RECAPTURING THE ABILITY TO HEAR WITH OUR EYES

When we fail to recall that Shakespeare's scripts were designed initially to provide words for people to hear in the theatre, we sometimes overlook a fact that is fundamental to the artistic structure of a work like *Macbeth*: that the messages a sequence of sounds convey through the ear are, if anything, even more significant than the messages a sequence of letters, punctuation marks, and white spaces on a printed page transmit through the eye. A telling illustration of this point, and of the potential for ambiguous or multiple implication in any Shakespearean script, may be found in the dethronement scene of *Richard II*. When Henry Bullingbrook asks the king if he is ready to resign his crown, Richard replies 'I, no no I; for I must nothing be.' Here the punctuation in the 1608 Fourth Quarto (the earliest text to print this richly complex passage) permits each *I* to signify either 'ay' or 'I' (*I* being the usual spelling for 'ay' in Shakespeare's time). Understanding *I* to mean 'I' permits additional play on *no*, which can be heard (at least in its first occurrence) as 'know'. Meanwhile the second and third soundings of *I*, if not the first, can also be heard as 'eye'. In the context in which this line occurs, that sense echoes a thematically pertinent passage from Matthew 18:9: 'if thine eye offend thee, pluck it out'.

But these are not all the implications *I* can have here. *I* it can also represent the Roman numeral for '1', which will soon be reduced, as Richard notes, to 'nothing' (o), along with the speaker's title, his worldly possessions, his manhood, and eventually his life. In Shakespeare's time, to become 'nothing' was, *inter alia*, to be emasculated, to be made a 'weaker vessel' (1 Peter 3:7) with 'no thing'. As the Fool in *King Lear* reminds another monarch who has abdicated his throne, a man in want of an 'I' is impotent, 'an O without a Figure' (I.iv.207). In addition to its other dimensions, then, Richard's reply is a statement that can be formulated mathematically, and in symbols that anticipate the binary system behind today's computer technology: '1, 0, 0, 1, for 1 must 0 be.'

Modern editions usually render Richard's line 'Ay, no; no, ay; for I must nothing be.' Presenting the line in that fashion makes good sense of what Richard is saying. But as we've seen, it doesn't make total sense of it, and it doesn't call attention to Richard's paradoxes in the same way that hearing or seeing three undifferentiated *I*'s is likely to have done for Shakespeare's contemporaries. Their culture was more attuned than ours is to the oral and aural dimensions of language, and if we want to appreciate the special qualities of their dramatic art we need to train ourselves to 'hear' the word-forms we see on the page. We must learn to recognize that for many of what we tend to think of as fixed linkages between sound and moaning (the vowel 'I', say, and the word 'eye'), there were alternative linkages (such as the vowel 'I' and the words 'I' and 'Ay') that could be just as pertinent to what the playwright was communicating through the ears of his theatre patrons at a given moment. As the word *audience* itself may help us to remember, people in Shakespeare's time normally spoke of 'hearing' rather than 'seeing' a play.

In its text of *Richard II*, the Everyman edition reproduces the title character's line as it appears in the early printings of the tragedy. Ideally the orthographic oddity of the repeated *I*'s will encourage today's readers to ponder Richard's utterance, and the play it epitomizes, as a characteristically Shakespearean enigma.

OTHER ASPECTS OF THE EVERYMAN TEXT

Now for a few words about other features of the Everyman text.

One of the first things readers will notice about this edition is its bountiful use of capitalized words. In this practice as in others, the Everyman exemplar is the First Folio, and especially the works in the Folio sections billed as 'Histories' and 'Tragedies'.* Everyman makes no attempt to adhere to the Folio printings with literal exactitude. In some instances the Folio capitalizes words that the Everyman text of the same passage lowercases; in other instances Everyman capitalizes words not uppercased in the Folio. The objective is merely to suggest something of the flavour, and what appears to have been the rationale, of Renaissance capitalization, in the hope that today's audiences will be made continually aware that the works they are contemplating derive from an earlier epoch.

Readers will also notice that instead of cluttering the text with stage directions such as '[Aside]' or '[To Rosse]', the Everyman text employs unobtrusive dashes to indicate shifts in mode of address. In an effort to keep the page relatively clear of words not

---

* The quarto printings employ far fewer capital letters than does the Folio. Capitalization seems to have been regarded as a means of recognizing the status ascribed to certain words (*Noble*, for example, is almost always capitalized), titles (not only King, Queen, Duke, and Duchess, but Sir and Madam), genres (tragedies were regarded as more 'serious' than comedies in more than one sense), and forms of publication (quartos, being associated with ephemera such as 'plays', were not thought to be as 'grave' as the folios that bestowed immortality on 'works', writings that, in the words of Ben Jonson's eulogy of Shakespeare, were 'not of an age, but for all time').

supplied by the original printings, Everyman also exercises restraint in its addition of editor-generated stage directions, Where the dialogue makes it obvious that a significant action occurs, the Everyman text inserts a square-bracketed phrase such as '[Fleance escapes.]'. Where what the dialogue implies is subject to differing interpretations, however, the Everyman text provides a facing-page note to discuss the most plausible inferences.

Like other modern editions, the Everyman text combines into 'shared' verse lines (lines divided among two or more speakers) many of the part-lines to be found in the early publications of the plays. One exception to the usual modern procedure is that Everyman indents some lines that are not components of shared verses. At times, for example, the opening line of a scene stops short of the metrical norm, a pentameter (five-foot) or hexameter (six-foot) line comprised predominantly of iambic units (unstressed syllables followed by stressed ones). In such cases Everyman uses indentation as a reminder that scenes can begin as well as end in mid-line (an extension of the ancient convention that an epic commences *in medias res*, 'in the midst of the action'). Everyman also uses indentation to reflect what appear to be pauses in the dialogue, either to allow other activity to transpire (as happens in *Macbeth*, II.iii.87, when a brief line 'What's the Business?' follows a Folio stage direction that reads 'Bell rings. Enter Lady.') or to permit a character to hesitate for a moment of reflection (as happens a few seconds later in the same scene when Macduff responds to a demand to 'Speak, speak' with the reply 'O gentle Lady, / 'Tis not for you to hear what I can speak').

Everyman preserves many of the anomalies in the early texts. Among other things, this practice pertains to the way characters are depicted. In *A Midsummer Night's Dream*, for example, the ruler of Athens is usually identified in speech headings and stage directions as 'Theseus', but sometimes he is referred to by his title as 'Duke'. In the same play Oberon's merry sprite goes by two different names: 'Puck' and 'Robin Goodfellow'.

Readers of the Everyman edition will sometimes discover that characters they've known, or known about, for years don't appear in the original printings. When they open the pages of the Everyman edition of *Macbeth*, for example, they'll learn that Shakespeare's audiences were unaware of any woman with the title 'Lady Macbeth'. In the only authoritative text we have of the Scottish tragedy, the protagonist's spouse goes by such names as 'Macbeth's Lady', 'Macbeth's Wife', or simply 'Lady', but nowhere is she listed or mentioned as 'Lady Macbeth'. The same is true of the character usually designated 'Lady Capulet' in modern editions of *Romeo and Juliet*. 'Capulet's Wife' makes appearances as 'Mother', 'Old Lady', 'Lady', or simply 'Wife'; but she is never called 'Lady Capulet', and her husband never treats her with the dignity such a title would connote.

Rather than 'correct' the grammar in Shakespeare's works to eliminate what modern usage would categorize as solecisms (as when Mercutio says 'my Wits faints' in *Romeo and Juliet*), the Everyman texts leaves it intact. Among other things, this principle applies to instances in which archaic forms preserve idioms that differ slightly from related modern expressions (as in the clause frequently 'you are too blame', where 'too' functions as an adverb and 'blame' is used, not as a verb, but as an adjective roughly equivalent to 'blameworthy').

Finally, and most importantly, the Everyman edition leaves unchanged any reading in the original text that is not manifestly erroneous. Unlike other modern renderings of Shakespeare's works, Everyman substitutes emendations only when obvious problems can be resolved by obvious solutions.

The Everyman Text of *Measure for Measure*

Modern editions of *Measure for Measure* derive from the printing of the tragicomedy that appeared seven years after Shakespeare's death in the 1623 First Folio. So far as we know, there was no quarto issue of the play during the author's lifetime. In general the Folio text of the play is one that inspires confidence. From all indications most if not all of the copy behind it was prepared by scrivener Ralph Crane, and he probably based his rendering of the drama on a slightly edited theatre promptbook that had been prepared from the playwright's final draft of the script.

Crane was evidently responsible for polished versions of several Shakespearean works, among them *The Two Gentlemen of Verona*, *The Merry Wives of Windsor*, *The Winter's Tale*, *The Tempest*, and at least parts of *2 Henry IV*, *Timon of Athens*, and *Cymbeline*. The texts in which he appears to have had a hand are all competently divided into acts and scenes, and in most cases (including *Measure for Measure*) they are followed by rosters of *dramatis personae*. At the same time they are marked by a proclivity to 'massed entry' stage directions (scene-commencing stage directions in which all the characters who will figure in a given sequence are listed at the outset rather than as they appear), and occasionally by mid-scene stage directions that are slightly out of sync with the timing the dialogue would suggest.

As a scribe, Crane seems to have been prone to heavier than usual punctuation. He frequently employs full stops, colons, and semicolons in places where modern usage would call either for commas or for no pointing at all. He tends to bracket parenthetical words, appositives, and exclamations. And he resorts to far more hyphens than we would opt for today (as illustrated by phrases such as 'Allhallond–Eve' at II.i.135, 'grosse-selues' at II.ii.88, 'tested-gold' at II.ii.150, 'Morne-praier' at II.iv.72, 'skyie-influences' at III.i.9, and 'moated-Grange' at III.i.279). In a way that anticipates current practice, he inserts apostrophes to mark the elision of words or syllables (as in ' 'Pray' for 'I pray' at II.ii.2, and ' 'Save' for 'God save' at II.ii.26). He also uses apostrophes to identify metrical contractions (as in spellings like 'I'am' in contexts where the conventions of iambic pentameter would call for a gliding sound with the metrical value of the single-syllable 'I'm').

Like other twentieth-century editions of *Measure for Measure*, the Everyman text disregards any features in the Folio printing that seem attributable solely to Crane's eccentricities as a scribe. Whenever a peculiar Folio form might be regarded as authentically Shakespearean, however, the Everyman text reproduces it. In accordance with this principle, Everyman retains a number of anomalies that other editions emend, among them such forms as *Meeter* (whose primary sense here is 'metre') in I.ii.23, *coheard* (where the context appears to call for 'cohered') in II.i.11, *Suborbs* (a thematically pertinent dialectal variant of 'suburbs') in II.i.66, *Prewyns* (a suggestive variant of 'prunes') in II.i.95, *fowl* (where we would expect 'foul') in II.ii.129, *recide* ('reside', but perhaps with a hint of the meanings associated with 'recede') in III.i.119, *wreakless* ('reckless') in IV.ii.153, *Shoo-Tie* ('shoe-tie') in IV.iii.19, *unpre-par'd* ('unprepar'd') in IV.iii.72, *reliver* (usually emended to 'redeliver') in IV.iv.6, and *marvaile* ('marvel') in V.i.383. In keeping with its customary procedure, Everyman also preserves such spellings as *abhominable* ('abominable'), *despight* ('despite'), *divelish* ('devilish'), *hether* and *thether* ('hither' and 'thither'), *prethee* ('prithee'), *shew* ('show'), *Sirrha* ('sirrah'), *travail'd* ('travell'd'), and *waigh* ('weigh').

Everyman retains most of the speech headings and other character designations to be found in the First Folio printing; among other things, this means that 'Mistress Over-done' is usually identified in the text (as opposed to the facing-page notes) as 'Bawd', and that 'Pompey' is usually identified in the text as 'Clown'. Meanwhile, Everyman preserves the act–scene divisions of the First Folio *Measure for Measure*. As a consequence, what most of today's editions treat as one scene (I.ii) appears in the Everyman text as two, I.ii and I.iii, with the result that Act I has five scenes rather than the four that have been customary since the nineteenth century. By the same token what most of today's editions divide into two scenes (III.i and III.ii) is treated in the Everyman text as the single unbroken scene, III.i, that appears in the Folio printing.

In a few instances Everyman emends the First Folio text. In the lines singled out below, the first entry, in boldface type, is the reading to be found in Everyman and (usually) in today's editions; the second entry is the reading (modernized in this listing) to be found in the First Folio.

I.i.	7	**that:** that, (Most of today's editions retain the Folio's comma.)
	15	**bear?** bear.
	34	**touch'd** tonch'd
I.ii.	35	**three-pil'd Piece** three pild-piece
I.iii.	10	**Liberty:** liberty
I.v.	5	**Sisters stood** Sisterstood (Most editions emend to 'sisterhood', following the 1632 Second Folio.)
	62	**Fast.** fast
II.i.	135	**All-hallond Eve** Allhallond-Eve
	170	**Right, Constable; what** right (Constable) what
II.ii.	38	**it?** it,
	71	**Vein** vain
	88	**gross Selves** gross-selves
	150	**tested Gold** tested-gold
II.iv.	72	**Morn Prayer** Morn-prayer
	77	**me be** be
	160	**Report** reporr
III.i.	9	**skyie Influences** skyie-influences
	279	**moated Grange** moated-Grange
	525	**Undertaking, there** undertaking. There
IV.i.	3	**Day,** day
	56	**Haste:** haste
IV.ii.	63	**yare** y'are
IV.iii.	105	**Form,** form.
IV.v.	6	**Flavius'** Flavia's
	10	**first.** first
V.i.	43	**Strange!** strange?
	55	**Absolute** absolute:
	206	**Enough** Enoug
	309	**Looker-on** looker on
	417	**with all** withall
	491	**yours.** yours

In a number of instances Everyman adheres to, or construes, the text of the First Folio *Measure for Measure* in ways that set it apart from other twentieth-century editions of the play. In the roster that follows, the first entry, in boldface type, is the reading to be found in the Everyman rendering of the text; the second entry is the reading adopted by some, if not most, modern editions. Unless otherwise specified, the first entry also represents the Folio reading.

I.i.	20	**Powre** power (so also in I.i.78, I.v.77, IV.ii.87, IV.iii.137)
	47	**Mettle** metal (so also in II.iv.49)
	64	**inforce** enforce
I.ii.	12	**Why?** Why,
	16	**ralish** relish
	23	**Meeter** metre
	26	**I** Ay (so also in II.i.117, 160, II.ii.148, IV.ii.37)
	36	**Lyst** list
	37	**pil'd** pilled
	48	**I have** 1 GENTLEMAN I have
	52	**Dollours** dollars *or* dolors
	103	**Burger** burgher
	118	**withdraw?** withdraw.
I.iii.	6	**Waight** weight (compare IV.ii.31, V.i.111)
	19	**Mortality** morality
	32	**onely** only (so also in I.iv.25, 50, II.iv.5, 124, 167, III.i.3, 161, 200, 246, 256, 522, IV.i.42)
	44	**strait** straight (so also in I.v.86, II.i.9)
	48	**inrolled** enrolled
	68	**Reason,** reason
I.iv	5	**, then** than
	10	**Youth,** youth
		Cost, cost
	14	**travail'd** travell'd
	20	**Weeds** steeds *or* jades
	27	**More** Becomes more
	43	**in it** *or* me
I.v.	7	**Ho?** Ho!
		Place. place!
	15	**him.** him. [*Exit.*]
	18	**steed** stead (so also in III.i.262)
	40	**thus,** thus:
	55	**Giving-out were** givings-out were *or* giving-out was
	79	**loose** lose (so also in III.i.7, V.i.72, 421)

II.i.
1 **Scar-crow** scarecrow
11 **coheard** coher'd
12 **our** your
20 **Sworn-twelve** sworn twelve
34 **to morrow** tomorrow (compare II.ii.7, 83, 84, 107,
145, 157, 160, II.iii.16, 36, 39, II.iv.169, III.i.59,
101, 105, 169, 465, 505, 580, IV.i.17, IV.ii.7, 24, 58,
69, 98, IV.iii.63, 68, 132, 145, 160)
39 **Brakes** breaks
66 **Suborbs** suburbs
70 **Sir?** sir,
95 **Prewyns** prunes (so also in II.i.107, 116)
185 **her,** her
204 **borne** born (so also in II.ii.99, III.i.194, 357, 384)

II.ii.
2 **'Pray** Pray
6 **for't?** for't!
26 **'Save** Save (so also in II.ii.162)
29 **'Please** Please
60 **longs** 'longs
98 **now** new
101 **here** ere
live live,
113 **never** ne'er
129 **fowl** foul (compare II.ii.174, II.iv.115, III.i.211)
154 **Sun rise** sunrise
160 **Prayers cross** prayer's cross'd
Hower hour
174 **fowlly** foully

II.iii.
25 **Offence-full** offenceful
29 **least** lest (so also in III.i.73)
39 **to morrow?** tomorrow!

II.iv.
9 **fear'd** sere *or* sear'd
49 **Mettle** metal (compare I.i.47)
54 **and** or
76 **so crafty** so, crafty *or* so craftily
81 **en-shield** enciel'd
95 **all-building** all-binding
115 **fowl** foul
124 **Fedary** feodary
143 **conceive** conceive,

III.i.
29 **thee, fire,** thee sire

31 **Sapego** serpigo
44 **ho?** how!
52 **them to hear me speak** me to hear them speak
63 **divelish** devilish
67 **Through** Though
87 **outward sainted** outward-sainted
89 **emmew** enew *or* ennew
92 **Prenzie,** precise (so also in III.i.95)
   Angelo? Angelo!
94 **damnest** damnedst
119 **bath** bathe
   recide reside (compare III.i.279)
127 **Perjury** penury
137 **think,** think?
211 **fowl** foul (compare II.ii.129)
220 **Oath** by oath
242 **World?** world!
243 **live?** live!
258 **Time** place
259 **Place** time
262 **steed** stead (compare I.v.18)
265 **here** hear
279 **recides** resides (compare III.i.119)
293 **Fox and** fox on
296 **'Bless** Bless
309 **Abhominable** abominable
310 **eat away** eat, array
334 **extracting** extracting it
340 **worse?** worse!
356–57 **Bawd borne** bawd-born
364 **Bondage** bondage;
   patiently: patiently,
403 **Generative** ungenerative
408 **Man?** man!
414 **never** have never
445 **dear** dearer
453 **Name?** name.
480 **Brown-bread** brown bread
491 **kind?** kind!
517 **Sea** See
522 **and as it** and it
540 **prepar'd?** prepar'd.
574 **Side?** side!

	578	things? things!
IV.i.	16	any body anybody
	17	to day; today?
	53	have so have *or* oft have *or* I have
	61	quest quests
	63	Dream dreams
IV.ii.	4	Wive's wife's
	31	waigh weigh (compare I.iii.6)
	48	CLOWN If If
	91	sildom seldom
	93	Hast haste (compare IV.v.11)
	100	Happely Happily
	105	DUKE PROVOST
		Lord's Lordship's
	106	PROVOST And And *or* DUKE And
	147	apparant apparent
	153	wreakless reckless
	183	Guide, guide: *or* guide.
	191	bar'd (bar'de F1) bared
IV.iii.	6	nine Score ninescore
	18	Forth-Light Forthright
	19	Shoo-Tie (shootie F1) Shoe-tie
	72	unpre-par'd unprepar'd
	94	yond yonder
	105	Weal- well-
	137	Wisdom, wisdom
	182	Medler medlar (compare V.i.144)
IV.iv.	2	manner, manner.
	6	reliver redeliver
	24	it? it!
	26	me? me!
	27	of a so
IV.v.	8	Valencius Valentius
	11	Varrius, Varrius;
IV.vi	4	vail veil
V.i.	13	we your we our *or* me your
	15	Curtesies courtesies
	32	here. hear!
	64	ere e'er (so also in V.i.348, 368)
	95	vild vile

111   **waigh'd** (compare I.iii.6)
131   **me?** me!
144   **Medler** meddler (compare IV.iii.182)
148   **villainously,** villainously;
158   **Noble Man** nobleman
167   **shew your Face** show her face
172   **Wife?** Wife!
210   **promis'd** promised
218   **affianced** affianc'd
273   **Gentlewoman,** gentlewoman
284   **How?** How!
290   **Fox;** fox?
305   **What?** What!
        Unjust? Unjust!
323   **Duke.** Duke?
325   **Sir:** Sir?
379   **Vassail** vassal
383   **marvaile** marvel
410   **Husband?** husband! *or* husband.
416   **Confutation** confiscation
532   **that** that's

MEASURE FOR MEASURE

NAMES OF THE ACTORS

Vincentio, DUKE OF VIENNA

ANGELO, the Deputy
ESCALUS, an ancient Lord
VARRIUS, a Gentleman, friend to the Duke

CLAUDIO, a young Gentleman
ISABELLA, Sister to Claudio
MARIANA, betrothed to Angelo
JULIET, beloved of Claudio

FRANCISCA, a Nun
LUCIO, a Fantastic
Two other like Gentlemen
PROVOST
FRIAR THOMAS
FRIAR PETER
JUSTICE

ELBOW, a simple Constable
FROTH, a foolish Gentleman
BAWD [MISTRESS OVER-DONE]
CLOWN [POMPEY], Servant to Mistress Over-done
ABHORSON, an Executioner
BARNARDINE, a dissolute Prisoner

LORDS
OFFICERS
CITIZENS
SERVANTS
A BOY

Note: The roster provided here is adpated from that supplied at the end of the text of *Measure for Measure* in the First Folio.

I.i.   The opening scene takes place at the Duke's palace in Vienna.

2   **Of . . . unfold**   to disclose the principles of good rule [to you].

3   **would . . . Discourse**   would make it appear that I am merely in love with the sound of my own voice.

4   **put to know**   compelled to acknowledge.
      Science   knowledge, understanding.

5   **Lists of all Advice**   limits (boundaries) of any counsel.

6   **Strength**   powers of wisdom and expertise.

7–8   **to . . . work**   [to entrust the dukedom] to your capability ('Sufficiency') and virtue ('Worth'), and let them perform their functions.

9–10   **Terms . . . Justice**   procedures for administering the laws justly. The Duke may also be referring to the terms (quarterly sessions) of the judicial calendar.

10   **y'are**   you are.
      pregnant in   filled with (informed about, expert in). Line 52 hints at the same 'quick' (life-filled) 'Condition'. In due course other senses of *pregnant* will become important.

11   **Art and Practice**   theoretical understanding and practical experience.

12   **our Commission**   my formal charge to you (a written statement of the responsibilities I leave in your hands). The Duke employs the royal plural (symbolic of a ruler's position as the epitome of his realm).

13   **warp**   deviate (literally, twist, distort, or go at cross purposes).

15   **Figure of us**   image or representative of me as Duke.
      bear   carry, (a) as a posture or 'bearing', (b) as an ensign carrying a banner, and (c) as a coin or piece of wax stamped with the royal insignia.

16   **special Soul**   careful deliberation (to the depths of my being).

17   **Elected . . . supply**   selected him to preside in my absence. Here *supply* means 'fill' or 'substitute for'.

18   **Lent him our Terror**   bestowed on him the awe inspired by my office, the power to instil fear by enforcing the laws vigorously.

ACT I

Scene 1

Enter Duke, Escalus, Lords.

DUKE   Escalus.

ESCALUS   My Lord.

DUKE   Of Government the Properties to unfold
Would seem in me t' affect Speech and Discourse,
Since I am put to know that your own Science
Exceeds in that the Lists of all Advice   5
My Strength can give you. Then no more remains
But that: to your Sufficiency, as your Worth is able,
And let them work. The Nature of our People,
Our City's Institutions, and the Terms
For Common Justice y'are as pregnant in   10
As Art and Practice hath enriched any
That we remember. There is our Commission,
From which we would not have you warp.
   – Call hither,
I say, bid come before us, Angelo.

                                    [Exit a Lord.]

– What Figure of us think you he will bear?   15
For you must know, we have with special Soul
Elected him our Absence to supply,
Lent him our Terror, dress'd him with our Love,

19   **his Deputation**   his position as my deputy (substitute).
        Organs   instruments, means. Subsequent events will give this
        word ironic implications. The same will be true of *Figure* and
        bear (line 15), *supply* (line 17), *undergo* (line 22), *come,*
        know, Pleasure (line 25), *go forth* (line 33), *finely touch'd*
        (line 34), *Part* (line 40), and *at full* (line 42).

20   **Powre**   power. But elsewhere in Shakespeare this spelling can
        also mean 'pour' (see *Macbeth*, I.v.28, IV.i.18), and that sense
        anticipates the imagery of lines 28–35; compare line 78, and
        see IV.iii.137.

22   **undergo . . . Honour**   have such bounteous power and dignity
        placed on him.

25   **Pleasure**   will, wishes.

26   **Character**   literally, engraving or inscription.

28   **Belongings**   possessions, qualities. The Duke echoes the
        Parables of the Talents (Matthew 25:14–30) and the Candle
        (Luke 8:16–18).

29   **so proper**   in so proprietary a way as to allow you. Here
        proper, like *own*, refers to that which pertains to the
        individual self; but it is also applicable to that which is
        'suitable' or 'correct'.

33   **'twere all alike**   it would be the same.

34–35 **Spirits . . . Issues**   human spirits are endowed with fine qualities
        not to spend upon themselves but to 'go forth' (line 33) and
        bear fruit. The Duke alludes to the 'virtue', the 'Strength' (line
        6), that went forth from Jesus to heal the woman with 'an
        issue of blood' who 'touched' him (Luke 8:40–48). Here *fine*
        can mean 'refined'. *Issues* can refer both to currency (compare
        lines 15, 26, 47–49) and to the seminal emissions that
        produce issue (offspring). And *touch'd* can mean 'tested', as in
        lines 47–49 and in II.ii.150.

36   **Scruple**   a tiny measurement (one twenty-fourth of an ounce).

37–38 **determines . . . Creditor**   allocates to herself the benefits that
        accrue to a lender. Those benefits include both gratitude and
        profitable productivity (line 39).

40   **my . . . advertise**   deliver and disseminate my advice in his own
        voice.

And given his Deputation all the Organs
Of our own Powre. What think you of it?   20
ESCALUS   If any in Vienna be of Worth
  To undergo such ample Grace and Honour,
  It is Lord Angelo.

Enter Angelo.

DUKE   Look where he comes.
ANGELO   Always Obedient to your Grace's Will,
  I come to know your Pleasure.
DUKE   Angelo: 25
  There is a kind of Character in thy Life
  That to th' Observer doth thy History
  Fully unfold. Thy Self and thy Belongings .
  Are not thine own so proper as to waste
  Thy Self upon thy Virtues, they on thee.   30
  Heaven doth with us as we with Torches do,
  Not light them for themselves: for if our
    Virtues
  Did not go forth of us, 'twere all alike
  As if we had them not. Spirits are not finely
    touch'd
  But to fine Issues; nor Nature never lends   35
  The smallest Scruple of her Excellence
  But like a thrifty Goddess she determines
  Her self the Glory of a Creditor,
  Both Thanks and Use. But I do bend my Speech
  To one that can my Part in him advertise.   40

42   **In . . . Self**   While I'm away, act as if you were the Duke himself.

43–44 **Mortality . . . Heart**   The Duke means 'you have it in your power to execute or show leniency to lawbreakers'. In time, however, this sentence will apply to Angelo in a way he little anticipates.

45   **first in Question**   entitled to initial consideration for this role. **Secondary**   second in command; support.

47   **Mettle**   virtue; but with wordplay on *metal* (here a stamped coin). Lines 47–49 build upon the figures in lines 15, 26, 34–35.

50   **leaven'd**   thoroughly deliberated (like slow-rising, yeasted dough). *Figure* (line 48) echoes line 15.

52   **of . . . Condition**   of such a pregnant (pressing) urgency. Compare line 10.

53   **prefers it self**   gives precedence (priority) to its own concerns. **unquestion'd**   unconsidered, unattended to. Compare line 45.

55   **importune**   demand (literally, beseech admission to a 'port' or door). See the note to line 63.

57   **befall**   happen to. The Duke's phrasing will prove apt.

60   **bring . . . way**   escort you some distance on your route.

63   **any Scruple**   the smallest concern or doubt (compare line 36). **Scope**   breadth and depth of oversight (authority).

64   **inforce**   enforce, execute. But *inforce* can also mean 'coerce' (literally, 'force in'), and *qualify* (adapt or modify) can refer to more than one way of applying 'the Laws / As to your Soul seems good'.

66   **privily**   privately, secretly (so as to avoid notice). The Duke's phrasing anticipates V.i.267–69, where *privately* relates to the privates; it also looks forward to the play's later references to the mysteriousness of a magistrate who can be described as 'the old fantastical Duke of Dark Corners' (IV.iii.161–63).

67   **stage . . . Eyes**   display myself to them (a line first spoken, of course, by an actor staging himself in the theatre).

68   **Though it do well**   either (a) though it serves a purpose [to appear in public], or (b) though it is gratifying [to hear their greetings].

Hold therefore, Angelo:
In our Remove be thou at full our self.
Mortality and Mercy in Vienna
Live in thy Tongue and Heart. Old Escalus,
Though first in Question, is thy Secondary.   45
Take thy Commission.
ANGELO   Now, good my Lord,
  Let there be some more Test made of my Mettle
  Before so Noble and so Great a Figure
  Be stamp'd upon it.
DUKE   No more Evasion.
  We have with a leaven'd and prepared Choice   50
  Proceeded to you: therefore take your Honours.
  Our Haste from hence is of so quick Condition
  That it prefers it self, and leaves unquestion'd
  Matters of needful Value. We shall write to you,
  As Time and our Concernings shall importune,   55
  How it goes with us, and do look to know
  What doth befall you here. So fare you well:
  To th' hopeful Execution do I leave you
  Of your Commissions.
ANGELO   Yet give leave, my Lord,
  That we may bring you something on the way.   60
DUKE   My Haste may not admit it,
  Nor need you, on mine Honour, have to do
  With any Scruple. Your Scope is as mine own,
  So to inforce or qualify the Laws
  As to your Soul seems good. Give me your Hand,   65
  I'll privily away. I love the People,
  But do not like to stage me to their Eyes.
  Though it do well, I do not relish well

69   **Aves vehement**   enthusiastic acclaim. *Ave* means 'hail' in Latin, and it was associated with 'Ave Caesar' (a salute to any 'Caesar' or ruler).

70   **safe Discretion**   secure judgement.

71   **affect it**   like it (excessively) and seek it out. Compare line 3.

76   **free**   frank, candid; unhindered.

77   **look . . . Place**   learn what the limits of my authority are to be. Escalus probably wishes (a) to read the 'Commission' (line 12) the Duke has given him, and (b) to hear what 'Powre' (line 78) Angelo plans to delegate to his subordinate or 'Secondary' (line 45).

82   **Touching that Point**   concerning that matter. *Touching* echoes lines 34–35. *Point* anticipates II.i.15 and III.i.255–56.

I.ii   This scene occurs either at or near Mistress Over-done's inn in Vienna.

2   **Composition**   an agreement or treaty.

3   **fall upon**   will join in making war upon. *Fall* echoes I.i.57.

7   **conclud'st**   Lucio plays on two senses of *conclude*: (a) finish, bring to a close, and (b) settle, resolve, bring to an agreement.
    sanctimonious   hypocritically devout (wrapped in sanctity). Compare *The Tempest*, IV.i.16, where the word means 'holy' or 'sanctified'.

9   **Commandements**   a common (four-syllable) Renaissance spelling for *commandments*.
    Table   tablet, register.

11   **raz'd**   erased, 'scrap'd' (line 9). Compare V.i.13.

Their loud Applause and Aves vehement;
Nor do I think the man of safe Discretion   70
That does affect it. Once more fare you well.
ANGELO   The Heavens give Safety to your Purposes.
ESCALUS   Lead forth, and bring you back in
   Happiness.
DUKE   I thank you, fare you well.   *Exit.*
ESCALUS   I shall desire you, Sir, to give me
   leave   75
To have free Speech with you. And it concerns
   me
To look into the Bottom of my Place:
A Powre I have, but of what Strength and Nature
I am not yet instructed.
ANGELO   'Tis so with me. Let us withdraw together,   80
And we may soon our Satisfaction have
Touching that Point.
ESCALUS   I'll wait upon your Honour.
                                          Exeunt.

Scene 2

Enter Lucio, and two other Gentlemen.

LUCIO   If the Duke, with the other Dukes, come
   not to Composition with the King of Hungary,
   why then all the Dukes fall upon the King.
1 GENTLEMAN   Heaven grant us its Peace, but
   not the King of Hungary's.   5
2 GENTLEMAN   Amen.
LUCIO   Thou conclud'st like the sanctimonious
   Pirate that went to Sea with the Ten
   Commandements, but scrap'd one out of the Table.
2 GENTLEMAN   'Thou shalt not Steal'?   10

12–14 **to . . . Functions** whose effect would be to prevent the pirates from doing their jobs. Compare I.ii.116–17 of *1 Henry IV*, where Falstaff says that ' 'tis no Sin for a Man to labour in his Vocation' and uses 1 Corinthians 7:20 to override the commandment forbidding theft (Exodus 20:15).

14 **put forth** embark. Compare I.i.4, 32–35, 73.

15–16 **Thanksgiving before Meat** prayer of thanksgiving before a meal ('Grace', line 21, echoing I.i.22, 24). *Meat* refers to any kind of food.

16 **ralish** relish, savour.
Petition request, plea. The First Gentleman probably refers to prayers such as 'God save our Queen and Realm, and send us peace in Christ'. He may also be alluding to 'the peacemakers' blessed in Matthew 5:9.

23 **In Meeter?** In metrically versified grace? The Folio's *Meeter* ('metre') may involve a bawdy pun, perhaps one that plays on *Grace* as the name of a prostitute who was *said* ('done') 'a dozen times'.

24 **Proportion** form (with wordplay on 'metre', another meaning of *Proportion*).

26 **I** either (a) I [think], or (b) Ay.

26–27 **despight of all Controversy** notwithstanding all the theological debates about the significance and operations of Divine Grace.

30–31 **there . . . us** a variation on 'we were cut from the same cloth'.

32–33 **the Lists and the Velvet** the boundaries or selvages (plain border strips of a bolt of cloth) and the velvet to be used for a gentleman's garment. *Velvet* was a term for the female genitalia, and by extension for a whore ('French Velvet', line 38), if not a whoremonger. Compare *Love's Labour's Lost*, III.i.201–8. *List* probably alludes to the male member.

35 **three-pil'd Piece** both (a) a piece of cloth with a pile (nap) of triple thickness, and (b) a 'Piece' (whore) 'pil'd' under three thicknesses of men. The Gentleman goes on to pun on *pill'd* (made bald), a state that resulted from the 'French disease' (syphilis), alluded to in line 38.

36 **Lyst** list (possibly punning on *lyest*, with reference to sexual 'lying').

LUCIO   Ay, that he raz'd.

1 GENTLEMAN   Why? 'twas a Commandement to
command the Captain and all the rest from their
Functions: they put forth to Steal. There's
not a Soldier of us all that in the Thanksgiving   15
before Meat do ralish the Petition well that
prays for Peace.

2 GENTLEMAN   I never heard any Soldier
dislike it.

LUCIO   I believe thee: for I think thou never   20
wast where Grace was said.

2 GENTLEMAN   No? A dozen times at least.

1 GENTLEMAN   What? In Meeter?

LUCIO   In any Proportion, or in any Language.

1 GENTLEMAN   I think, or in any Religion.   25

LUCIO   I, why not? Grace is Grace, despite of
all Controversy: as, for example, thou thy
self art a wicked Villain, despight of all
Grace.

1 GENTLEMAN   Well: there went but a   30
pair of Shears between us.

LUCIO   I grant: as there may between the Lists
and the Velvet. Thou art the List.

1 GENTLEMAN   And thou the Velvet; thou art
good Velvet; thou'rt a three-pil'd Piece, I   35
warrant thee. I had as lief be a Lyst of an

37   **English Kersey**   a plain woollen cloth (here symbolizing an
       Englishman).

38   **feelingly**   penetratingly, to the point. Compare *King Lear*,
       IV.vi.147.

42   **drink after thee**   drink from the same cup as you (to avoid
       contracting the painful mouth lesions your venereal disease
       has 'Tainted' you with).

S.D.   **Bawd**   madam (proprietess of a bawdy-house, a brothel). We
       later learn (II.i.211) that the Bawd's name is Mistress
       Over-done.

47   **Madam Mitigation**   a madam who mitigates (relieves) desire.
       Many editions reassign Lucio's second sentence ('I . . . to – ')
       to the First Gentleman, assuming that Lucio would not admit
       to having purchased any 'Diseases' (both prostitutes and the
       infections they carry) himself.

52   **Dollours**   both (a) dollars (coins from Germany or Spain), and
       (b) dolours, pains. Compare *The Tempest*, II.i.14–18.

55   **French Crown**   both (a) a French coin, and (b) the bald head
       resulting from the 'French disease'. See lines 34–42.

56   **figuring**   (a) reckoning up, counting, (b) attributing by means of
       figures of speech, and (c) imagining. Compare *Figure* in I.i.15,
       46–49.

57   **Sound**   'Free', not 'Tainted' by infection (line 46); sounded
       (plumbed, tested) and proven to be in sound health. See the
       note to I.i.34–35. In line 59 Lucio gives the word another
       implication: sounding (resounding or echoing).

59–60 **Thy . . . Hollow**   Another name for syphilis was 'Neapolitan
       Bone-ache' (*Troilus and Cressida*, II.iii.21–22). *Impiety* here
       means 'sinfulness', wanton disregard of the teaching that
       one's body is to be kept pure of corruption, since it is 'the
       temple of the Holy Ghost' (see 1 Corinthians 3:15–20).

61   **How now**   a greeting to Mistress Over-done.

62   **profound Sciatica**   deep pain. Sciatica, an ailment of the hips
       and thighs, was once associated with syphilis; the term now
       applies to neuritis.

67   **Marry**   indeed. This word originally referred to the Virgin
       Mary. Here, as frequently elsewhere, Shakespeare employs it
       in a context that relates to the sense *marry* normally carries.

English Kersey as be pil'd, as thou art pil'd,
for a French Velvet. Do I speak feelingly now?

LUCIO   I think thou dost, and indeed with most
painful Feeling of thy Speech. I will, out of   40
thine own Confession, learn to begin thy Health;
but, whilst I live, forget to drink after thee.

1 GENTLEMAN   I think I have done my self
wrong, have I not?

2 GENTLEMAN   Yes, that thou hast, whether   45
thou art Tainted or Free.

Enter Bawd.

LUCIO   Behold, behold, where Madam Mitigation
comes. I have purchas'd as many Diseases under
her Roof as come to —

2 GENTLEMAN   To what, I pray?   50

LUCIO   Judge.

2 GENTLEMAN   To three thousand Dollours a
Year.

1 GENTLEMAN   Ay, and more.

LUCIO   A French Crown more.   55

1 GENTLEMAN   Thou art always figuring Diseases
in me; but thou art full of Error, I am Sound.

LUCIO   Nay, not, as one would say, Healthy; but
so Sound as things that are Hollow. Thy Bones
are Hollow; Impiety has made a Feast of thee.   60

1 GENTLEMAN   — How now, which of your Hips
has the most profound Sciatica?

BAWD   Well, well: there's one yonder arrested,
and carried to Prison, was worth five thousand
of you all.   65

2 GENTLEMAN   Who's that, I pray thee?

BAWD   Marry Sir, that's Claudio, Signior Claudio.

72 **after . . . Fooling** enough of (let's put behind us) all this levity.

77 **since** ago.

78 **precise** faithful, reliable. Compare I.iv.50.

80–81 **something . . . purpose** somewhat close to the remarks we exchanged to similar effect. The audience has not heard this 'Speech'.

82–83 **agreeing . . . Proclamation** in accord with what one might expect, given 'the Proclamation' (another subject about which the audience has yet heard nothing).

86 **Sweat** probably the sweating of syphilitics being treated in heated powdering tubs.
   the Gallows men being hanged.

87 **Custom-shrunk** left with a shortage of customers.

90 **done** committed. The Clown (Pompey, as we learn in II.i.225) gives the verb a copulative sense. See the note to line 23.

93 **Groping . . . River** Engaging in illicit 'fishing'. Here *peculiar* probably means 'private' in both a sexual and a legal sense (pertaining to fishing where it is forbidden without authorization); but the word could also refer to 'one's own' (in this case Claudio's betrothed), and thus to an act that would not normally be subject to prosecution. See the notes to I.i.29, 66.

95 **with Maid** with child (*Maid* here referring to the offspring of the skate, a flat saltwater fish with a long tail). The Clown is playing on *made* (synonymous with 'done', line 90) to emphasize that Claudio has made a 'Woman' out of a 'Maid' (virgin).

99 **Houses** bawdy-houses ('Houses of Resort', line 105).
   Suburbs residential districts outside the city walls. Southwark, the London suburb south of the Thames, was outside the jurisdiction of the City and was as notorious for its brothels as for theatres like the Globe.

1 GENTLEMAN   Claudio to Prison? 'Tis not so.

BAWD   Nay, but I know 'tis so: I saw him arrested,
saw him carried away; and which is more, within   70
these three Days his Head to be chopp'd off.

LUCIO   But, after all this Fooling, I would not
have it so. Art thou sure of this?

BAWD   I am too sure of it: and it is for getting
Madam Julietta with Child.   75

LUCIO   Believe me, this may be: he promis'd to
meet me two Hours since, and he was ever
precise in Promise-keeping.

2 GENTLEMAN   Besides, you know, it draws
something near to the Speech we had to such a   80
purpose.

1 GENTLEMAN   But most of all agreeing with
the Proclamation.

LUCIO   Away: let's go learn the Truth of it.

Exit [with Gentlemen].

BAWD   Thus, what with the War, what with the   85
Sweat, what with the Gallows, and what with
Poverty, I am Custom-shrunk.

Enter Clown.

– How now? What's the News with you?

CLOWN   Yonder Man is carried to Prison.

BAWD   Well: what has he done?   90

CLOWN   A Woman.

BAWD   But what's his Offence?

CLOWN   Groping for Trouts, in a peculiar River.

BAWD   What? Is there a Maid with Child by him?

CLOWN   No: but there's a Woman with Maid by him: 95
you have not heard of the Proclamation, have
you?

BAWD   What Proclamation, Man?

CLOWN   All Houses in the Suburbs of Vienna must
be pluck'd down.   100

102   **stand for Seed**   remain standing (uncut, not 'pluck'd down') to
       provide seed for the next growing season. The Clown puns on
       another kind of 'stand' (erection) that issues forth in 'Seed'.
       Compare I.iii.71, and see the notes to I.i.19, 34–35.

103   **Burger**   burgher, citizen.

108   **indeed**   both (a) indeed, and (b) in deed, as in lines 39–40 (see
       the note to line 90, and compare *Othello*, III.iii.98–100, and
       Hamlet, I.ii.178).

110   **Counsellors**   The Clown dignifies Mistress Over-done's
       professional services by comparing them to those of other
       kinds of advisors. He probably means 'Coun-sellers', with
       Coun- playing on *cunnus* (the Latin term for the female
       pudendum) and functioning in the same way as *count*, *con-*,
       com- and similar word-forms elsewhere in Shakespeare.
       Compare *Hamlet*, III.ii.122, and *All's Well That Ends Well*,
       III.vii.5, 32, IV.iii.70–73.

111   **change your Place**   both (a) relocate your place of business, and
       (b) exchange (sell) your 'place'. Compare I.iii.45 and II.iv.93.
       Change echoes lines 108–9.

113   **Tapster**   barman, bartender (here a euphemism for 'pimp').

114–   **worn . . . Service**   The Clown implies that the 'Service' Mistress
15   Over-done has provided for the 'Commonwealth' (line 109) is
       comparable to military service in terms of the sacrifices it
       requires. The affliction he refers to may allude to the
       proverbial image of blindfolded Cupid (a symbol sometimes
       displayed outside Elizabethan brothels, as Benedick notes in
       Much Ado About Nothing, I.i.259–63); but it probably also
       refers to the debilities brought on by venereal disease.

116   **considered**   given special favour. See the note to line 110.
       Withdraw (line 118) recalls I.i.80–82; in both passages it
       hints at the 'Satisfaction' that issues from 'Touching that
       Point' at the 'Bottom of' a 'Place' (I.i.77–82). See the note to
       I.iii.45.

I.iii   The scene shifts to the street outside Mistress Over-done's inn.
       Most editions ignore the Folio's scene division and continue
       the previous scene. But the *Exeunt* at I.ii.120 indicates that
       the Bawd and the Clown 'withdraw' (line 118) to clear the
       stage momentarily.

4   **by Special Charge**   by explicit order.

BAWD   And what shall become of those in the City?

CLOWN   They shall stand for Seed. They had gone
down too, but that a wise Burger put in for
them.

BAWD   But shall all our Houses of Resort in the   105
Suburbs be pull'd down?

CLOWN   To the Ground, Mistress.

BAWD   Why here's a Change indeed in the
Commonwealth: what shall become of me?

CLOWN   Come, fear not you: good Counsellors lack   110
no Clients. Though you change your Place, you
need not change your Trade: I'll be your
Tapster still. Courage, there will be Pity
taken on you: you that have worn your Eyes
almost out in the Service, you will be   115
considered.

BAWD   What's to do here, Thomas Tapster? Let's
withdraw?

CLOWN   Here comes Signior Claudio, led by the
Provost to Prison; and there's Madam Juliet.   120

Exeunt.

Scene 3

*Enter Provost, Claudio, Juliet, Officers, Lucio,
and two Gentlemen.*

CLAUDIO   Fellow, why dost thou show me thus to
th' World?
Bear me to Prison, where I am committed.

PROVOST   I do it not in Evil Disposition,
But from Lord Angelo by Special Charge.

5   **Demigod**   an allusion to the commonplace that a ruler is God's deputy.

6   **by Waight**   in accordance with the weight of our purchases (compare I.ii.48–49). *Waight*, a common Shakespearean spelling for *weight*, sometimes plays on *wait*; for his transgression, Claudio will now 'wait upon' Angelo's 'Honour' (I.i.82).

6–8   **Make . . . Just**   Claudio's phrasing echoes Romans 9:15–18, 'I will have mercy on whom I will have mercy . . . Therefore hath he mercy on whom he will have mercy, and on whom he will he hardeneth.' Claudio means that if Heaven's 'Authority' chooses to make us 'pay down' (put on the scales of Justice) the full 'Waight' of punishment for 'our Offence', he is simply doing what 'The Words of Heaven' declare to be 'Just'.

11   **Surfeit . . . Fast**   overindulgence leads to strict dieting. Compare line 29.

12   **Scope**   'Liberty' (line 10), freedom (as in I.iv.35). But compare I.i.63, where the word means 'supervision' or 'rule'. Other meanings of *scope* are also pertinent here, among them (a) aim, intent, (b) pursuit of an object of desire, (c) skill in aiming or shooting, (d) reach or range, and (e) power or potency. *Use* echoes I.i.35–39.

14   **ravin**   consume ravenously (greedily).
     their proper Bane   poison especially designed for them. *Bane* can also mean 'curse' (ban), 'evil', or 'destruction'; compare *Hamlet*, III.ii.283. *Proper* recalls I.i.28–30.

18   **I . . . lief**   I would just as willingly.

19   **Foppery of Freedom**   foolishness that freedom permits.

26   **look'd after**   watched and apprehended (an echo of the sense of *Scope* introduced in I.i.63). Lucio's phrasing emphasizes that Claudio is not being 'look'd after' (watched over and cared for) in the positive sense.

27   **true Contract**   public declaration of intent to marry. Such a 'Contract' was legally binding (and thus amounted to a 'true' marriage), even though the Church called for a religious rite before bestowing its full blessing on any consummation of the union. *Stands* (line 26) echoes I.ii.102.

CLAUDIO   Thus can the Demigod Authority   5
  Make us pay down, for our Offence, by Waight
  The Words of Heaven; on whom it will, it will,
  On whom it will not, so; yet still 'tis Just.
LUCIO   Why how now, Claudio? Whence comes this
    Restraint?
CLAUDIO   From too much Liberty, my Lucio, Liberty: 10
  As Surfeit is the Father of much Fast,
  So every Scope by the Immoderate Use
  Turns to Restraint. Our Natures do pursue,
  Like Rats that ravin down their proper Bane,
  A Thirsty Evil, and when we Drink, we Die.   15
LUCIO   If I could speak so wisely under an Arrest,
  I would send for certain of my Creditors; and
  yet, to say the truth, I had as lief have the
  Foppery of Freedom as the Mortality of
  Imprisonment. What's thy Offence, Claudio?   20
CLAUDIO   What but to speak of would offend again.
LUCIO   What, is't Murder?
CLAUDIO   No.
LUCIO   Lechery?
CLAUDIO   Call
  It so.
PROVOST   Away, Sir, you must go.
CLAUDIO   One Word, good Friend. – Lucio, a Word
    with you.
LUCIO   A Hundred, if they'll do you any good.   25
  Is Lechery so look'd after?
CLAUDIO   Thus stands it
  With me. Upon a true Contract I got
  Possession of Julietta's Bed.
  You know the Lady; she is fast my Wife,

30–31 **Save . . . Order** except that we have yet to perform the
ceremony and make the public announcement required to
conform with 'outward Order'.

32 **Propagation of a Dow'r** the producing (literally, 'breeding') of
a dowry (the property or money provided to a bride's
husband). Here as elsewhere, *onely* means 'only'.

33 **Friends** parents or other relatives.

35 **made . . . us** persuaded them to consent to our marriage.

36 **mutual Entertainment** deeply exchanged 'hospitality'.
Compare *The Tempest*, I.ii.463, II.i.14–18.

37 **Character too gross** handwriting or stamping that is too large,
obvious, coarse, and rude. Compare I.i.26, 46–48. *Gross*
anticipates II.ii.88, II.iv.83.

40 **Whether . . . Newness** whether because of his infatuation with
the brilliance of his newly bestowed glory.

42 **A Horse . . . ride** Claudio's image suggests that Angelo is a
stern horseman who wishes to deploy 'the Spur' to break the
will of a spirited steed (with analogies to a man 'taming' a
woman). He goes on to suggest that Angelo simply wants to
earn a 'Name' (reputation) for 'command'.

44 **strait** (a) constrictingly (strictly and painfully), (b) straight
(unbendingly, sharply), and (c) straightway (immediately). See
the note to I.v.86.

45 **in his Place** simply an aspect of the office itself (rather than a
characteristic of the tyrant who currently 'fills it up', line 46).
Compare I.i.17, 77, and I.ii.111. Like *Spur*, *Place* can carry
genital implications, and by II.iv.93 those implications will be
protruding themselves in ways that cannot be ignored.

47 **stagger in** both (a) stumble over (unable to resolve my
questions), and (b) stagger like a spent horse.

48 **Awakes . . . Penalties** wakes up and applies to me all the
punishments called for in an 'Act' (law) that has been lying
asleep on the books. The Folio's *inrolled* (enrolled, legally
inscribed and registered) suggests the kind of posture that
'fills' a receptive female 'Place'; meanwhile *Penalties* hints at
the phallic sense *Pen* conveys in *The Merchant of Venice*,
V.i.236–37, and in *All's Well That Ends Well*, II.i.69–78.
Awakes anticipates II.ii.95.

Save that we do the Denunciation lack   30
Of outward Order. This we came not to
Onely for Propagation of a Dow'r
Remaining in the Coffer of her Friends,
From whom we thought it meet to hide our Love
Till Time had made them for us. But it chances   35
The Stealth of our most mutual Entertainment
With Character too gross is writ on Juliet.
LUCIO   With Child, perhaps?
CLAUDIO   Unhappily even so.
And the new Deputy, now for the Duke,
Whether it be the Fault and Glimpse of Newness,   40
Or whether that the Body Public be
A Horse whereon the Governor doth ride,
Who, newly in the Seat, that it may know
He can command, lets it strait feel the Spur:
Whether the Tyranny be in his Place   45
Or in his Eminence that fills it up,
I stagger in. But this new Governor
Awakes me all th' inrolled Penalties
Which have, like unscour'd Armour, hung by th' Wall

50 **Zodiacs** years (the time required for the passing of each zodiac). Compare I.iv.21, where the Duke mentions 'fourteen Years' of leniency.

55 **tickle** precariously. See the note to *Troilus and Cressida*, II.ii.9. *Stands* (line 54) echoes line 26.

59 **Service** favour. Compare I.ii.115.

60 **should . . . enter** is scheduled to enter a convent.

61 **Approbation** 'probation' (V.i.73) or novitiate; status as a novice in a convent.

64 **strict Deputy** stringent Deputy. See the note to line 44.
her . . . him try him (appeal to him) in her own person. *Assay* (test, attempt) recalls I.i.34–35, 47–49, I.ii.57.

66 **prone . . . Dialect** stationary and silent discourse. Claudio refers to a type of non-verbal communication that results solely from his sister's maidenly charisma (the charm that constitutes a special gift of her 'Youth'). The word *prone*, which usually means 'lying down', derives from the Latin word *pronus*, one of whose meanings is 'projecting forward'. Compare I.i.34–35, 80–82, I.ii.116 (see note), I.iii.44, 48.

67 **move men** Claudio means 'persuade men to relent'; but his phrasing in lines 65–69 suggests that her 'speechless Dialect' may appeal to more than the Deputy's sense of pity.
prosperous Art the kind of skill that promises and then propagates success (see the note to line 32). The word *Art* is often associated with the use of charms or magic, and Claudio's phrasing thus looks forward to Prospero's 'Art' in *The Tempest*. Meanwhile *prosperous* is a word whose *pro-* prefix hints at the same kind of 'jutting before' implicit in *prone*. Compare III.i.274, and see *Troilus and Cressida*, II.ii.129–37, 189.

68 **Reason** logic. But *Reason* was pronounced like *raisin* in Shakespeare's time, and here that suggests the 'raising' of a man susceptible to Isabella's power to 'move' him and arouse 'great Hope' (lines 67, 65). For related wordplay on *Reason*, see *The Merchant of Venice*, III.v.43–44, and *All's Well That Ends Well*, I.iii.29–40.

So long that nineteen Zodiacs have gone round   50
And none of them been worn; and for a Name
Now puts the drowsy and neglected Act
Freshly on me. 'Tis surely for a Name.
LUCIO   I warrant it is. And thy Head stands so
tickle on thy Shoulders that a Milkmaid, if she   55
be in love, may sigh it off. Send after the
Duke, and appeal to him.
CLAUDIO   I have done so, but he's not to be
        found.
I prethee, Lucio, do me this kind Service.
This day my Sister should the Cloister enter,   60
And there receive her Approbation.
Acquaint her with the Danger of my State;
Implore her, in my Voice, that she make Friends
To the strict Deputy; bid her self assay him,
I have great Hope in that; for in her Youth   65
There is a prone and speechless Dialect
Such as move men; beside, she hath prosperous
        Art
When she will play with Reason, and Discourse,
And well she can persuade.
LUCIO   I pray she may:

70–71 **the Encouragement . . . Imposition** the encouragement of others in plights similar to yours, who otherwise would be subject to similar punishment. *Imposition* (accusation) literally means 'placing something in or on'. It thus relates to *stand* (line 71, echoing line 54) and *Tick-tack* (line 74), a game in which pegs are fitted into holes. Compare the phrasing in I.i.16–20, 46–49, 63–65, I.iii.40–47.

I.iv This scene takes place in a monastery in Vienna.

1 **throw away** dismiss, disregard.

2 **dribbling . . . Love** The Duke is alluding to Cupid's arrow, here depicted as too feeble to reach or penetrate its mark. But *dribbling Dart* can also refer to a man's 'arrow'. Compare the 'wayward Boy' and 'Dan Cupid' imagery in *Love's Labour's Lost*, III.i.180–210, and the 'drivelling Love' simile in *Romeo and Juliet*, II.iii.98–100.

3 **Bosom** breast (here referring specifically to the heart). Again the Duke's phrasing suggests additional possibilities; *bosom* can refer to the womb, and by extension to the seat of erotic desire (as in II.ii.137 and in *King Lear*, IV.v.25–26, V.i.10–13), and a 'Complete Bosom' is one that is proof (armed) against invasion by sexual temptation.

5 **Grave and Wrinkled** in keeping with the solemnity and wisdom of age. The Duke implies that he is too 'shrunk' (I.ii.87) by age to be aroused by burning passion.
   Aims and Ends desires and goals (with allusion to the genital 'arrows' and 'targets' of hot-blooded young people). Here *then* has 'than' as its primary meaning, but in time 'then' will prove pertinent to a 'Purpose' the Duke little imagines himself susceptible to at this point in the action.

8 **the Life Removed** a secluded, contemplative way of life. Compare *The Tempest*, I.ii.72–77, 89–97.

9 **held . . . Assemblies** placed little value on being in public gatherings. See I.i.66–71.

10 **Where . . . keeps** where lavish-spending young gallants display themselves with senseless luxury. Here *Bravery* refers to vainglorious ostentation.

12 **Stricture** strict self-discipline. Compare *strict* in line 19, and see I.iii.64.
   firm Abstinence resolute self-denial. In other contexts *firm* means 'stiff'. Compare I.iii.39–47.

as well for the Encouragement of the like, which   70
else would stand under grievous Imposition, as
for the enjoying of thy Life, who I would be
sorry should be thus foolishly lost at a Game
of Tick-tack. I'll to her.
CLAUDIO   I thank you, good Friend Lucio.   75
LUCIO   Within two Hours.
CLAUDIO   – Come, Officer, away.
Exeunt.

Scene 4

Enter Duke and Friar Thomas.

DUKE   No: holy Father, throw away that Thought,
Believe not that the dribbling Dart of Love
Can pierce a Complete Bosom. Why I desire thee
To give me Secret Harbour hath a Purpose
More Grave and Wrinkled, then the Aims and Ends   5
Of burning Youth.
FRIAR   May your Grace speak of it?
DUKE   My holy Sir, none better knows than you
How I have ever lov'd the Life Removed,
And held in Idle Price to haunt Assemblies
Where Youth, and Cost, witless Bravery keeps.   10
I have deliver'd to Lord Angelo
(A Man of Stricture and firm Abstinence)

13   **My . . . Place**   all the power that resides in my position. *Place* echoes I.iii.45.

14   **travail'd**   travelled.

15   **strew'd**   spread, sown (like seeds scattered on a field). Compare I.ii.102.

20   **Bits**   the metal mouthpieces on a horse's bridle, allowing the rider to curb or control its 'headstrong' movements. *Bits* echoes *biting* and reinforces *strict* (which means 'stretched tight') in line 19.
     Weeds   The preceding images lead us to expect *steeds* (an emendation that some editions supply). But *Weeds* picks up on *strew'd* in line 15 and looks forward to such potentially related words as *slip* (which means 'shoot' or 'scion' when used as a noun, as in III.i.139), *o'ergrown*, and *Twigs* in lines 21–24. The meaning of *Weeds* is not limited to unwanted plants; the word can also refer to garments, such as the 'witless Bravery' of the headstrong 'Youth' described in line 10.

23   **fond**   foolish, overindulgent.

24   **bound up**   both (a) gathered and tied together into a bundle, and (b) tied up (restrained), line 32.

26   **For Terror**   to frighten them. *Use* recalls I.i.35–39, I.iii.9–13.

28   **Dead to Infliction**   too long inactive to be inflicted on anyone now.
     to . . . dead   are as much as dead in their own eyes.

30–31 **quite . . . Decorum**   totally awry goes all sense of order. *Liberty* (unruly licence), line 29, recalls I.iii.10.

33   **Dreadful**   fearful, inspiring awe and respect. *Scope* echoes I.iii.12.

36   **gall**   chafe (as from a whipping with 'Twigs of Birch', line 24).

38   **have . . . Pass**   are passed over (allowed to trespass unimpeded and unpunished) by a permissive ruler.

41   **in th' Ambush of**   under the cover of. *Impos'd* (line 40) recalls I.iii.71.

My absolute Power and Place here in Vienna,
And he supposes me travail'd to Poland
(For so I have strew'd it in the Common Ear,   15
And so it is receiv'd). Now, pious Sir,
You will demand of me, why I do this.

FRIAR   Gladly, my Lord.

DUKE   We have strict Statutes, and most biting
    Laws
    (The needful Bits and Curbs to headstrong
        Weeds),   20
    Which for this fourteen Years we have let slip,
    Even 'ke an o'ergrown Lion in a Cave
    That goes not out to prey. Now, as fond
        Fathers,
    Having bound up the threat'ning Twigs of Birch
    Onely to stick it in their Children's Sight   25
    For Terror, not to Use, in time the Rod
    More mock'd than fear'd, so our Decrees,
    Dead to Infliction, to themselves are dead,
    And Liberty plucks Justice by the Nose,
    The Baby beats the Nurse, and quite athwart   30
    Goes all Decorum.

FRIAR   It rested in your Grace
    To unloose this tied-up Justice when you
        pleas'd;
    And it in you more Dreadful would have seem'd
    Than in Lord Angelo.

DUKE   I do fear, too Dreadful.
    Sith 'twas my Fault to give the people Scope,   35
    'Twould be my Tyranny to strike and gall them
    For what I bid them do: for we bid this be done
    When Evil Deeds have their permissive Pass,
    And not the Punishment. Therefore indeed, my
        Father,
    I have on Angelo impos'd the Office,   40
    Who may in th' Ambush of my Name strike home,

43   **do in Slander** act in such a way as to make me seem tyrannical. Compare lines 39–43 with *Macbeth*, III.i.116–31.

    Sway scope, exercise of authority. But of course *sway* can also mean (a) swerve, (b) lean, (c) swing or vacillate, and (d) totter. Compare *King Lear*, I.i.138–39, I.ii.55.

44   **as 'twere** as if I were.

45   **Visit** pay ministerial calls (see II.iii.3–5, III.i.46, 540–41, 560, and compare *The Tempest*, II.i.11) to provide comfort and spiritual guidance. But *Visit* can also refer to afflictions to test the virtuous (as with Job), to chastise the wayward, or to punish the wicked. See the note to *Hamlet*, II.ii.25, and compare *The Merchant of Venice*, III.v.14–15, and *Antony and Cleopatra*, IV.xv.68.

46   **Supply . . . Habit** provide me with the monastic cloth of your order. *Supply* recalls I.i.17.

47   **formally** in proper form, in both (a) appearance, and (b) manner. See V.i.227, and compare *Antony and Cleopatra*, II.v.40.

48   **Moe** more.

50   **precise** exacting, sharply scrupulous. Compare I.ii.78.

51   **Stands . . . Envy** maintains a strong defence, either (a) armed with Envy (malice), or (b) armed against Envy (enmity or evil intent). Compare I.ii.102, I.iii.54, 71.

53   **Is . . . Stone** is more inclined to bread than stone. The Duke's implication is that Angelo is so lacking in normal appetites and passions ('Blood') that he seems more like a marble statue than a living, breathing human being. The Duke's imagery recalls Matthew 7:9, where Jesus says, 'Or what man is there of you, whom if his son ask bread, will he give him a stone?' Compare I.v.56–62 and III.i.399–402. *Purpose* echoes line 4; in the process it suggests that we should be alert to whether the 'Power' the Duke's new 'Habit' affords him will 'change' his 'Purpose' in any way.

I.v.   Having just seen the Duke enter a monastery, we now observe Isabella's arrival at a convent.

6   **Saint Clare** a thirteenth-century nun who founded an order whose members ('Votarists', line 5) subjected themselves to a rule of extreme austerity. *Restraint* (line 4) recalls I.iii.11–13; *stood* echoes I.iv.50–51.

And yet my Nature never in the Fight
To do in Slander. And to behold his Sway
I will, as 'twere a Brother of your Order,
Visit both Prince and People. Therefore I
    prethee   45
Supply me with the Habit, and instruct me
How I may formally in Person bear
Like a true Friar. Moe Reasons for this Action
At our more Leisure shall I render you;
Onely this one, Lord Angelo is precise,   50
Stands at a guard with Envy, scarce confesses
That his Blood flows, or that his Appetite
Is more to Bread than Stone; hence shall we see
If Power change Purpose, what our Seemers be.

                                                        Exeunt.

Scene 5

Enter Isabella and Francisca, a Nun.

ISABELLA   And have you Nuns no farther Privileges?
NUN   Are not these large enough?
ISABELLA   Yes truly; I speak not as desiring more,
    But rather wishing a more strict Restraint
    Upon the Sisters stood, the Votarists of   5
    Saint Clare.
LUCIO *within*   Ho? Peace be in this Place.
ISABELLA   Who's that which calls?
NUN   It is a Man's Voice. Gentle Isabella,

9   **know . . . him** find out what brings him here. The Nun's phrasing is unintentionally equivocal: *know* frequently refers to physical intimacy (see V.i.194–95, 204–5), and *Business* is a word that often has sexual implications in Shakespeare's plays. Compare *All's Well That Ends Well*, II.i.86, *Hamlet*, I.v.126, *Romeo and Juliet*, II.iii.56–58, and *Troilus and Cressida*, III.i.40–44, V.i.88. The words *Turn* (see the note to IV.ii.62) and *Key* (see IV.i.30–31) reinforce the erotic suggestiveness of the Nun's instruction to her newest charge.

10   **Unsworn** not pledged to uphold all the rules of the order.

15   **I . . . him** Most editions insert an *Exit* after this line; but it is conceivable that the Nun simply steps aside and remains silently present while Isabella speaks with Lucio; see lines 8–14.

17   **Hail, Virgin** Lucio's greeting echoes two *Aves*, (a) the kind referred to by the Duke in I.i.69, and (b) the 'Hail, thou that art highly favoured' with which the angel Gabriel announced himself to the Virgin Mary in Luke 1:28.
    Cheek-roses rosy-coloured cheeks. The rosebud was a traditional symbol of unspoiled beauty. It could also symbolize ardour and pride, however, as in *A Midsummer Night's Dream*, III.i.94.

18   **steed** both (a) stead, help, and (b) steed (bear, like a high-spirited horse). See III.i.262, and compare I.iii.39–47, I.iv.19–20.

19   **to the sight** into the presence. Like his greeting in line 17, Lucio's phrasing borders on impudence. Compare *Hamlet*, IV.iv.4–7, IV.vii.44–45. His tone suggests that he is less than reverential about the rules of the order of Saint Clare (as outlined in lines 11–14), and Isabella tactfully chides him for it in line 38.

23   **The rather for** all the more quickly so because.

26   **Not . . . you** not to try your patience with a tedious narrative.

30–31 **make . . . Story** don't try to make me look ridiculous (and thus provide yourself a tale to amuse your friends with later) by persuading me to believe something as incredible as this.

32   **my familiar Sin** my habitual vice (familiarity).

Turn you the Key, and know his Business of him.
You may, I may not; you are yet Unsworn.   10
When you have vow'd, you must not speak with
    Men
But in the presence of the Prioress;
Then if you speak, you must not show your Face;
Or if you show your Face, you must not speak.
He calls again: I pray you answer him.   15
ISABELLA   Peace and Prosperity: who is't that
    calls?

[Enter Lucio.]

LUCIO   Hail, Virgin, if you be, as those Cheek-
    roses
Proclaim you are no less: can you so steed me
As bring me to the sight of Isabella,
A Novice of this Place, and the fair Sister   20
To her unhappy brother Claudio?
ISABELLA   Why her unhappy Brother? Let me ask,
The rather for I now must make you know
I am that Isabella, and his Sister.
LUCIO   Gentle and Fair: your Brother kindly greets
    you.   25
Not to be weary with you, he's in Prison.
ISABELLA   Woe me, for what?
LUCIO   For that which, if my self might be his
    Judge,
He should receive his Punishment in Thanks:
He hath got his Friend with Child.
ISABELLA   Sir, make   30
Me not your Story.
LUCIO   'Tis true:
I would not (though 'tis my familiar Sin

33   **Lapwing** A bird proverbial for its deceptiveness, the lapwing
      kept predators from its nest by singing far away from it.

33–34 **to . . . Heart** to mock with a tongue unrelated to my real
      feelings.

35   **en-skied** elevated to a celestial realm. *Sainted* (holy) recalls
      I.ii.7–8.

36   **Renouncement** denial of the pleasures of the senses.

40   **Fewness and Truth** to speak briefly and honestly. Compare line
      26.

43   **Seedness** seed-time, when new crops are sown. Compare
      I.ii.102, I.iv.15, 20.
      Fallow unplanted fields.

44   **teaming Foison** bounteous harvest.

45   **Expresseth . . . Husbandry** presses out (and thus reveals for all
      to see) its full tillage and cultivation. *Husbandry* refers to the
      tillage and 'planting' of a husband (here likened to a farmer).
      Compare the stamp imagery in I.i.46–49 and I.iii.35–37.

48   **Adoptedly** by 'adoption' or affectation (a secondary sense of
      'Affection', line 49).
      change either (a) modify, as with nicknames, or (b) exchange.
      Compare I.ii.111, I.iv.53–54.

49   **vain though apt** idle (playful) though nevertheless fitting.

50   **Point** matter at issue; what brings me to see you. *Point* recalls
      I.i.82.

52–53 **Bore . . . Action** led many young men to think that some
      military engagement was afoot (hinted at in I.ii.1–5).
      Compare *Macbeth*, III.i.79, where the title character tells the
      Murderers that they were 'borne in hand' (led on deceitfully)
      by Banquo.

54   **Nerves of State** sinews (inner councils) of the government.
      Compare *Troilus and Cressida*, III.iii.188–96.

55–56 **His . . . Design** what he put out for public consumption was at
      variance with what he was actually planning to do. Lucio's
      words echo lines 32–34; they also recall I.iv.40–43 and
      I.v.14–16. *Place* echoes I.iv.13, I.v.7.

57   **full line** complete rein (reign). Compare I.i.42, I.iii.39–47, and
      I.iv.19–23.

With Maids to seem the Lapwing, and to jest
Tongue far from Heart) play with all Virgins so.
I hold you as a thing en-skied and sainted,   35
By your Renouncement, an immortal Spirit,
And to be talk'd with in Sincerity,
As with a Saint.
ISABELLA   You do blaspheme the Good, in mocking me.
LUCIO   Do not believe it. Fewness and Truth, 'tis
    thus,   40
Your Brother and his Lover have embrac'd:
As those that feed grow full, as blossoming
    Time,
That from the Seedness the bare Fallow brings
To teeming Foison, even so her plenteous Womb
Expresseth his full Tilth, and Husbandry.   45
ISABELLA   Some one with Child by him? My cousin
    Juliet?
LUCIO   Is she your Cousin?
ISABELLA   Adoptedly, as Schoolmaids change their
    Names
By vain though apt Affection.
LUCIO   She it is.
ISABELLA   Oh, let him marry her.
LUCIO   This is the Point.   50
The Duke is very strangely gone from hence;
Bore many Gentlemen, my self being one,
In hand, and hope of Action; but we do learn,
By those that know the very Nerves of State,
His Giving-out were of an infinite Distance   55
From his true-meant Design. Upon his Place,
And with full line of his Authority,
Governs Lord Angelo, a Man whose Blood
Is very Snow-broth, one who never feels

60 **wanton . . . Sense** sensual impulses normal to humanity. *Motions* recalls the phrase 'move men' in I.iii.67. *Blood* (line 58) echoes I.iv.50–53. *Snow-broth* (line 59) means 'melted snow'.

61 **rebate** 're-abate' (repel, suppress); make dull or 'blunt'. *Rebate* can also mean 'draw back' (as when a falconer brings a bating (excited, wing-beating) hawk to rest on his fist. See the note on *withdraw* at I.ii.116.
Edge sharp desire. Compare *Hamlet*, III.ii.273–74.

63 **Use** usage (habits that have become the norm). *Use* echoes I.iv.26; *Liberty* recalls I.iii.10–20, I.iv.19–29; meanwhile line 62 recalls I.iv.7–10.

64 **run . . . Law** scampered past the goblin-like Law. Compare I.iv.19–31.

66 **heavy Sense** oppressive import (as rigorously and severely interpreted). Lucio is contrasting one kind of 'Sense' (meaning) with another, the kind of 'Sense' (sensations and desires) referred to in line 60.

68 **the Rigour . . . Statute** the most rigid (hard, unbending) application of the law in question. Compare I.iv.50–51.

71 **Pith** core, essence, kernel. *Business* echoes line 9. Lines 69–71 will prove ironic.

73 **Has** he has.
censur'd judged and sentenced.

77 **Assay** try, endeavour to use. See the notes to I.iii.64, I.iv.45. *Powre* (power) recalls I.i.20, 78, and anticipates IV.ii.87, IV.iii.137.

78–80 **Our . . . attempt** Compare Helena's remarks on 'strange Attempts' in *All's Well That Ends Well*, I.i.233–46. *Loose* (line 79) can mean either (a) unleash (compare I.iv.31–32) and thus surrender to chance, or (b) lose.

81 **sue** ask, plead (as in a court of law).

The wanton Stings and Motions of the Sense,   60
But doth rebate and blunt his natural Edge
With Profits of the Mind: Study and Fast.
He (to give fear to Use and Liberty,
Which have, for long, run by the hideous Law
As Mice by Lions) hath pick'd out an Act   65
Under whose heavy Sense your Brother's Life
Falls into Forfeit. He arrests him on it,
And follows close the Rigour of the Statute
To make him an Example. All Hope is gone
Unless you have the Grace, by your fair Prayer,   70
To soften Angelo. And that's my Pith of
    Business
'Twixt you and your poor Brother.
ISABELLA   Doth he so,
    Seek his Life?
LUCIO   Has censur'd him already,
    And, as I hear, the Provost hath a Warrant
    For's Execution.
ISABELLA   Alas, what poor   75
    Ability's in me to do him good.
LUCIO   Assay the Powre you have.
ISABELLA   My Power? Alas, I doubt.
LUCIO   Our Doubts are Traitors,
    And makes us loose the Good we oft might win
    By fearing to attempt. Go to Lord Angelo,   80
    And let him learn to know, when Maidens sue,

82 **give like Gods** Lucio probably means 'remain aloof', like the Olympian Gods as depicted in Epicurean philosophy. Another possibility is that he means that men who answer prayers exhibit a magnanimity that parallels the pardon bestowed by the Gods. Later Isabella will employ this second notion when she tells Angelo that rulers are most God-like (in a sense derived from Christian rather than pagan theology) when they imitate Divine Grace (see II.ii.60–64, 74–80). Portia makes the same argument in her famous speech on 'the Quality of Mercy' in IV.i.187–208 of *The Merchant of Venice*.

83 **Petitions** requests. Compare I.ii.14–17.

84 **theirs** Maidens'.
as they as if they.

85 **owe** own.

86 **strait** straight away, immediately. The spelling in the Folio text suggests that Isabella intends to perform her errand in a way that is 'strait' (in strict conformity with the restraints she has chosen to impose upon herself by entering a nunnery). Like *strict*, *strait* derives ultimately from the Latin verb *stringere*, whose meanings range from 'draw tight' or 'tie firmly' (as in I.iv.19–21) to 'strip', 'draw a weapon', 'press together', 'compress', 'touch', 'move', and 'wound'. Compare I.iii.44.

87 **staying** delaying.
but than.
Mother Mother Superior, Prioress (line 12).

89 **Soon at Night** by early evening.

90 **my Success** how I fare; the outcome of my mission (whether or not it is successful in the usual modern sense).

Men give like Gods; but when they weep and kneel,
All their Petitions are as freely theirs
As they themselves would owe them.
ISABELLA   I'll see what I can do.
LUCIO   But speedily.   85
ISABELLA   I will about it strait;
    No longer staying but to give the Mother
    Notice of my Affair. I humbly thank you:
    Commend me to my Brother. Soon at Night
    I'll send him certain Word of my Success.   90
LUCIO   I take my leave of you.
ISABELLA   Good Sir, adieu.   *Exeunt.*

II.i   This scene takes place in a Viennese courtroom.

1   **Scar-crow** scarecrow. Lines 1–4 echo such earlier passages as I.iii.39–53, I.iv.19–31, and I.v.63–69.

2   **fear** frighten.

3   **let . . . Shape** let it remain unmoving and unchanging (and thus reveal itself as merely a scarecrow, not a real 'Terror').
    Custom long-standing familiarity. Compare I.ii.85–87.

4   **Their Perch** a place where they feel comfortable sitting (not at all frightened away by it). *Terror* recalls I.i.18.

5   **Keen** sharp (like a surgeon's knife). See the second note to I.v.61.

6   **fall** let drop (like a heavy bludgeon or other blunt instrument). *Fall* echoes I.i.57.

9   **strait** strict, straitlaced. Compare I.v.86. The sound of this word suggests implications similar to those of *prone* (I.iii.66).

10   **Affections** sensual impulses. See I.v.48–49.

11   **coheard** cohered, convened, matched (literally, stuck together). The Folio spelling, here retained, suggests wordplay on *heard*, and possibly on *herd*. Compare III.i.52–53.
    Place both (a) situation, and (b) position. Here *Place* hints at a potential genital sense (compare I.ii.111, I.iii.45, I.v.6, 56, and II.iv.93), as does *misplaces* in II.i.92.

12–13 **Or . . . Purpose** or if acting out a male drive common to us all had been able to gain you what you desired. Shakespeare frequently uses the word *resolute* to describe the impassioned courage of a man who acts on the promptings of impulse rather than hesitating in response to questions raised by 'the Pale Cast of Thought' (see *Hamlet*, III.i.80–85 and IV.iv.36–63). *Acting* echoes I.iii.51–53, I.v.63–66, *Blood* I.v.58–59, *Purpose* I.iv.53–54.

15   **Err'd . . . him** gone astray in the same way that you now judge him so severely for doing. By the word *Point* Escalus probably means 'point of law' (statute); compare I.v.50. But for other implications, see the notes to IV.iii.66 of *All's Well That Ends Well* and I.v.126 of *Hamlet*. *Censure* recalls I.v.73.

19   **passing** passing judgement. See the second note to I.iv.38. *Fall* (line 18) means 'submit to temptation'; compare line 6.

ACT II

Scene 1

Enter Angelo, Escalus, and Servants, Justice.

ANGELO We must not make a Scar-crow of the Law,
Setting it up to fear the Birds of Prey,
And let it keep one Shape till Custom make it
Their Perch and not their Terror.

ESCALUS   Ay, but yet
Let us be Keen, and rather cut a little   5
Than fall and bruise to Death. Alas, this
      Gentleman,
Whom I would save, had a most noble Father.
Let but your Honour know
(Whom I believe to be most strait in Virtue)
That in the working of your own Affections   10
(Had Time coheard with Place, or Place with
      Wishing,
Or that the resolute Acting of our Blood
Could have attain'd th' Effect of your own
      Purpose)
Whether you had not sometime in your Life
Err'd in this Point which now you censure him   15
And pull'd the Law upon you.

ANGELO 'Tis one thing to be tempted, Escalus,
Another thing to fall. I not deny
The Jury passing on the Prisoner's Life
May in the Sworn-twelve have a Thief or two   20
Guiltier than him they try. What's open made
      to Justice,

23   **pass** both (a) enact, and (b) enforce. See line 19, and compare *King Lear*, III.vii.24–27. Angelo's point is that, once legislated, the laws have no knowledge of how they are executed.

        pregnant manifest (as the state of a woman in the most advanced stage of pregnancy is open to the eye). See the second note to I.i.10.

27–28 **You . . . Faults** you cannot excuse or lessen the degree of his guilt merely because I, the judge, have erred in the same manner. The word *extenuate* literally means 'make thin', and it is related to *extend*, 'stretch out'. *Faults* recalls I.iv.35–37. Here, as frequently elsewhere, *for* means 'because'.

30   **Let . . . Death** let the sentence I give another be the pattern for my own execution. *Censure* (judge), line 29, echoes line 15.

31   **And . . . partial** and let nothing intrude to give me partial (preferential) treatment. Angelo's phrasing is unintentionally suggestive. The word *partial* derives from *part* (a word that frequently carries genital associations), and the other words in the phrase cohere with those associations. See I.i.39–40 and II.i.64, 219, and compare *Hamlet*, I.v.124–29, and *All's Well That Ends Well*, I.i.148–49, II.i.92, II.iii.267–68, II.iv.47–50.

35   **Confessor** the priest to hear his confession. One of the duties of a provost (head jailer) was to assure that condemned prisoners were spiritually prepared to proceed from this life to the next.

36   **the . . . Pilgrimage** the end of his earthly journey.

38   **Some . . . fall** Escalus probably means that some people rise to the height of Fortune's wheel by doing evil, whereas others fall by doing good. But Escalus' words are by no means limited to a single interpretation, and in due course they will prove to be a sentence (a maxim of proverbial wisdom, from the Latin *sententia*) of wide applicability in *Measure for Measure*. *Fall* echoes lines 6, 18.

That Justice seizes. What knows the Laws
That Thieves do pass on Thieves? 'Tis very
    pregnant,
The Jewel that we find, we stoop and take't
Because we see it; but what we do not see,   25
We tread upon, and never think of it.
You may not so extenuate his Offence
For I have had such Faults; but rather tell me,
When I that censure him do so offend,
Let mine own Judgement pattern out my Death   30
And nothing come in partial. Sir, he must die.

                    Enter Provost.

ESCALUS   Be it as your Wisdom will.
ANGELO   Where is the Provost?
PROVOST   Here, if it like your Honour.
ANGELO   See that Claudio
    Be executed by nine to morrow morning.
    Bring him his Confessor, let him be prepar'd,   35
    For that's the utmost of his Pilgrimage.
                                        Exit Provost.
ESCALUS   Well: Heaven forgive him, and forgive
    us all.
    Some rise by Sin, and some by Virtue fall.

39–40 **Some . . . alone** The simplest interpretation of this
much-debated sentence is 'some make large breaches (breaks)
in the ice and run away unharmed and unpunished (without
having to answer for their deed), while others pay with their
lives for a tiny crack in the surface'. *Brakes* usually means
'thickets' in Shakespeare, and *Ice* is often a symbol of virginity
or frigidity (as in I.v.59 and III.i.399–402). It is thus possible
that 'Brakes of Ice' is meant to hint at (a) the 'Brakes' of
chaste maidens, or (b) a thicket-like residue of slivers from
shattered ice. Here *Fault* refers to a misdeed; but its literal
meaning (crack or breach) frequently associates it with the
female genitalia. See lines 27–28, and compare *King Lear*,
I.i.16.

43 **common Houses** a euphemism for houses of prostitution.
Compare I.ii.99–106.
Commonweal (commonwealth) recalls I.ii.108–9.

48 **lean upon** Elbow means 'am upheld by' or 'rely upon'. But
another sense ('encroach upon' or 'impose a burden upon')
proves equally apt. Given the way Elbow 'misplaces' (line 92)
the adjective *poor* (humbling the Duke rather than expressing
the modesty of his incompetent Constable in lines 46–47), his
elbow does indeed 'lean upon' Vienna's chief magistrate of
'Justice'.

54 **precise** Elbow probably means 'real'; his phrasing echoes the
adjective the Duke has applied to Angelo in I.iv.50.

55–56 **void . . . World** lacking in all the impiety in the world. No
doubt inadvertently, Elbow's malapropism echoes 1 John
2:15–17. In its inept attempt to describe the 'Benefactors'
('well-doers,' as opposed to 'evil-doers') Elbow has arrested,
moreover, it offers an unwittingly 'wise' (line 58) portrayal of
the unworldly Angelo and of what 'good Christians ought to
have'. Compare V.i.432–34, and see the note to *A
Midsummer Night's Dream*, IV.i.214–18.

62 **out at Elbow** literally, exposed at the elbow. The Clown
(Pompey) takes a proverbial expression for witlessness and
suggests that this 'Elbow' is 'out' (out of things to say)
because he can't even understand his own name. Compare
line 48.

Some run from Brakes of Ice, and answer none,
And some condemned for a Fault alone.   40

Enter Elbow, Froth, Clown, Officers.

ELBOW Come, bring them away. If these be good
People in a Commonweal, that do nothing but use
their Abuses in common Houses, I know no Law.
Bring them away.

ANGELO How now, Sir, what's your Name? And
what's the matter?   45

ELBOW If it please your Honour, I am the poor
Duke's Constable, and my name is Elbow. I do
lean upon Justice, Sir, and do bring in here
before your good Honour two notorious
Benefactors.   50

ANGELO Benefactors? Well: what Benefactors are
they? Are they not Malefactors?

ELBOW If it please your Honour, I know not well
what they are. But precise Villains they are,
that I am sure of, and void of all Profanation   55
in the World, that good Christians ought to
have.

ESCALUS — This comes off well: here's a wise
Officer.

ANGELO Go to. What Quality are they of? Elbow   60
is your name? Why dost thou not speak, Elbow?

CLOWN He cannot, Sir: he's out at Elbow.

ANGELO What are you, Sir?

64 **parcel Bawd**   partial (part-time) pimp. See the note to line 31.
    Elbow is finally answering Angelo's question (line 60) about
    Pompey's 'Quality' (position or vocation).

66 **Suborbs**   suburbs. Elbow inadvertently anticipates the 'suborbs'
    referred to in line 115. Lines 65–66 recall I.ii.99–100, 105–7,
    and II.i.16.

67 **professes a Hot-house**   claims to be operating a bath-house.

70 **detest**   Elbow means 'protest' (profess), as in V.i.333, or 'attest'
    (vow).

75 **therefore**   for that reason.

79 **Naughty House**   a house of ill repute. Whether or not Elbow
    recognizes it, *Naught* ('no thing') is a term for the female
    genitalia. See the notes to *Romeo and Juliet*, II.iii.130, *A
    Midsummer Night's Dream*, IV.ii.14, and *Hamlet* III.ii.123,
    IV.ii.29–31.

82 **cardinally given**   Elbow means 'given to carnality' (the lusts of
    the flesh). See V.i.204–5. But *cardinally* is a reminder that
    prostitutes of Shakespeare's time apparelled themselves in red.
    Mistress Quickly commits a similar malapropism in
    II.iii.35–36 of *Henry V* when she takes *incarnate* to be a
    reference to the red 'Carnation'.

90 **Varlets**   Either Elbow doesn't realize that this is an insulting
    term (a corruption of *valets* that had come to mean 'villains'),
    or he is transposing it with the term he 'misplaces' (line 92),
    misapplies, when he addresses Pompey as an 'Honourable
    Man' (compare *Julius Caesar*, III.ii.79–159).

95 **stew'd Prewyns**   boiled prunes (here depicted as something a
    pregnant woman craves). Brothels (frequently referred to as
    'stews', as in *Richard II*, V.iii.15, and *2 Henry IV*, I.ii.60–61)
    were proverbial for serving stewed prunes, which seem to
    have been regarded both as an aphrodisiac and as a preventive
    against venereal disease. Pompey asks for the Court's
    indulgence before he mentions such an indelicate item.
    'Stewed prunes' was a euphemism for 'whores'.

ELBOW   He, Sir? A Tapster, Sir; parcel Bawd; one
that serves a bad Woman; whose House, Sir, was   65
(as they say) pluck'd down in the Suborbs; and
now she professes a Hot-house; which, I think,
is a very Ill House too.

ESCALUS   How know you that?

ELBOW   My Wife, Sir? whom I detest before Heaven,   70
and your Honour.

ESCALUS   How? Thy Wife?

ELBOW   Ay Sir: whom I thank Heaven is an Honest
Woman —

ESCALUS   Dost thou detest her therefore?   75

ELBOW   I say, Sir, I will detest my self also,
as well as she, that this House, if it be not
a Bawd's House, it is pity of her Life, for it
is a Naughty House.

ESCALUS   How dost thou know that, Constable?   80

ELBOW   Marry Sir, by my Wife, who, if she had
been a Woman cardinally given, might have been
accus'd in Fornication, Adultery, and all
Uncleanliness there.

ESCALUS   By the Woman's means?   85

ELBOW   Ay Sir, by Mistress Over-done's means: but
as she spit in his Face, so she defied him.

CLOWN   Sir, if it please your Honour, this is not
so.

ELBOW   Prove it before these Varlets here, thou   90
Honourable Man, prove it.

ESCALUS   — Do you hear how he misplaces?

CLOWN   Sir, she came in great with Child; and
longing (saving your Honour's reverence) for
stew'd Prewyns; Sir, we had but two in the   95

96–   **which . . . Dishes**   Pompey is probably being equivocal. Words
100   like *distant* (which means 'standing apart') and *stood*
       probably have the implications implicit in I.ii.102. *Fruit Dish*
       and *China-dishes* are common ('three Pence') and expensive
       ('good') prostitutes. Compare *2 Henry IV*, III.ii.25. And
       Prewyns probably plays on such senses as 'prow-ins' and
       'privy-in' (*prewa* being an older form of *privy*, here hinting at
       male 'privates').

103   **not . . . Pin**   not at all (not worth a thing). But like *Point* in the
       next line, *Pin* can also have the same phallic implications as
       Prewyns, a sense reinforced by the phrase 'therein in the
       Right' (one meaning of *right* being 'erect') and by the play on
       long in 'longing' (lines 94, 107). See the note on *Penalties* at
       I.iii.48. *Point* recalls I.v.50.

115   **cracking the Stones**   Pompey is probably referring not only to
       the stones of the 'foresaid Prewyns' but to the kinds of
       'Stones' hinted at in *A Midsummer Night's Dream*, V.i.193,
       The Merchant of Venice, II.viii.20–24, and *2 Henry IV*,
       III.ii.355.

117   **I**   both (a) I, and (b) Ay. Compare I.ii.26.

119   **such a one**   Pompey probably means 'three Pence' (a whore).
       But *one* (1) is often phallic; see the notes to *Macbeth*, I.v.73,
       Romeo and Juliet, II.iii.72–73, *A Midsummer Night's Dream*,
       V.i.311, *Julius Caesar*, I.ii.154, III.i.66, 69, *King Lear*,
       I.iv.207, and *The Two Gentleman of Verona*, I.i.115 and
       II.v.30–31.

120   **the thing . . . of**   The 'thing' Froth knows of is venereal disease.
       Compare I.ii.47–62, 85–87, 114–16.

125   **done**   In this context, Escalus' verb resonates with the sense the
       verb carries in I.ii.90–91; Pompey plays on that meaning in
       line 150. Similarly, in lines 126–30 *come* carries reminders of
       the same orgasmic sense as in II.iv.47–50 of *All's Well That
       Ends Well*.

House, which at that very distant time stood,
as it were, in a Fruit Dish, a Dish of some
three Pence. Your Honours have seen such
Dishes: they are not China-dishes, but very
good Dishes.   100
ESCALUS   Go to, go to: no matter for the Dish,
Sir.
CLOWN   No indeed, Sir, not of a Pin; you are
therein in the Right; but to the Point. As I
say, this Mistress Elbow, being (as I say)   105
with Child, and being Great-bellied, and
longing (as I said) for Prewyns; and having
but two in the Dish (as I said), Master Froth
here, this very Man, having eaten the rest
(as I said), and (as I say) paying for them   110
very honestly – for, as you know, Master Froth,
I could not give you three Pence again.
FROTH   No indeed.
CLOWN   Very well: you being then, if you be
remembered, cracking the Stones of the   115
foresaid Prewyns –
FROTH   I, so I did indeed.
CLOWN   Why, very well: I telling you then (if you
be remembered) that such a one, and such a one
were past cure of the thing you wot of, unless   120
they kept very good Diet, as I told you –
FROTH   All this is true.
CLOWN   Why very well then.
ESCALUS   Come: you are a tedious Fool; to the
Purpose; what was done to Elbow's Wife, that he   125

126   **cause**   reason. But *cause* is often synonymous with *case* (both
words deriving from the Latin *causa*), as in line 145. For the
genital implications of *case*, see *Romeo and Juliet*,
II.iii.50–60, III.iii.84, IV.iii.185–86.

    Come me   Here *me* exemplifies what grammarians call the
'ethic dative', a construction that means something like 'to
me' and gives a statement a degree of personal immediacy it
would otherwise lack. Compare I.iii.48. In line 128 Pompey's
reply suggests that he is mis-taking Escalus' order to be a
demand for the same thing that was supposedly 'done to'
Elbow's wife.

133   **Pound**   pounds. In view of the other wordplay in this scene, it
appears likely that Pompey is referring not only to his friend's
income but also to the number of 'poundings' that make him
come to a 'froth' each year. See *The Two Gentleman of
Verona*, I.i.105–12, for similar wordplay on *Pound*. An
income of eighty pounds would have been four times what a
well-compensated schoolmaster would have earned in
Shakespeare's time. Lines 131–35 echo lines 6–7.

    Hallowmas   All Saints' Day (1 November). Pompey implies
that a man whose father died on this holiday must be
virtuous. Pompey may be referring, however, to a Hallowmas
when Froth's father 'died' orgasmically after a 'Pound'
supplied by one of the 'good Dishes' under his supervision.

135   **All-hallond Eve**   Halloween, 31 October. For pertinent
implications of *Holland* (another name for 'the Low
Countries', a nether region alluded to in *Hamlet*, III.ii.122),
see 2 *Henry IV*, II.ii.21–27.

138   **the Bunch of Grapes**   a room in Mistress Over-done's inn. Then
as now, grapes were suggestive of bacchanalian release.

140   **open**   public. Such a room would be 'good for Winter' (line
141) because a fire would burn there at all times.

158   **mark**   observe, note. *Purpose* recalls I.iv.53–54.

hath cause to complain of? Come me to what was
done to her.

CLOWN Sir, your Honour cannot come to that yet.

ESCALUS No Sir, nor I mean it not.

CLOWN Sir, but you shall come to it, by your   130
Honour's leave. And I beseech you, look into
Master Froth here, Sir, a Man of four-score
Pound a Year; whose Father died at Hallowmas –
was't not at Hallowmas, Master Froth?

FROTH All-hallond Eve.   135

CLOWN Why very well: I hope here be Truths. He,
Sir, sitting (as I say) in a lower Chair, Sir,
'twas in the Bunch of Grapes – where indeed
you have a delight to sit, have you not?

FROTH I have so, because it is an open Room, and   140
good for Winter.

CLOWN Why very well then: I hope here be Truths.

ANGELO All this will last out a Night in Russia
When Nights are longest there: I'll take my
     leave,
And leave you to the Hearing of the Cause,   145
Hoping you'll find good Cause to whip them all.

ESCALUS I think no less. Good morrow to your
     Lordship.   *Exit [Angelo].*
– Now Sir, come on: what was done to
Elbow's Wife, once more?

CLOWN Once, Sir? There was nothing done to her   150
once.

ELBOW I beseech you, Sir, ask him what this
Man did to my Wife.

CLOWN I beseech your Honour, ask me.

ESCALUS Well Sir, what did this Gentleman to her?   155

CLOWN I beseech you, Sir, look in this Gentleman's
Face. – Good Master Froth, look upon his Honour;
'tis for a good Purpose. – Doth your Honour mark
his Face?

160   I   both 'I' and 'Ay', as in line 117.

165   **suppos'd . . . Book**   literally, laid upon a Bible. Pompey is
       probably engaging in further bawdy wordplay. Meanwhile, he
       is parodying Elbow's tendency to 'misplace' words (line 92);
       the expected term here would be *depos'd* (sworn).

166   **worst thing**   Pompey is probably punning on *thing*, with the
       suggestion that if Froth's face is the 'worst thing about him',
       and his face is harmless, then his other 'thing' has to be
       innocent of the charges Elbow is trying to bring forward.
       Escalus is probably going along with the jest when he says
       'He's in the Right' in line 170 (see the note to line 103). *Thing*
       echoes line 120.

168   **Constable's Wife**   Pompey is probably having fun at the
       expense of Elbow's title. *Constable* can be dissected into a
       syllable alluding to the female genitalia (see the note to
       I.ii.110) and two syllables (*-stable*) that derive from the Latin
       verb *stare*, to stand (see the notes to I.ii.102, I.iii.27, 70–71,
       I.iv.51). The word seems to have been a common subject of
       bawdy jokes in Shakespeare's time. In *All's Well That Ends
       Well* the Clown plays on *Constable* in one of his interchanges
       with the Countess: 'Have you, I say, an Answer of such
       Fitness for all Questions? . . . From below your Duke to
       beneath your Constable, it will fit any Question' (II.ii.30–33).

172   **and . . . you**   if you please.

173   **respected**   Elbow probably means 'suspected' or 'detected'
       (accused publicly, as in III.i.414–15). Compare *Much Ado
       About Nothing*, IV.ii.80–81, where another constable,
       Dogberry, asks, 'Doost thou not suspect my Place?' The literal
       meaning of *respected* is 'looked at' (compare lines 156–57
       and V.i.198–99, 438–40), and that sense can refer to the kind
       of looking that would make a 'respected Woman' suspect in
       the eyes of some beholders; see I.iii.26, where Lucio asks, 'Is
       Lechery so look'd after?' and V.i.359–63, where Angelo notes
       that his master 'like Powre Divine' has 'look'd upon' his
       'Passes'.

175–   **By . . . all**   By telling the truth, Pompey sends the poor Elbow
76   into paroxysms of exasperation.

ESCALUS   I, Sir, very well. 160

CLOWN   Nay, I beseech you mark it well.

ESCALUS   Well, I do so.

CLOWN   Doth your Honour see any Harm in his Face?

ESCALUS   Why no.

CLOWN   I'll be suppos'd upon a Book, his Face is 165
the worst thing about him. Good then: if his
Face be the worst thing about him, how could
Master Froth do the Constable's Wife any Harm?
I would know that of your Honour.

ESCALUS   He's in the Right, Constable; what say 170
you to it?

ELBOW   First, and it like you, the House is a
respected House; next, this is a respected
Fellow; and his Mistress is a respected Woman.

CLOWN   By this Hand, Sir, his Wife is a more 175
respected person than any of us all.

ELBOW   Varlet, thou liest; thou liest, wicked
Varlet. The time is yet to come that she was
ever respected with Man, Woman, or Child.

CLOWN   – Sir, she was respected with him before 180
he married with her.

ESCALUS   – Which is the Wiser here, Justice or
Iniquity? – Is this true?

ELBOW   O thou Caitiff; O thou Varlet; O thou

54

185 **Hannibal** Elbow may mean 'cannibal'. But in fact 'Hannibal' is amusingly apt, both as the name of a brilliantly successful general (247–183 BC) with much higher standing than Pompey the Great (who was defeated by Julius Caesar in 48 BC), and as the name of a tactician proverbial for the use of his wits to escape from the difficulties he got into.

189– **mine . . . thee** you arrested on the charge of physical assault.
90 Again the Constable's ineptitude proves apt. *Action* is frequently used with sexual implication (see *All's Well That Ends Well*, IV.iii.28–30), and *Batt'ry* could well refer to a 'pounding' with a 'bat' (see the note to line 133). *Action* recalls line 12; *poor* (line 188) echoes lines 46–47 and anticipates lines 209, 234.

191 **If . . . Ear** if he struck you on the ear (that is, battered you in the legal sense). Escalus' phrasing permits bawdy interpretations of *took* (a word that could mean the same thing as *do* and *make*) and *Box* (another word for *case*, as in V.i.15 of *Troilus and Cressida* and in II.iii.296 of *All's Well That Ends Well*).

192 **Slander** Escalus' point is that what Elbow has called 'Batt'ry' is actually 'Slander'. But since slander (false accusation) is an assault on the 'Ear', Escalus' phrasing is particularly appropriate. *Marry* (lines 193, 200) recalls I.ii.67.

195 **Caitiff** base villain (literally, captive).

198 **continue . . . Courses** keep on with his present activities. There is probably wordplay on *continue* (see the note to line 168), a word whose Latin forebear, *continuare*, lends itself to such pertinent meanings as 'extend', 'draw out', 'occupy', and 'join together'.

204 **borne** (a) carried, (b) born, and (c) reared.

213 **Over-done . . . last** both (a) having acquired the name 'Over-done' by virtue of her last marriage [to Master Overdone], and (b) over- 'done' by her last husband. Compare lines 125–27, 150–51.

214 **hether** hither.

wicked Hannibal; I respected with her, before I   185
was married to her? – If ever I was respected
with her, or she with me, let not your Worship
think me the poor Duke's Officer. – Prove this,
thou wicked Hannibal, or I'll have mine Action
of Batt'ry on thee.   190

ESCALUS   If he took you a Box o'th' Ear, you
might have your Action of Slander too.

ELBOW   Marry I thank your good Worship for it:
what is't your Worship's pleasure I shall do
with this wicked Caitiff?   195

ESCALUS   Truly, Officer, because he hath some
Offences in him that thou wouldst discover if
thou couldst, let him continue in his Courses,
till thou knowst what they are.

ELBOW   Marry I thank your Worship for it. – Thou   200
seest, thou wicked Varlet now, what's come upon
thee. Thou art to continue now, thou Varlet,
thou art to continue.

ESCALUS   Where were you borne, Friend?

FROTH   Here in Vienna, Sir.   205

ESCALUS   Are you of four-score Pounds a Year?

FROTH   Yes, and 't please you, Sir.

ESCALUS   So. – What Trade are you of, Sir?

CLOWN   A Tapster, a poor Widow's Tapster.

ESCALUS   Your Mistress' name?   210

CLOWN   Mistress Over-done.

ESCALUS   Hath she had any more than one Husband?

CLOWN   Nine, Sir: Over-done by the last.

ESCALUS   Nine? – Come hether to me, Master Froth.

215–
16
acquainted with   associating with. Here *acquainted* has connotations that relate to the real occupation of 'Tapsters' such as
Pompey; it can carry the same implications as *know*, and its
root word, *quaint*, is another variant on the most vulgar term
(from Latin *cunnus*) for the female genitalia. See the note to
line 168, and compare *Twelfth Night*, I.iii.54–55, *Much Ado
About Nothing*, V.i.341–42, and Sonnet 89, lines 8–12.

216   **draw you**   (a) dry you out (by drawing forth and thus draining
you of your 'froth' or liquor), and (b) drag you to execution.
Escalus plays on the phrase 'hang, draw, and quarter', a
reference to the practice of disembowelling and cutting to
pieces the corpses of hanged traitors. See *King John*,
II.i.506–8.

217   **hang them**   lead them to be hanged as well (with wordplay on
the kind of 'hanging', copulation, that acquaintance with
'Tapsters' promotes). See *Love's Labour's Lost*, V.ii.600.

219   **For . . . part**   as far as I am concerned (with wordplay on the
kind of 'part' that hangs). See the note to line 31.

221   **drawn in**   enticed (in the sense that leads him to 'come', line
220, echoing lines 123–30). See the note on *withdraw* at
I.ii.116.

228   **Bum**   buttocks (evidently Pompey's surname). But here Escalus
is also using the word with phallic import, perhaps by
association with *bum-blade*, a large sword, or *bum-dagger*.

230   **Pompey the Great**   the Roman general (106–48 BC) and
triumvir defeated by Julius Caesar at the battle of Pharsalia.
Great   both (a) large, and (b) enlarged, tumescent, like a
lecherous satyr. Compare *Love's Labour's Lost*, V.i.137–51,
V.ii.499–506, 514–18, 666–72.

231   **colour**   camouflage, disguise.

235   **live**   earn a living. *Poor* (line 234) echoes lines 188 and 209 and
anticipates line 245; here it means both 'modest' and
'impoverished'.

242   **geld and splay**   castrate and spay.

246   **to't**   copulate. Compare *King Lear*, IV.vi.113–14.
take order for   make arrangements for (by sterilizing or
exercuting), see to.

Master Froth, I would not have you acquainted   215
with Tapsters; they will draw you, Master
Froth, and you will hang them. Get you gone,
and let me hear no more of you.

FROTH   I thank your Worship. For mine own part,
I never come into any Room in a Tap-house, but   220
I am drawn in.

ESCALUS   Well: no more of it, Master Froth.
Farewell.   *[Exit Froth.]*
– Come you hether to me, Master Tapster.
What's your name, Master Tapster?

CLOWN   Pompey.   225

ESCALUS   What else?

CLOWN   Bum, Sir.

ESCALUS   Troth, and your Bum is the greatest
thing about you, so that in the Beastliest
Sense you are Pompey the Great. Pompey, you   230
are partly a Bawd, Pompey, howsoever you colour
it in being a Tapster, are you not? Come, tell
me true, it shall be the better for you.

CLOWN   Truly Sir, I am a poor Fellow that would
live.   235

ESCALUS   How would you live, Pompey? By being a
Bawd? What do you think of the Trade, Pompey?
Is it a Lawful Trade?

CLOWN   If the Law would allow it, Sir.

ESCALUS   But the Law will not allow it, Pompey;   240
nor it shall not be allowed in Vienna.

CLOWN   Does your Worship mean to geld and splay
all the Youth of the City?

ESCALUS   No, Pompey.

CLOWN   Truly Sir, in my poor Opinion they will   245
to't then. If your Worship will take order for

247 **Drabs** whores.
     Knaves wanton young men. Compare *The Tempest*,
     II.i.146–48.

250 **Heading** beheading. Escalus' term allows for wordplay on
     other senses of *Heading* and *Hanging* (a) raising and
     horizontally suspending male 'heads', and (b) taking
     'maidenheads' (a sense deriving from *hang* as a word that can
     mean 'hook', 'attach to', or 'cling to'). See the note to line
     217, and compare the discussion of different types of hanging
     in IV.ii.33–64. Also see the note to II.iv.178.

252 **for . . . together** over a period of ten years (with wordplay on
     the sense of *together* implied by 'offend that way').

253 **to . . . Heads** to place an order for an additional supply of
     heads. Compare *King Lear*, IV.vi.117.

255 **after** for a price of.
     a Bay the portion of a house defined by a single gable. *Three
     Pence* echoes lines 97–98, 112.

258– **requital of** repayment for.
59

261 **not for** not even for so trifling a charge as.

262 **beat . . . Tent** drive you off the battlefield and into retreat.

263 **a shrewd . . . you** as harsh in my treatment of you as Julius
     Caesar was to Pompey the Great. Escalus is also using *Caesar*
     in the generic sense, to refer to himself as a representative of
     the ruler. Here *shrewd* means both (a) cunning, and (b)
     curse-like (from *shrewd* as an aphetic form of *beshrewed*
     'cursed').

263– **plain dealing** unvarnished, direct speech. As it happens,
64   Escalus' phrase is not unrelated to the kind of 'dealing'
       (transaction) Pompey does for a 'Trade' (line 270); see *The
       Comedy of Errors*, II.ii.91–94, *Love's Labour's Lost*,
       IV.iii.371, and *The Merchant of Venice*, III.v.60–61, where
       plain means 'naked'.

269 **let . . . Jade** let the lowly carter whip his worthless, recalcitrant
     horse.

273 **place** position, office. Compare line 11, and see the notes to
     lines 168, 173.

the Drabs and the Knaves, you need not to fear
the Bawds.

ESCALUS   There is pretty Orders beginning, I can
tell you: it is but Heading and Hanging.   250

CLOWN   If you Head and Hang all that offend that
way but for ten Year together, you'll be glad
to give out a Commission for more Heads. If
this Law hold in Vienna ten Year, I'll rent the
Fairest House in it after three Pence a Bay. If   255
you live to see this come to pass, say Pompey
told you so.

ESCALUS   Thank you, good Pompey; and in requital
of your Prophecy, hark you, I advise you let me
not find you before me again upon any Complaint   260
whatsoever; no, not for dwelling where you do.
If I do, Pompey, I shall beat you to your Tent,
and prove a shrewd Caesar to you. In plain
dealing, Pompey, I shall have you whipp'd. So
for this time, Pompey, fare you well.   265

CLOWN   I thank your Worship for your good
Counsel. – But I shall follow it as the Flesh
and Fortune shall better determine.
Whip me? No, no, let Carman whip his Jade,
The Valiant Heart's not whipp'd out of his
      Trade.   *Exit.*   270

ESCALUS   Come hether to me, Master Elbow;
come hither, Master Constable. How long
have you been in this place of Constable?

ELBOW   Seven Year, and a half, Sir.

275   **thought**   inferred, concluded.
       Readiness   both (a) skilled preparedness, and (b) eagerness.
       Continued (line 274) echoes lines 196–203.

279   **Pains**   effort, difficult.

280   **put . . . upon't**   force you to perform this duty so frequently.
       Constables were elected, normally on an annual basis.

281   **Ward**   jurisdiction, administrative district (synonymous with
       'Parish', line 289).
       sufficient . . . it   qualified to do the job.

283   **Wit**   intelligence, competence. Like *Will* (see the second note to
       II.ii.27, and see Sonnets 135–36), *Wit* can refer to erotic
       ingenuity and to the genitalia of either gender; compare
       Romeo and Juliet, I.i.212, I.iii.42, *As You Like It*,
       IV.i.168–87, and *The Merchant of Venice*, III.v.52–60.
       Meanwhile *matters* can refer to what the Cobbler calls
       'Women's matters' in *Julius Caesar*, I.i.27.

284–   **to . . . them**   to let me serve in their stead.
85

285   **some piece**   a small amount.

286   **go . . . all**   take care of the whole job myself.

287   **Look you**   see that you. Escalus is desperate for new officers.

293   **Dinner**   the main midday meal.

294   **for**   about.

297   **looks**   appears to be.

298   **still**   always, ever.
       the . . . Woe   the nourisher of more grief [by failing to deal with
       the initial problem]. In lines 296–98 Escalus tries to persuade
       himself that Angelo's policies are in fact wise ones.

ESCALUS   I thought by the Readiness in the Office,   275
you had continued in it some time. You say
seven Years together.

ELBOW   And a half, Sir.

ESCALUS   Alas, it hath been great Pains to you:
they do you wrong to put you so oft upon't.   280
Are there not Men in your Ward sufficient to
serve it?

ELBOW   'Faith Sir, few of any Wit in such matters.
As they are chosen, they are glad to choose me
for them. I do it for some piece of Money, and   285
go through with all.

ESCALUS   Look you bring me in the Names of
some six or seven, the most sufficient of your
Parish.

ELBOW   To your Worship's House, Sir?   290

ESCALUS   To my House. Fare you well. *[Exit Constable.]*
— What's a' clock, think you?

JUSTICE   Eleven, Sir.

ESCALUS   I pray you home to Dinner with me.

JUSTICE   I humbly thank you.

ESCALUS   It grieves me for the Death
Of Claudio, but there's no Remedy.   295

JUSTICE   Lord Angelo is Severe.

ESCALUS   It is but Needful.
<u>Mercy is not it self that oft looks so:</u>
<u>Pardon is still the Nurse of Second W</u>oe.
But yet, poor Claudio. There is no Remedy.
Come, Sir.   *Exeunt.*   300

II.ii   This scene takes place in an anteroom of the Courtroom.

1   **hearing . . . Cause**   hearing (judging) a case.
    come straight   come right away. Like so much of the language
    in this play, the Servant's phrasing suggests that even the most
    straitlaced of characters may prove to be subject to 'Motions
    of the Sense' at odds with 'Profits of the Mind' (I.v.60, 62).
    See the notes to II.i.9 and II.i.125, 221, and compare the
    phrasing in II.i.31.

3   **His Pleasure**   what he (Angelo) would have me do. *Know*
    recalls I.v.9 and *know / His Pleasure* echoes. I.i.25.
    relent   melt (literally, become soft and pliable).

4   **He . . . Dream**   his (Claudio's) offence is so minor that it is no
    more reprehensible than the misdeeds people merely dream
    about doing.

5   **Sects**   groups of people (sections of the population).
    smack . . . Vice   are subject to the appetite that leads to this sin.
    Compare *The Merchant of Venice*, II.ii.17–19, where
    Launcelet says that his 'Father did something smack,
    something grow to; he had a kind of Taste'.

7   **to morrow**   tomorrow. But here, as elsewhere in Shakespeare,
    the Renaissance spelling permits additional meanings. If
    Claudio is executed, he will 'die to morrow' in at least two
    senses: (a) he will be dead to the morrow (unable to witness
    its arrival with his mortal eyes), and (b) he will die to achieve
    a different kind of morrow (the afterlife). Compare *Macbeth*,
    I.v.60–63, II.iii.59.

9   **Rash**   hasty, impulsive.

10   **Under your good Correction**   if you'll pardon my saying so.
    The Provost's phrasing hints at more than the kind of 'good
    correction' (virtuous discipline) he has in mind. The Latin
    root of *correct* (*correctus*, from *com-*, together, and *regere*,
    lead or rule straight) is the same as that for *erect*, *direct*, and
    rector (see *All's Well That Ends Well*, IV.iii.55–77, especially
    lines 66–69), and here it suggests what Lucio will later call the
    'downright way of Creation' (III.i.396–97).

Scene 2

Enter Provost, Servant.

SERVANT   He's hearing of a Cause; he will come
straight,
I'll tell him of you.
PROVOST   'Pray you do.   *[Exit Servant.]*
                                    – I'll know
His Pleasure, may be he will relent. Alas,
He hath but as offended in a Dream;
All Sects, all Ages, smack of this Vice, and he   5
To die for't?

Enter Angelo.

ANGELO   Now, what's the matter, Provost?
PROVOST   Is it your will Claudio shall die
to morrow?
ANGELO   Did not I tell thee yea? Hadst thou not
Order?
Why dost thou ask again?
PROVOST   Lest I might be too Rash:
Under your good Correction, I have seen   10

11–12 **Judgement . . . Doom**   the judge has regretted the sentence he imposed. The Provost's phrasing is subject to a second interpretation as well: 'the judge has been led to lament the doom he has brought upon himself'.

12   **Go to**   forget it and begone.

13   **mine**   my concern and responsibility.
      Office   duty.

14   **Place**   post, job. Compare line 18 and II.i.273.
      spar'd   Angelo means 'dispensed with'; but *spar'd* can also mean 'exempted from the penalty you would otherwise suffer'.

16   **groaning**   moaning (with labour pains). *Groaning* is a word that can also refer to the throes that led to Juliet's condition (see *Hamlet*, III.ii.272–74, where Ophelia calls the Prince 'keen' and he tells her 'It would cost you a Groaning to take off mine Edge'), and that sense is reinforced by the suggestive phrase *fitter place* (see the second note to II.i.11) in line 18.

17   **Dispose of**   remove. *Dispose* recalls I.iii.3.

20   **access to**   an audience with. Here *access* is accented on the second syllable. The same phrasing occurs in II.iv.18.
      Sister   This designation is a reminder that Isabella is subject to the demands of two different callings: (a) her love for her brother, and (b) her forthcoming vows to the Order of Saint Clare.

22   **of a Sister-hood**   a member of an order of nuns. The Folio hyphen provides a reminder of the hood that would be part of a nun's habit.

24   **Fornicatress**   The harshness of this name for Juliet is an indication of the severity of Angelo's moral indignation.

26   **Order**   authorization. Compare line 8. *Needful* echoes I.i.54, I.iv.20.

27   **Y'are welcome**   you are welcome to my presence. Angelo addresses Isabella, who has probably knelt to express her reverence and indicate her gratitude for the privilege of speaking with the Deputy.
      what's your Will?   what business brings you to me? *Will* means 'desire', and it often refers to erotic promptings. It can also be a word for the genitalia of either gender. Compare I.i.24–25, I.iii.5–8, II.i.32, and see line 34.

When, after Execution, Judgement hath
Repented o'er his Doom.

ANGELO   Go to; let that
Be mine, do you your Office, or give up
Your Place, and you shall well be spar'd.

PROVOST   I crave your Honour's Pardon.   15
What shall be done, Sir, with the groaning
      Juliet?
She's very near her Hour.

ANGELO   Dispose of her
To some more fitter place, and that with speed.

[Enter Servant.]

SERVANT   Here is the Sister of the man condemn'd,
Desires access to you.

ANGELO   — Hath he a Sister?   20

PROVOST   Ay my good Lord, a very virtuous Maid,
And to be shortly of a Sister-hood,
If not already.

ANGELO   — Well, let her be admitted.

                                   [Exit Servant.]
— See you the Fornicatress be remov'd;
Let her have needful but not lavish Means.   25
There shall be Order for't.

Enter Lucio and Isabella.

PROVOST   'Save your Honour.

28 **woeful** sorrowful. But *woe* and *woo* are closely associated, and
    at times interchangeable, in Shakespeare (see the note to
    Romeo and Juliet, III.iv.8), and in a way she couldn't imagine
    Isabella will prove to be a wooful suitor (see I.iii.60–69).

31 **meet . . . Justice** be struck down by the Justice's executioner.
    Isabella's phrasing inadvertently hints at other ways in which
    women sometimes meet 'Blows'. Compare I.ii.287–90 of
    Troilus and Cressida.

34 **At . . . Not** Isabella's words recall the psychomachia (battle for
    control of the soul) that the Apostle Paul describes in Romans
    7:15–25, where he notes that 'the good that I would I do not,
    but the evil which I would not, that I do'. See the notes to
    lines 20, 27, and compare line 53.

36 **let . . . Fault** let it be his sin that is condemned.

37 **moving Graces** the gift to inspire compassion. Compare I.iii.67
    and I.v.69–71.

39 **condemn'd** judged to be a sin (by definition), and condemned
    by God. Lines 38–39 echo line 19.

40 **Mine . . . Function** mine would be nothing more than an empty
    role.
    Cipher 'nothing' or 'zero'.

41–42 **whose . . . Actor** which are already defined as crimes calling for
    specific penalties before a given 'Actor' is brought before me
    to be judged. Compare II.i.12–13, 189–90. *Fine* can mean
    both (a) penalty, and (b) end, finish. And *stands* is a reminder
    of the nature of the 'Fault' at issue in this case; see the notes
    to I.ii.102, II.i.168.

46 **a Pin** nothing more than a pin. Compare II.i.103.

53 **Look what** whatever, that which. See the note to II.i.173. The
    phrase *will not* echoes line 34.

ANGELO   Stay a little while. —Y'are welcome:
  what's your Will?

ISABELLA   I am a woeful Suitor to your Honour,
  'Please but your Honour hear me.

ANGELO   Well: what's your Suit?

ISABELLA   There is a Vice that most I do abhor,
  And most desire should meet the Blow of Justice,
  For which I would not plead, but that I must,
  For which I must not plead, but that I am
  At War, 'twixt Will and Will Not.

ANGELO   Well: the Matter?   30

ISABELLA   I have a Brother is condemn'd to die;
  I do beseech you let it be his Fault,
  And not my Brother.

PROVOST   — Heaven give thee moving Graces.

ANGELO   Condemn the Fault and not the Actor of it?   35
  Why every Fault's condemn'd ere it be done:
  Mine were the very Cipher of a Function
  To fine the Faults, whose Fine stands in Record,
  And let go by the Actor.   40

ISABELLA   Oh just but severe Law:
  I had a Brother then; Heaven keep your Honour.

LUCIO   — Give't not o'er so: to him again, entreat him,
  Kneel down before him, hang upon his Gown.
  You are too Cold: if you should need a Pin,   45
  You could not with more tame a Tongue desire it.
  To him, I say.

ISABELLA   — Must he needs die?

ANGELO   Maiden, no Remedy.

ISABELLA   Yes: I do think that you might pardon
  him,
  And neither Heaven nor Man grieve at the Mercy.   50

ANGELO   I will not do't.

ISABELLA   But can you if you would?

ANGELO   Look what I will not, that I cannot do.

54   **do't** Here and elsewhere in this exchange, the verb *do* reverberates with unintended echoes of the sense implicit in I.ii.90, II.i.125, 148–51.

57   **Cold** dispassionate (as in 2 *Henry IV*, V.ii.97, and *Hamlet*, I.ii.77).

59   **call it again** call it back, retract it.

60   **Ceremony** emblem of office.
       Great Ones rulers, majestic personages. *Great* recalls II.i.230.
       longs 'longs, belongs. See the note to II.i.103.

61   **deputed Sword** the justice a ruler wields as God's deputy.

62   **Marshal's Truncheon** the baton symbolizing military authority. Like *Sword*, this word suggests more than one kind of 'Ceremony that to Great Ones longs' (line 60). It also hints at more than one way to be 'stern' (stiff, rigid, hard, unyielding, line 66).

65   **slipp'd** misstepped. Compare I.iv.21.

68   **Potency** power, authority. This word reminds us of Claudio's proven potency, and it hints at Angelo's potential to be 'like him' (line 65).

71   **Vein** strain, style, approach. Another sense of *vein* is relevant to Lucio's insistence that Isabella 'touch' Angelo and thereby heat his icy 'Blood' (see I.v.58–59). The Folio spelling, *Vain*, hints that Isabella is beginning to 'touch' Angelo in a way that relates to the kind of 'Pride' (arousal) depicted in Sonnet 151, lines 7–12.

72   **Forfeit . . . Law** condemned lawbreaker.

75   **Vantage** both (a) advantage, and (b) highest vantage point ('Top of Judgement', line 77). Isabella alludes to such biblical passages as Isaiah 53:6, Romans 3:21–26 and Matthew 6:14–15. *Remedy* (line 76), an echo of II.i.294–99, is another term for the cure a merciful God 'found out' (discovered) for a fallen and therefore forfeited human race.

80   **Man new made** This phrase refers to the concept of spiritual rebirth as expressed in John 3:3, Colossians 3:9–10, and Ephesians 2:1–10 and 4:22–25. Lines 74–78 recall what Escalus has said in II.i.8–16; line 80 echoes I.i.46–49, I.ii.94–95, I.iii.35–38, I.v.41–45, 58–62.

ISABELLA   But might you do't, and do the World no
     Wrong,
   If so your Heart were touch'd with that Remorse   55
   As mine is to him?
ANGELO   He's sentenc'd, 'tis too late.
LUCIO — You are too Cold.
ISABELLA   Too late? Why no: I that do speak a Word
   May call it again. Well, believe this:
   No Ceremony that to Great Ones longs   60
   (Not the King's Crown, nor the deputed Sword,
   The Marshal's Truncheon, nor the Judge's Robe)
   Become them with one half so good a Grace
   As Mercy does. If he had been as you,
   And you as he, you would have slipp'd like him,
   But he like you would not have been so stern.
ANGELO   Pray you be gone.
ISABELLA   I would to Heaven I had
   Your Potency and you were Isabel.
   Should it then be thus? No: I would tell what 'twere
   To be a Judge, and what a Prisoner.   70
LUCIO — Ay, touch him: there's the Vein.
ANGELO   Your Brother is a Forfeit of the Law,
   And you but waste your Words.
ISABELLA   Alas, alas:
   Why all the Souls that were were Forfeit once,
   And he that might the Vantage best have took   75
   Found out the Remedy. How would you be
   If he which is the Top of Judgement should
   But judge you as you are? Oh think on that,
   And Mercy then will breathe within your Lips
   Like Man new made.
ANGELO   Be you content, fair Maid: 80
   It is the Law, not I, condemn your Brother.
   Were he my Kinsman, Brother, or my Son,
   It should be thus with him: he must die
      to morrow.

84   **sudden**   [too] soon. Isabella gives the word the connotations it
         often has elsewhere: (a) rash, impetuous (see line 9), and (b)
         violent, tyrannical, as in *Macbeth*, IV.iii.59.

86   **of Season**   of the requisite size and maturity.

86–88 **Shall . . . Selves?**   Shall we present to Heaven a dish that has
         been prepared with less thought and care than those we
         provide for our own corporeal selves? Here *serve* compares
         preparing meals and waiting on tables to the kind of spiritual
         service (reverent obedience) that Christians 'minister' to God
         as His faithful subjects. *Respects* means both (a)
         consideration, and (b) courteous deference; compare
         II.i.172–88. And *gross* (an echo of I.iii.37) means both (a)
         physical, and (b) corrupt (manifesting all the characteristics of
         'the flesh' as defined in Romans 7:15–25 and Galatians 5:17).

94   **th' Edict infringe**   transgress the statute. Here *Edict* is accented
         on the second syllable.

95   **answer'd**   been judged and punished. The implications of
         'answer' in passages such as II.ii of *All's Well That Ends Well*
         charge 'answer'd for his Deed' with a suggestiveness that will
         soon prove pertinent.
         Now 'tis awake   By the end of the scene, this assertion will take
         on meanings not intended by the speaker at present. *Awake*
         recalls I.iii.47–49.

97   **Glass**   the kind of crystal used for divination (forecasting the
         future). Compare *Macbeth*, IV.i.118, where the eighth king in
         the procession presented to the title character bears such a
         glass.
         shews   shows. But here as elsewhere, the Folio spelling hints at
         the possibility of wordplay on an aphetic (frontally
         abbreviated) form of *eschews* (shuns, spurns). Compare *The
         Tempest*, III.i.81.

98   **Remissness new conceiv'd**   newly hatched forms of neglect
         (disregard of the law). Again, Angelo's wording will prove
         ironic.

99   **borne**   both (a) born, and (b) carried, nurtured. Compare
         II.i.204. Brutus uses a similar hatching image in II.i.28–34 of
         Julius Caesar.

100   **successive Degrees**   heirs, offspring. Angelo's concept of
         anticipatory 'Pity' (line 101) echoes what Escalus has said in
         II.i.297–98. Compare lines 38–42.

ISABELLA   To morrow? Oh that's sudden: spare him,
  spare him,
He's not prepar'd for Death. Even for our
  Kitchens   85
We kill the Fowl of Season. Shall we serve
  Heaven
With less Respect than we do minister
To our gross Selves? Good, good my Lord,
  bethink you:
Who is it that hath died for this Offence?
There's many have committed it.   90
LUCIO   – Ay, well said.
ANGELO   The Law hath not been dead, though
  it hath slept:
Those many had not dar'd to do that Evil
If the first that did th' Edict infringe
Had answer'd for his Deed. Now 'tis awake,   95
Takes note of what is done, and like a Prophet
Looks in a Glass that shews what future Evils
(Either now or by Remissness new conceiv'd,
And so in Progress to be hatch'd and borne)
Are now to have no successive Degrees,   100
But here they live to end.
ISABELLA   Yet shew some Pity.
ANGELO   I shew it most of all when I shew Justice:
  For then I pity those I do not know,

[handwritten marginal note: not parallel in comparison]

104 **Which . . . gall**   whom an unpunished crime would later injure. *Gall* recalls I.iv.36–37.

113 **Jove**   Isabella depicts the 'Thunderbearer' (Zeus in Greek mythology, Jove or Jupiter in Roman) as an emblem of divine wrath and its petty human imitations. The second *Jove* in this line probably refers to Jove's earthly deputies, the 'powers that be' who are 'ordained of God' (Romans 13:1). Compare I.iii.5, where Claudio describes Angelo as 'the Demigod Authority', and V.i.362, where Angelo likens the Duke to 'Powre Divine'. Such 'Great Men' (lines 112, 128, echoing line 60) need to remember that, for all their sway, they remain servants of Heaven, since 'there is no power but of God' (Romans 13:1), and that power is delegated only for 'brief' stewardships (line 119); see the note to I.i.28, and compare Luke 12:42–48. Line 112 (a part line) is here indented to indicate a brief pause before Isabella resumes speaking.

114 **pelting**   both (a) paltry, and (b) missile-throwing (pelting in the usual modern sense).

116– **Merciful . . . Myrtle**   Heaven itself reserves the mightiest 'Bolt'
18   for the hard, stubborn 'Oak' rather than unleashing all its wrath on the pliant, defenceless little 'Myrtle'. Compare *Coriolanus*, V.iii.149–53, and *The Tempest*, V.i.44–46.

119 **brief**   Isabella is thinking of the short lifespan of 'Proud Man'; but her adjective also applies to Angelo's deputyship.

120 **what . . . assur'd**   both (a) what he should know with most certainty, and (b) what he feels most sure he does know. Isabella implies that Angelo is a victim of 'Security' (the *pleonexia*, unwarranted self-confidence, and *atê*, blindness, that accompanies *hubris*, the overreaching arrogance that precipitates a fall in Greek tragedy). Compare *Julius Caesar*, II.iii.9.

121 **Glassy**   fragile, easily shattered, like the mirror that symbolizes vanity. Compare line 97 and see the first note to II.iv.128.

122 **fantastic**   ludicrous; reflecting nothing but an ape's antics.

123– **who . . . Mortal**   who if they shared our susceptibility to
24   impulsive emotions (centred in the 'Spleen') would (a) laugh the way mortals do, and (b) laugh themselves to death.

126 **coming**   responding. See the second note to line 1.

Which a dismiss'd Offence would after gall,
And do him Right that, answering one foul Wrong,   105
Lives not to act another. Be satisfied;
Your Brother dies to morrow; be content.

ISABELLA   So you must be the first that gives this
    Sentence,
And he, that suffers. Oh it is excellent
To have a Giant's Strength; but it is tyrannous   110
To use it like a Giant.

LUCIO   — That's well said.

ISABELLA   Could Great Men thunder
As Jove himself does, Jove would never be quiet:
For every pelting petty Officer
Would use his Heaven for Thunder, nothing but
    Thunder.   115
— Merciful Heaven, thou rather with thy sharp
And sulphurous Bolt splits the unwedgeable
And gnarled Oak than the soft Myrtle. But Man,
Proud Man, dress'd in a little brief Authority,
Most ignorant of what he's most assur'd   120
(His Glassy Essence), like an angry Ape,
Plays such fantastic Tricks before high Heaven
As makes the Angels weep: who, with our Spleens,
Would all themselves laugh Mortal.

LUCIO   — Oh to him, to him, Wench: he will relent,   125
He's coming, I perceive't.

74

127   **We . . . Self**   We cannot presume to weigh others by our own
       judgement and virtue. See the note to line 140. *Wit* (line 128)
       recalls II.i.283.

129   **But . . . Profanation**   but in lesser men the most impudent
       irreverence. *Fowl* (foul) echoes lines 85–86; *Profanation*
       recalls II.i.54–57.

131– **That . . . Blasphemy**   What in the captain can be excused as a
32   result of choler (the humour that prompts outbursts of anger)
       would be considered the most egregious effrontery in a
       low-ranking soldier.

133   **Art . . . that?**   Are you [a mere maiden] so wise as to know
       that?
       on't   of it. But *on it* is also pertinent to what is happening to
       Angelo at this moment; see the first half of line 126.

136– **Medicine . . . Top**   antidote in the very nature of its position
37   that heals itself, righting an error (in the same way that a layer
       of new skin seals over a sore or wound). Compare *Hamlet*,
       III.iv.142–46. *Top* echoes line 77.

140   **A natural Guiltiness**   a sin-prone nature. Implicit here and in
       line 127 is Jesus' admonition in the Sermon on the Mount:
       'Judge not, that ye be not judged. For with what judgement ye
       judge, ye shall be judged: and with what measure ye mete, it
       shall be measured to you again. And why beholdest thou the
       mote that is in thy brother's eye, but considerest not the beam
       that is in thine own eye?' (Matthew 7:1–5).

143   **Sense**   Angelo probably means 'reason' (good sense) in both
       uses of this word, but *breeds* (both 'mates' and 'begets')
       suggests a second meaning (defined in the note to I.v.60)
       'that's like my Brother's Fault'.

148   **I**   both 'I', and 'Ay', as in II.i.160. Given Angelo's newly
       awakened sensibility, *Heaven* probably conveys images of the
       kind of earthly paradise alluded to in *All's Well That Ends
       Well*, IV.iii.61–62, where we hear that Helena 'made a Groan
       of her last Breath, and now she sings in Heaven'.

PROVOST   — Pray Heaven she win him.

ISABELLA   We cannot weigh our Brother with our
 Self.
 Great Men may jest with Saints: 'tis Wit in
  them,
 But in the Less fowl Profanation.

LUCIO   — Thou'rt i'th' right, Girl, more o' that.   130

ISABELLA   That in the Captain's but a Choleric
 Word
 Which in the Soldier is flat Blasphemy.

LUCIO   — Art avis'd o' that? More on't.

ANGELO   Why do you put these Sayings upon me?

ISABELLA   Because Authority, though it err like
 others,   135
 Hath yet a kind of Medicine in it self
 That skins the Vice o'th' Top. Go to your
  Bosom,
 Knock there, and ask your Heart what it doth
  know
 That's like my Brother's Fault. If it confess
 A natural Guiltiness such as is his,   140
 Let it not sound a Thought upon your Tongue
 Against my Brother's Life.

ANGELO   — She speaks, and 'tis
 Such Sense that my Sense breeds with it.
 — Fare you well.

ISABELLA   Gentle my Lord, turn back.

ANGELO   I will bethink me: come again to morrow. 145

ISABELLA   Hark, how I'll bribe you: good my Lord,
 turn back.

ANGELO   How? Bribe me?

ISABELLA   I, with such Gifts that Heaven shall
 share with you.

LUCIO   — You had marr'd all else.

[handwritten: Angelo tempted by Virtue of Isabel]

150 **fond . . . tested gold** foolishly prized shekels (Hebrew coins) of
pure gold (having been 'tested' by the touchstone for
authenticity). See I.i.34–35, 46–49, 82. But another kind of
sickle (a keen-edged cutting implement) is relevant to the now
'marr'd' nature of 'precise' Angelo. See the notes to I.v.61,
II.i.5, 103, 228, II.ii.46. The sound of *tested gold* gives *Stones*
(line 151, echoing II.i.115) a genital suggestiveness that
'breeds with' (line 143) Angelo's own 'Suborbs' (II.i.66). In
the process it imparts to *fond* (which recalls I.iv.23) a hint
that Isabella's 'Bribe' will involve erotic fondling. This hint is
reinforced by *turn* in lines 144, 146; see the note to IV.ii.62.

151– **Or . . . them** or precious stones (gems), whose price is either
52 high or low as our subjective standards of value determine.
Isabella's remarks inadvertently call to mind another meaning
of *Stones* (see the note to line 150) and another kind of
'Fancy' (infatuation). These suggestions are reinforced by the
words *up, enter,* and *rise* in lines 153–54. *Heaven* echoes line
148.

154 **preserved** both (a) untouched, cloistered, and (b) saved,
redeemed. Compare I.v.35.

155 **fasting** self-denying, austere, dedicated. But to an imagination
aroused by sensual appetite, *fasting* (an echo of I.v.62) could
well suggest 'fast-sting' (see I.v.60) and 'fastening' (see the
notes to II.i.11, 250). *Maids* echoes I.ii.94–95. *Temporal* (line
156) means 'of this world, subject to time'.

160 **cross** both (a) meet, converge, and (b) are at odds with
themselves, or with other prayers. Here *cross* can also mean
'thwart' or 'impede'. Angelo notes that Isabella's prayers for
his safety may be needed to counter the insincerity of his
recitation of 'lead us not into temptation, but deliver us from
evil' (Matthew 6:13).
Hower hour; here metrically disyllabic.

162 **'Save your Honour** God preserve your Honour. Isabella uses
Honour as a title of respect; but another sense of the word
(honourable character, honesty) is pertinent in ways that she
does not suspect.

166 **lying by** lying beside; with unintended hints of other senses of
lying. Fault (line 163) recalls II.i.39–40; and lines 164–65
echo lines 159–60 and II.i.17–18.

ISABELLA   Not with fond Sickles of the tested Gold,   150
Or Stones, whose Rate are either Rich or Poor
As Fancy values them; but with true Prayers
That shall be up at Heaven and enter there
Ere Sun rise; Prayers from preserved Souls,
From fasting Maids, whose Minds are dedicate   155
To nothing Temporal.
ANGELO   Well: come to me to morrow.
LUCIO   — Go to: 'tis well,
Away.
ISABELLA   Heaven keep your Honour safe.
ANGELO   — Amen.
For I am that way going to Temptation,
Where Prayers cross.
ISABELLA   At what Hower to morrow   160
Shall I attend your Lordship?
ANGELO   At any time 'fore Noon.
ISABELLA   'Save your Honour.
                         [Exit, with Lucio and Provost.]
ANGELO   — From thee: even from thy Virtue.
What's this? What's this? Is this her Fault, or
    mine?
The Tempter, or the Tempted, who sins most, ha?
Not she: nor doth she tempt. But it is I   165
That, lying by the Violet in the Sun,
Do as the Carrion does, not as the Flow'r,

168   **Corrupt . . . Season**   putrefy in the same beneficent sunlight that nourishes the flower. *Season* echoes lines 85–86.

170   **Lightness**   wantonness, licentious behaviour. Compare V.i.271–72.

171   **raze the Sanctuary**   defile a temple and turn it into 'Waste Ground'. *Raze* recalls I.ii.11.

172   **pitch our Evils**   either (a) throw our dung, or (b) erect our evil tents.

174   **fowlly**   both (a) foully, vilely, and (b) in a filthy, predatory, fowl-like manner. Compare line 129.

176   **Authority**   authorization, licence. Lines 175–77 recall II.i.18–31. *Authority* echoes lines 118–24, 135–37.

179   **dream on**   allow myself to fantasize about. Compare lines 3–4.

180   **cunning Enemy**   crafty Devil (Satan). See the note to II.i.215–16.
         Saint   man of holiness. Angelo refers to himself, and his noun recalls *Sanctuary* (line 171) and *preserved* (line 154). Compare I.v.6, 35.

181   **Hook**   Angelo likens himself to an unsuspecting fish. Lucio uses trout imagery with related implications in I.ii.93. See the note to II.i.250.

184   **Strumpet**   seductress, wanton.
         double Vigour   twofold power (both her wiles and her beauty).

185   **stir my Temper**   disturb my self-control. In Elizabethan psychology a person's 'Temper' maintained a proper balance among the four humours that made up his or her disposition, keeping the senses and passions subject to reason and judgement. In this passage another sense of *Temper* is also relevant: the kind of tempering (intense heating and cooling) that made steel hard and durable. In *1 Henry IV*, V.ii.92–94, Hotspur says 'here draw I / A Sword whose Temper I intend to stain / With the best Blood that I can meet withal'.

186   **subdues me quite**   conquers me completely.

187   **fond**   infatuated, foolish (unable to control their emotions). See line 150.

Corrupt with virtuous Season. Can it be
That Modesty may more betray our Sense
Than Woman's Lightness? Having Waste Ground
    enough,   170
Shall we desire to raze the Sanctuary
And pitch our Evils there? Oh fie, fie, fie:
What dost thou? Or what art thou, Angelo?
Dost thou desire her fowlly for those things
That make her good? Oh, let her Brother live.   175
Thieves for their Robbery have Authority
When Judges steal themselves. What, do I love
    her,
That I desire to hear her speak again?
And feast upon her Eyes? What is't I dream on?
– Oh cunning Enemy, that to catch a Saint   180
With Saints dost bait thy Hook. Most dangerous
Is that Temptation that doth goad us on
To Sin in loving Virtue; never could
The Strumpet, with all her double Vigour, Art,
And Nature, once stir my Temper; but this
    virtuous   185
Maid subdues me quite. Ever till now
When Men were fond, I smil'd and wond'red how.

                                              Exit.

II.iii   This scene takes place in the Viennese prison. From this point until the beginning of Act V the Duke appears only in the guise of a Friar.

3   **Bound . . . Charity**   obliged by my commitment to deeds of Christian love. *Will* (line 2) echoes II.i.283 (see note), II.ii.27, 34, 53. *Visit* recalls I.iv.44–45.

5–6   **Do . . . them**   grant me the privilege common to all men of the cloth and let me visit them.

9   **if . . . needful**   if you were to say that you needed more of me. *Needful* recalls II.ii.25.

11   **Flaws**   both (a) defects, faults (as in II.i.40, II.ii.163), and (b) sudden gusts (usually referring to wind, but here used metaphorically of passion).

12   **blister'd her Report**   blemished her reputation (like a whore whose shame has been branded on her forehead).

13   **got**   begot, conceived.

14   **fit**   suitable (but with a reminder of the kind of 'fitting' that got him into this situation). Compare II.ii.18 and II.iv.163, and see *All's Well That Ends Well*, II.ii.15–16.

17   **Stay**   wait. The Provost addresses Juliet.
       conducted   taken to the place provided for you to give birth to your child (in accordance with II.ii.16–18).

19   **bear the Shame**   both (a) bear the child that displays my shameful behaviour, and (b) endure the reproach my behaviour has earned me.
       patiently   penitently, without resistance or complaint.

20   **arraign**   make trial of (literally, accuse and bring to trial).

21   **Sound**   healthy, reliable, solid. Compare I.ii.56–60.

22   **hollowly put on**   worn insincerely. See I.ii.58–60.

Scene 3

Enter Duke and Provost.

DUKE   Hail to you, Provost, so I think you are.
PROVOST   I am the Provost. What's your Will,
   good Friar?
DUKE   Bound by my Charity, and my blest Order,
   I come to visit the afflicted Spirits
   Here in the Prison. Do me the common Right   5
   To let me see them, and to make me know
   The nature of their Crimes, that I may minister
   To them accordingly.
PROVOST   I would do more than that, if more were
   needful.

Enter Juliet.

   Look, here comes one, a Gentlewoman of mine   10
   Who, falling in the Flaws of her own Youth,
   Hath blister'd her Report; she is with Child,
   And he that got it, sentenc'd: a Young Man
   More fit to do another such Offence
   Than die for this.
DUKE   When must he die?
PROVOST   As I   15
   Do think, to morrow. – I have provided for you:
   Stay a while, and you shall be conducted.
DUKE   Repent you, Fair One, of the Sin you carry?
JULIET   I do; and bear the Shame most patiently.
DUKE   I'll teach you how you shall arraign your
   Conscience   20
   And try your Penitence, if it be Sound
   Or hollowly put on.
JULIET   I'll gladly learn.
DUKE   Love you the Man that wrong'd you?

26   **mutually**   reciprocally (from Latin *mutare*, to change or exchange). Compare I.iii.36.

27   **heavier kind**   a more serious nature (because of the double standard whereby a woman was held more culpable than the man she 'bore'). The word *heavier* is also a reminder of the burden Juliet carries in her womb.

29   **meet so**   appropriate that you do.
      least   lest. Compare III.ii.73.

30   **as that**   solely because.

31   **toward our selves**   motivated solely by our regret that we got caught.

32   **as we love it**   because of our love of Heaven. *Spare* echoes II.ii.14–15.

33   **But . . . Fear**   but because of our fear of divine wrath. *Stand* recalls II.ii.41.

34–35 **I . . . Joy**   I repent what I have done, not because I have suffered for it, but simply because it was evil; and I am glad to bear my penance (and my child) as a mark of my gratitude for God's grace.

35   **There rest**   Remain in that healthy spiritual condition.

37   **with Instruction**   with wise counsel to prepare his soul for death. Compare I.i.78–79, I.iv.46–48.

38   **Benedicite**   [may God] bless you.

39   **injurious**   both (a) unjust, illicit, and (b) harmful, inflicting injury.

40   **respites**   grants (as a reprieve).
      Life   Juliet is probably thinking of her own life (the fact that she is being spared execution, even though her lover 'must die'), but she is also referring to (a) the new life she carries in her womb, the fruit of 'injurious Love', and (b) the new life she has as a result of her redemption (see the note to II.ii.80).

41   **still**   both (a) yet, and (b) ever.

II.iv   This scene takes place at the Duke's palace in Vienna.

2   **To several Subjects**   in contrary directions. Compare II.ii.30–34, 159–60, and *Hamlet*, III.iii.36–72.

JULIET   Yes, as I love the Woman that wrong'd him.
DUKE   So then it seems your most Offence-full Act   25
  Was mutually committed.
JULIET   Mutually.
DUKE   Then was your Sin of heavier kind than his.
JULIET   I do confess it, and repent it, Father.
DUKE   'Tis meet so, Daughter; but least you do repent
  As that the Sin hath brought you to this Shame,   30
  Which Sorrow is always toward our selves,
    not Heaven,
  Showing we would not spare Heaven as
    we love it
  But as we stand in Fear –
JULIET   I do repent me as it is an Evil,
  And take the Shame with Joy.
DUKE   There rest.   35
  Your Partner, as I hear, must die to morrow,
  And I am going with Instruction to him.
  Grace go with you, *Benedicite.*   *Exit.*
JULIET   Must die to morrow? Oh injurious Love,
  That respites me a Life whose very Comfort
  Is still a dying Horror.   40
PROVOST   'Tis Pity of him.   *Exeunt.*

Scene 4

Enter Angelo.

ANGELO   When I would pray, and think, I think, and
    pray
  To several Subjects: Heaven hath my empty Words,

84

3   **Invention** creative imagination. *Invent* means 'come upon, discover'.

6–7   **swelling . . . Conception** Angelo describes his growing inclination to evil in terms that relate to both tumescence (line 16, where 'Horn' is phallic) and pregnancy. *Conception* recalls II.ii.98.

7   **The . . . studied** both (a) the way of life, and (b) the principles of government to which I devoted all my attention. Like *stay* (II.iii.17) and *Constable* (see the note to II.i.168), *State* derives from the Latin verb *stare*, to stand.

9   **grown . . . tedious** either (a) grown timid and tiresome, or (b) to be avoided because it has now become laborious or boring. Compare I.iv.23–31. Most editions substitute *sere* (arid) for the Folio's *fear'd*.
       Gravity weightiness of purpose and dignity of manner.

10   **Place** position, high office. Compare II.ii.13–14, 18, and see the second note to II.i.11.

11   **with Boot** for advantage.
       change both (a) exchange, (b) change away from.
       idle Plume frivolous ornament of feathers on a hat or helmet (a traditional emblem of pride).

12   **for Vain** as if it were nothing (vanity), like a weathervane. Compare II.ii.71.

13   **Case** external appearance, which awes 'Fools' and deceives 'the Wiser'. Like *Place*, *Case* can refer to the genitalia; see *Romeo and Juliet*, II.iii.56–62. *Habit* (clothing, manner) recalls I.iv.46.

16–17 **Let's . . . Crest** Let's place the motto 'Good Angel' on the Devil's horn where it belongs, rather than continuing to abide by 'Form' (custom, convention) and regarding such 'False Seeming' as limited to his 'Crest' (heraldic emblem). If Satan can transform himself into 'an angel of light' (2 Corinthians 11:14), Angelo implies, it follows that if you uncase (unmask) a man named 'Angel' you will discover a 'Devil' with an unruly 'Horn' beneath his saintly 'Habit'. *Blood* recalls II.i.12 and anticipates line 20; compare I.v.58–62.

Whilst my Invention, hearing not my Tongue,
Anchors on Isabel (Heaven in my Mouth,
As if I did but onely chew his Name,   5
And in my Heart the strong and swelling Evil
Of my Conception). The State whereon I studied
Is like a good thing being often read,
Grown fear'd and tedious; yea, my Gravity,
Wherein (let no man hear me) I take Pride,   10
Could I, with Boot, change for an idle Plume
Which the Air beats for Vain. – Oh Place, oh Form,
How often dost thou with thy Case, thy Habit,
Wrench Awe from Fools, and tie the Wiser Souls
To thy False Seeming? – Blood, thou art Blood.   15
Let's write Good Angel on the Devil's Horn;
'Tis not the Devil's Crest. – How now? Who's
    there?

Enter Servant.

SERVANT   One Isabel, a Sister, desires access
    To you.

19 **Teach** show. Angelo's verb calls attention to a private equivocation in his reply, which can mean 'show her how to get "access" to me'. *Sister* recalls II.ii.19–22; *access* (line 18) echoes II.ii.20.

20 **muster** gather (like an army of troops being called into formation).

21 **unable . . . self** incapable of functioning normally itself (because it is overwhelmed with more blood than it can manage). *Parts* recalls I.i.39–40, II.i.219.

23 **Fitness** health (here, blood supply). Compare II.iii.14.

24 **foolish Throngs** crowds of unthinking people.
 swounds swoons, faints.

27 **general Subject to** ordinary subjects (common people) of.

28 **Quit . . . Part** leave their own places, forsake their roles. See lines 21–22.
 obsequious Fondness well-intended but obstructive homage. *Fondness* echoes II.ii.150, 187.

29 **untaught** untrained, disruptive. *Offence* (line 30) recalls I.ii.92, I.iii.6, 20, II.i.27, 197, II.ii.89, 104 and II.iii.14, 25, and anticipates II.iv.86.

31 **know your Pleasure** learn how you have decided to respond to my suit. In the reflections that follow in lines 32–33, Angelo gives *know* a personal meaning (see the note to I.v.9) that relates to a very different kind of 'Pleasure'. Compare I.i.25, where Angelo uses almost exactly the same phrasing; also see II.i.194–95, II.ii.2–3. *Come* recalls II.ii.1, 126; see the notes to II.i.125, 221, III.i.259–60.

33 **Than . . . 'tis** either (a) than to have you ask me what it is (because Angelo is still not able to claim the shameful desires he now feels), or (b) than to have to demand that you give me 'what 'tis'.

35 **Heaven . . . Honour** Isabella is prepared to accept Angelo's 'Pleasure' and leave. Her prayer for 'your Honour' recalls II.ii.162. *Long* (line 37) is a reminder of Angelo's 'swelling Evil' (line 6); see the notes to II.i.103 and II.iv.101.

41 **fitted** prepared for what he must face. See lines 23, 163, and compare lines 39–41 with II.ii.84–86.

42 **sicken not** not surrender to fear or despair.

ANGELO　Teach her the way.　　　　　*[Exit Servant.]*
　　　　　　　　　　　　　　　– Oh Heavens,
Why does my Blood thus muster to my Heart,　　　20
Making both it unable for it self
And dispossessing all my other Parts
Of necessary Fitness?
So play the foolish Throngs with one that
　　swounds:
Come all to help him, and so stop the Air　　　25
By which he should revive. And even so
The general Subject to a well-wish'd King
Quit their own Part, and in obsequious Fondness
Crowd to his Presence, where their untaught
　　Love
Must needs appear Offence.　　　　　30

Enter Isabella.

　　　　　　　　　– How now, Fair Maid?
ISABELLA　I am come to know your Pleasure.
ANGELO　That you might know it would much
　　better please me
Than to demand what 'tis.
Your Brother cannot live.
ISABELLA　Even so: Heaven keep your Honour.　　　35
ANGELO　Yet may he live a while; and it may be
As long as you, or I; yet he must die.
ISABELLA　Under your Sentence?
ANGELO　Yea.
ISABELLA　When, I beseech you: that in his
　　Reprieve,
　　　　　　　　　　　　　　　　　　　40
Longer or shorter, he may be so fitted
That his Soul sicken not.

45   **already made**   fully formed. Compare II.ii.80.
       remit   pardon.

46   **saucy Sweetness**   impudent lasciviousness (with wordplay on
       the kind of sauce that pleases the palate). Compare the use of
       sweet in line 55.
       coin Heaven's Image   make new 'coins' (offspring) in God's
       likeness (an allusion to Genesis 1:26).

47   **In . . . forbid**   with illegal (counterfeit) means of engraving.
       Compare I.i.46–49 and I.iii.35–37.

49   **Mettle**   both (a) metal, and (b) spirit, virtue, as in I.i.47.
       restrained Means   restricted (forbidden) instruments.

51   **set down**   decreed (with an echo of Angelo's stamping imagery).

52   **pose you**   pose (put) a question to you. What Angelo would like
       to do is hinted at in this phrase, which literally means
       'position you'; *pose* suggests *impose* ('press' or 'imprint'),
       propose, and *depose* (obtain sworn testimony from), and
       quickly can mean (a) swiftly, (b) in a lively fashion, and (c)
       deeply, to the quick. See the note to V.i.189.

54   **and**   or.

58–59 **our . . . Accompt**   The sins we are compelled to do may be
       numbered, but we are not held accountable for them. *Stand*
       and *Accompt* (account) are both suggestive, as is *thing* in line
       61. See the notes to I.ii.102, 110, and II.i.79, 166.

60   **warrant that**   stand behind and adhere to the position I've just
       stated.

61   **Against**   in opposition to. But *Against* can also mean (a)
       towards, (b) in anticipation of, and (c) in contact with,
       adjoined to; all three senses charge *thing* with erotic
       implication.

64   **Charity**   love, compassion, grace (from the Latin *caritas*, a
       word roughly equivalent to the Greek *agape*). Compare
       II.iii.3.

65–67 **Please . . . Charity**   If it pleases you to 'save this Brother's Life'.
       I'll take responsibility for the deed myself, on the 'Peril' (risk)
       that it will not be judged a 'Sin at all', but an act of Christian
       love. Isabella assumes that Angelo is now proposing a
       different way to 'do't' ('redeem him', line 54). See the note on
       do't at II.ii.54.

ANGELO   Ha? Fie, these filthy Vices. It were as good
  To pardon him that hath from Nature stol'n
  A Man already made as to remit   45
  Their saucy Sweetness that do coin Heaven's Image
  In Stamps that are forbid. 'Tis all as easy
  Falsely to take away a Life true made
  As to put Mettle in restrained Means
  To make a false one.   50
ISABELLA   'Tis set down so in Heaven, but not in
  Earth.
ANGELO   Say you so: then I shall pose you quickly.
  Which had you rather, that the most just Law
  Now took your Brother's Life, and to redeem him
  Give up your Body to such sweet Uncleanness   55
  As she that he hath stain'd?
ISABELLA   Sir, believe this:
  I had rather give my Body than my Soul.
ANGELO   I talk not of your Soul: our compell'd Sins
  Stand more for Number than for Accompt.
ISABELLA   How say you?
ANGELO   Nay, I'll not warrant that: for I can speak   60
  Against the thing I say. Answer to this:
  I (now the Voice of the recorded Law)
  Pronounce a Sentence on your Brother's Life;
  Might there not be a Charity in Sin
  To save this Brother's Life?
ISABELLA   Please you to do't,   65
  I'll take it as a Peril to my Soul,
  It is no Sin at all, but Charity.
ANGELO   Pleas'd you to do't, at Peril of your Soul

69 **Were . . . Charity** would be equal weights of sin and sacrificial love. *Poise* echoes *pose*, line 52.

71 **bear't** be burdened with the blame for it. Even as she rejects Angelo's overture, Isabella uses a phrase that inadvertently leaves it hovering in the air. See the notes to II.iii.19, 27. So also with 'added to the Faults of mine', 'nothing of your Answer', and 'in nothing Good'. Line 72 echoes II.ii.152–54.

75 **Your . . . mine** you're not following my meaning. Compare II.ii.143.

76 **crafty** craftily (cleverly, like a coy seductress who only pretends to be 'good'). Compare *All's Well That Ends Well*, V.iii.208–17.

78 **graciously** as infused by divine grace.

79–82 **Thus . . . displayed** Thus cunning contrives to appear most wise and virtuous when it downplays its own merits, in the same way that dark veils that 'hide' beauty actually display it most ostentatiously. Here *tax* means 'take to task', reprove. *Proclaim* recalls I.v.17–18.

81 **en-shield** shielded, hidden. Many editions emend to *enciel'd*, 'heavenly'. Compare *en-skied* in I.v.35.

83 **gross** openly, nakedly. Compare I.iii.37 and II.ii.86–88. *Plain* recalls II.i.263–64.

87 **Accountant . . . Pain** subject to justice on that penalty. *Accountant* echoes line 59; *Pain* recalls II.i.279.

90–91 **As . . . Question** bearing in mind that I state this proposition hypothetically, solely for purposes of discussion. In line 92 *person* means 'individual'; but here its connotations are coloured by the meaning it has in other contexts: physical body, external appearance. See *A Midsummer Night's Dream*, IV.ii.11–12, *King Lear*, I.ii.182–84, *Hamlet*, IV.v.125, and *Love's Labour's Lost*, I.i.183–84, III.i.129–30. *Loss* and *Question* are both suggestive words in this context; compare *All's Well That Ends Well*, II.ii.13–35 (for a bawdy sense of *Question*) and III.ii.43–45 (for the 'Loss' men risk in 'Standing to't'). Meanwhile *subscribe* hints at the copulative sense implied in *All's Well That Ends Well*, II.i.77–78.

Were equal Poise of Sin and Charity.
ISABELLA   That I do beg his Life, if it be Sin,   70
Heaven let me bear it. You granting of my Suit,
If that be Sin, I'll make it my Morn Prayer,
To have it added to the Faults of mine,
And nothing of your Answer.
ANGELO   Nay, but hear me,
Your Sense pursues not mine: either you are
Ignorant   75
Or seem so crafty, and that's not good.
ISABELLA   Let me be Ignorant, and in nothing Good,
But graciously to know I am no Better.
ANGELO   Thus Wisdom wishes to appear most Bright
When it doth tax it self: as these Black Masques   80
Proclaim an en-shield Beauty ten times louder
Than Beauty could displayed. But mark me,
To be received plain, I'll speak more gross:
Your Brother is to die.
ISABELLA   So.   85
ANGELO   And his Offence is so, as it appears,
Accountant to the Law upon that Pain.
ISABELLA   True.
ANGELO   Admit no other way to save his Life
(As I subscribe not that, nor any other,   90
But in the loss of Question), that you, his
Sister,
Finding your self desir'd of such a person
Whose Credit with the Judge, or own great
Place,
Could fetch your Brother from the Manacles

95   **all-building** all-enabling, all-powerful; foundational. Most
editions emend *building* to *binding* (a word the context
encourages), but Angelo's phrasing is probably meant to be
another reminder of his 'all-building' 'great Place' (line 93).
See the notes to II.i.230, II.ii.60, 113 (on *great*), and I.iii.45,
II.i.11, II.iv.10 (on *Place*). *Treasures* (line 97) recalls *Hamlet*,
I.iii.31–32, where Laertes warns Ophelia not to 'open' her
'chast Treasure' (virginity) to the Prince.

98   **suppos'd** posited person (see line 52). The literal meaning of
suppose is sub-pose, place under (compare *subscribe*, 'write
under', line 90, and see the note about the penile sense of *pen*
at I.iii.48). The phrase *let him suffer* in this line is meant by
Angelo to refer to Claudio; but here it applies with equal
pertinence to 'this suppos'd', who will in fact 'suffer'
considerable agony before the situation he is now creating is
resolved.

101   **under . . . Death** sentenced to die. In this speech words like
under, *Impression* (literally, pressing in), *keen*, *Whips*, *strip*,
Bed, and *longing* are so evocative that their effect can only be
to inflame Angelo's passion and 'let him suffer' (line 98)
rather than extinguish his desire. *Keen* recalls II.i.5, *Whips*
II.i.269–70; *longing* echoes II.i.93–95, 105–7, 272–73,
II.ii.60, and II.iv.36–37, 38–42.

104   **That . . . for** that I have longed for like a dying patient.

110   **die for ever** be condemned to eternal perdition.

112   **slander'd so** defamed on the same basis (for its cruelty).
Compare I.iv.42–43, II.i.191–92.

113–   **Ignomy . . . Houses** Ignominy (shame) tendered as a ransom
14   and pardon rendered freely (by a magistrate who has to
sacrifice nothing and break no law, human or divine) are
totally different things. Isabella alludes to Mark 3:25, where
Jesus responds to the Scribes' charge that 'by the prince of the
devils casteth he out devils' by saying that 'if a kingdom be
divided against itself, that kingdom cannot stand.' And if a
house be divided against itself, that house cannot stand.'
Miranda echoes the same passage in *The Tempest*,
I.ii.455–57; compare *Richard II*, IV.i.145–47.

115   **fowl** foul (but with the additional implications noted in
II.ii.174).

Of the all-building Law, and that there were   *growing*
No Earthly Mean to save him but that either   *impatient* 95
You must lay down the Treasures of your Body
To this suppos'd or else to let him suffer:
What would you do?

ISABELLA   As much for my poor Brother as my self: 100
That is, were I under the terms of Death,
Th' Impression of keen Whips I'd wear as
     Rubies,
And strip my self to Death as to a Bed
That longing have been sick for, ere I'd yield
My Body up to Shame.   105

ANGELO   Then must your Brother die.

ISABELLA   And 'twere the Cheaper Way:
Better it were a Brother died at once
Than that a Sister, by redeeming him,
Should die for ever.   110

ANGELO   Were not you then as cruel as the
     Sentence
That you have slander'd so?

ISABELLA   Ignomy in Ransom and free Pardon
Are of two Houses: lawful Mercy
Is nothing kin to fowl Redemption.   115

ANGELO   You seem'd of late to make the Law a
     Tyrant,

measure
Kin
saintly?
Puritanical?

117   **Sliding** fall, slip. Compare II.ii.65. *Sliding* is probably used here as an abbreviated form for *backsliding*, 'sinning'; see Jeremiah 3:6–12.

118   **Merriment** something to be laughed at and dismissed as lightly as a harmless jest. Compare I.v.31, 39. *Merriment* hints at 'marry-meant'; see the note to I.iii.27.

121   **something** somewhat, to some degree.

122   **For his Advantage** in giving the benefit of the doubt to him. *Advantage* echoes II.ii.74–76.

123   **Frail** weak, susceptible to temptations of the flesh.

124   **onely** only, solely, as in I.iii.32, I.iv.25, 50, II.iv.5, 167.

124–   **If . . . Weakness** if doing so will assure that no confederate
25   owns and transmits the weakness you describe. Isabella refers both (a) to Angelo, as one who is on the verge of falling victim to the same vice as Claudio, and (b) to herself, if she should follow Juliet's example and produce successors. *Fedary* means both (a) confederate, and (b) feudatory (feudal, hereditary tenant), from the Latin *feodarius*. Line 126 recalls *Hamlet*, I.ii.146.

127   **Glasses** mirrors (emblems of vanity and the vice it provokes). See II.ii.95–101, 121.

128   **easy broke** easily broken. Compare II.i.95–100, and see *Richard II*, IV.i.262–93, and *Pericles*, IV.vii.155–57.
       make Forms render images of those whose 'Forms' they (a) reflect, and (b) reproduce as offspring. *Forms* echoes lines 12–15.

129–   **Men . . . them** Men wrong themselves [since they were created
30   by women] in taking advantage of the fragility of 'weaker vessels' (1 Peter 3:7) and thereby marring both God's creatures and the creation of new generations.

131   **Complexions** both (a) skins, features, and (b) constitutions, both physiological and psychological.

132   **credulous . . . Prints** impressionable, receptive to counterfeiting. *False Prints* echoes *Impression* (line 102); compare lines 43–47.

136   **arrest your Words** seize hold of your own argument.

And rather prov'd the Sliding of your Brother
A Merriment than a Vice.

ISABELLA   Oh pardon me,
My Lord; it oft falls out, to have what we
Would have, we speak not what we mean.   120
I something do excuse the thing I hate
For his Advantage that I dearly love.

ANGELO   We are all Frail.

ISABELLA   Else let my Brother die
If not a Fedary but onely he
Owe and succeed thy Weakness.   125

ANGELO   Nay, Women are Frail too.

ISABELLA   Ay, as the Glasses where they view
        themselves,
Which are as easy broke as they make Forms.
Women? Help, Heaven; Men their Creation mar
In profiting by them. Nay, call us ten times
        Frail,   130
For we are Soft, as our Complexions are,
And credulous to False Prints.

ANGELO   I think it well,
And from this Testimony of your own Sex
(Since I suppose we are made to be no Stronger
Than Faults may shake our Frames) let me be
        Bold: 135
I do arrest your Words. Be that you are,

137   **if . . . none** Angelo's phrasing echoes that of *Macbeth*, I.vii.46–47, where the title character says, 'I dare do all that may become a Man; / Who dares no more is none.'

139   **Warrants** assurances; representations, appearances. Compare line 60.

140   **destin'd Livery** the uniform or distinguishing dress that frail women are fated to wear. Compare *Romeo and Juliet*, II.i.46–51.

143   **conceive** understand (with the sexual sense only slightly secondary). See the note to lines 6–7.

147– **I . . . others** I know that a virtuous magistrate is permitted to
49   say things that sound evil in order to provoke the wicked to say or do something that will give them away. The Duke speaks similarly in III.i.160–65. *Fouler* echoes line 115. *Pluck* echoes I.ii.99–100.

151   **Little . . . believ'd** Isabella's point is that if Angelo is really speaking on his honour, he is only proving himself to be dishonourable. *Purpose* echoes I.iv.53–54 and II.ii.8–16; compare I.ii.80–81, I.iv.4, II.i.125, 158.

153   **proclaim** expose publicly. Compare lines 79–83. *Seeming* recalls I.iv.53–54.

155   **Or . . . aloud** Appropriately, this line is itself 'out-stretch'd' to two syllables more than the pentameter norm. Compare *Hamlet*, II.ii.276–78.

158   **Vouch** sworn testimony. *Place* echoes lines 93–95.

160   **stifle** choke, suffocate. See line 155.

161   **Calumny** slander (as one who has falsely accused a virtuous deputy).

162   **give . . . Rein** give my lustful spirit (disposition) both (a) free rein (like a racing steed that is being allowed to gallop at full speed), and (b) unlimited reign (ungoverned tyranny). Compare I.iii.39–47, I.iv.19–20.

163   **Fit . . . Appetite** Here *Fit*, *Consent*, and *sharp* are all aptly chosen words (see the notes to II.iii.14, I.ii.110, I.v.61, and II.i.5, 103, 228). *Appetite*, like *Will* (line 166), here refers to sensual desire. *Nicety* means 'coyness', pretended modesty.

That is, a Woman; if you be more, you're none.
If you be one (as you are well express'd
By all external Warrants), shew it now
By putting on the destin'd Livery.   140
ISABELLA   I have no Tongue but one; gentle my
    Lord,
Let me entreat you speak the former Language.
ANGELO   Plainly conceive I love you.
ISABELLA   My Brother did love Juliet,
And you tell me that he shall die for't.   145
ANGELO   He shall not, Isabel, if you give me
    Love.
ISABELLA   I know your Virtue hath a Licence
    in't,
Which seems a little fouler than it is
To pluck on others.
ANGELO   Believe me, on mine Honour.
My Words express my Purpose.   150
ISABELLA   Ha? Little Honour to be much believ'd,
And most pernicious Purpose. Seeming, Seeming.
I will proclaim thee, Angelo, look for't.
Sign me a present Pardon for my Brother,
Or with an out-stretch'd Throat I'll tell the
    World aloud   155
What Man thou art.
ANGELO   Who will believe thee, Isabel?
My unsoil'd Name, th' Austereness of my Life,
My Vouch against you, and my Place i'th'
    State,
Will so your Accusation over-weigh
That you shall stifle in your own Report,   160
And smell of Calumny. I have begun,
And now I give my Sensual Race the Rein:
Fit thy Consent to my sharp Appetite,

164– **prolixious ... for** prolific protestations of bashfulness, which
65   prompt the very desire they ostensibly eschew and thereby
      drive away what they come to plead for (and prevent your
      obtaining the pardon you seek). See lines 75–82, and compare
      II.ii.162–86. *Will* (line 166) recalls II.ii.27, 34.

167   **die the Death** be executed.

168   **Unkindness** both (a) cruelty (to Angelo, and thus to Claudio),
      and (b) unnaturalness (by refusing to act the part of the 'kind'
      of creature you are, as defined in lines 136–40). The phrase
      draw out echoes *out-stretch'd* (line 155); it recalls II.i.215–21.
      See the note on *long* at line 35.

169   **Sufferance** suffering, torture. See the notes to lines 98, 101.

170   **Affection** passion. Compare I.v.48–49, II.i.8–16.

172   **my ... True** my false testimony will carry more weight than
      your true. *O'erweighs* echoes line 159. Behind Angelo's
      phrasing is the image of a pair of scales, used to assure exact
      measure; see the note to II.ii.140, and compare IV.ii.31–32.
      Scales were also symbolic of Justice, of course, and it is a
      telling indication of how far Angelo has fallen that his
      imagery involves a perversion of the office he is pledged to
      uphold.

174   **perilous** threatening, treacherous.

176   **Approof** approval, justification (of an unlawful deed).

177   **make Curtsy to** bow (submit) to.

178   **Hooking** This image echoes Angelo's observation at the
      beginning of the scene that his 'Invention' 'Anchors on Isabel'
      (II.iv.4); it also recalls II.ii.180–81, where Angelo notes that
      'to catch a Saint' Satan 'with Saints does bait [his] Hook'. In
      this context, *Hooking* carries implications similar to those of
      Hanging (II.i.250).

180   **Prompture** prompting, urging, provocation.
      Blood here, as elsewhere, a synonym for *Will* (a genital term)
      and *Appetite*. But line 187 reminds us that the word could
      also refer to blood relationships. See the note to lines 16–17.

182   **tender** offer, lay (paralleling *stoop* in line 184).

Lay by all Nicety and prolixious Blushes
That banish what they sue for. Redeem thy
    Brother   165
By yielding up thy Body to my Will,
Or else he must not onely die the Death
But thy Unkindness shall his Death draw out
To ling'ring Sufferance. Answer me to morrow,
Or by the Affection that now guides me most,   170
I'll prove a Tyrant to him. As for you,
Say what you can: my False o'erweighs your
    True.   *Exit.*
ISABELLA   To whom should I complain? Did I tell
    this,
Who would believe me? O perilous Mouths,
That bear in them one and the selfsame Tongue,   175
Either of Condemnation or Approof,
Bidding the Law make Curtsy to their Will,
Hooking both Right and Wrong to th' Appetite,
To follow as it draws. I'll to my Brother;
Though he hath fall'n by prompture of the
    Blood,   180
Yet hath he in him such a Mind of Honour
That had he twenty Heads to tender down
On twenty bloody Blocks, he'd yield them up
Before his Sister should her Body stoop
To such abhorr'd Pollution.   185
Then Isabel, live Chaste, and Brother, die:

187   **More . . . Chastity** The certainty with which Isabella assures
herself that she is not called to be Claudio's 'keeper' in this
situation suggests that in her present state she would spurn
'the voice of [her] brother's blood' even if it cried unto her
'from the ground' (Genesis 4:9–10). To forestall that, she will
'fit his Mind to Death' (an echo of lines 163–69). *Rest* (line
189) recalls II.iii.35.

More than our Brother is our Chastity.
I'll tell him yet of Angelo's Request,
And fit his Mind to Death, for his Soul's Rest.

Exit.

III.i   This scene takes place in the prison.

2   **Medicine**   way of sustaining themselves. Claudio's words echo II.ii.135–37. *Onely* (only) recalls II.iv.124, 167.

4   **absolute for Death**   completely resolved to die (literally 'loosened from' everything other than death, as explained in line 7, where *loose* means both 'loose', release, and 'lose'). Compare lines 42–43.

8   **A Breath thou art**   you are no more (a) substantial, or (b) long-lived, than a breath. The Duke is probably alluding to Genesis 2:7, 'And the Lord God formed man of the dust of the ground, and breathed into his nostrils the breath of life; and man became a living soul.'

9   **Servile to**   a slave to.
      Skyie   heavenly. The Duke is referring to the commonplace that configurations of the planets and stars affected everything below the lunar sphere, including the operations of the human body and its humours. His phrasing recalls Lucio's description of Isabella as 'a thing en-skied and sainted' (I.v.35), and soon Claudio will discover that he is 'Servile to all the Skyie Influences' of his sister and what she will and will not do to rescue him from his death sentence.

10   **this Habitation**   both (a) the Earth, and (b) the body.
      thou keep'st   you dwell.

11   **Merely**   to put it in the starkest terms. Here *merely* means 'absolutely', 'purely'. Compare *Hamlet*, I.ii.136–37.
      Fool   plaything, victim, laughing-stock. Lines 11–13 allude to pictorial and dramatic representations of a court fool (jester) trying in vain to evade the clutches of a pursuing Death.

13   **still**   both (a) even so, and (b) always.

14   **Accommodations**   comforts, conveniences, and apparel. See *King Lear*, III.iv.105–14.

15   **nurs'd by Baseness**   derived from the lowest forms of matter and sustained by the least dignified of human activities.

17   **poor Worm**   lowly snake (whose tongue is like a 'tender Fork'). Compare *Antony and Cleopatra*, V.ii.240–79, *A Midsummer Night's Dream*, III.ii.71, and *King Lear*, IV.i.32–33.

18   **provok'st**   call forth, solicit.
      grossly   both (a) greatly, and (b) basely. This word echoes II.iv.83.

ACT III

Scene 1

Enter Duke, Claudio, and Provost.

DUKE   So then you hope of Pardon from Lord
  Angelo?
CLAUDIO   The Miserable have no other Medicine
  But onely Hope. I have hope to live, and am
  Prepar'd to die.
DUKE   Be absolute for Death:
  Either Death or Life shall thereby be the
    Sweeter.   5
  Reason thus with Life:
  If I do loose thee, I do loose a thing
  That none but Fools would keep. A Breath thou
    art,
  Servile to all the Skyie Influences
  That dost this Habitation where thou keep'st   10
  Hourly afflict. Merely, thou art Death's Fool,
  For him thou labour'st by thy Flight to shun
  And yet runn'st toward him still. Thou art not
    Noble,
  For all th' Accommodations that thou bear'st
  Are nurs'd by Baseness. Thou'rt by no means
    Valiant,   15
  For thou dost fear the soft and tender Fork
  Of a poor Worm. Thy best of Rest is Sleep,
  And that thou oft provok'st, yet grossly
    fear'st
  Thy Death, which is no more. Thou art not thy
    self,

21 **issue ... Dust** This is another allusion to Genesis 2:7 and 3:19, 'dust thou art, and unto dust shalt thou return'. *Issue* recalls I.i.34–35.

23 **Certain** stable, able to remain in a fixed disposition or resolve.

24–25 **For ... Moon** for your physical and psychological makeup alters as frequently and completely as the Moon (making each state or 'Effect' seem 'Strange' in relation to those that precede or follow it), and under the Moon's influence. *Complexion* echoes II.iv.131; *Effects* recalls II.i.13.

26 **Ingots** bars of gold or other metal.

29–30 **For ... Loins** For your own innards, which summon (arouse, or seek to arouse) you, kindle and discharge the simple outflowing of your own loins (genital region). *Mere* echoes line 11. Most editions emend *fire* to *sire* and move the Folio's comma to the end of line 29.

31 **Gout ... Rheum** swollen joints, skin disease (serpigo, ringworm), and excess fluids that afflict your system.

32 **nor** neither.

35 **Becomes as Aged** either (a) grows old [proves to be something you cannot possess], or (b) is so beset with disease that it makes you seem old. *Dreaming* (line 34) recalls II.ii.179.

36 **palsied Eld** enfeebled, shaky old age.

37 **Heat** vitality, vigour. See lines 29–30.
   Affection feeling, desire, passions.
   Limb effectual bodily movement.

38 **pleasant** a source of pleasure. Compare II.iv.31.
   yet it this thus far in this catalogue of afflictions. In line 39 *Yet* means 'nevertheless'.

40 **moe** more.
   Deaths pains that make us wish we were dead.

41 **That ... Even** which evens out (by conquering and thereby eliminating) all these odds (disadvantages, enemies). Lines 38–41 echo *Julius Caesar*, II.ii.32–37, III.i.99–106, and *Othello*, I.i.122.

For thou exists on many a thousand Grains   20
That issue out of Dust. Happy thou art not,
For what thou hast not still thou striv'st to
   get,
And what thou hast forget'st. Thou art not
   Certain,
For thy Complexion shifts to Strange Effects
After the Moon. If thou art Rich thou'rt Poor: 25
For like an Ass whose Back with Ingots bows,
Thou bear'st thy heavy Riches but a Journey
And Death unloads thee. Friend hast thou none:
For thine own Bowels which do call thee, fire
The mere Effusion of thy proper Loins,   30
Do curse the Gout, Sapego, and the Rheum
For ending thee no sooner. Thou hast nor Youth
   nor Age,
But as it were an after-Dinner's Sleep
Dreaming on both: for all thy blessed Youth
Becomes as Aged, and doth beg the Alms   35
Of palsied Eld. And when thou art Old and Rich,
Thou hast neither Heat, Affection, Limb, nor
   Beauty
To make thy Riches pleasant. What's yet in this
That bears the name of Life? Yet in this Life
Lie hid moe thousand Deaths; yet Death we fear,   40
That makes these Odds all Even.
CLAUDIO   I humbly thank you.

42   **To . . . die** I now realize that if I beg to live, what I am really requesting is death [which will release me to eternal 'Life', line 43, and free me from what only appears to be life]. Claudio's words echo such New Testament passages as John 12:25, 'He that loveth his life shall lose it; and he that hateth his life in this world shall keep it unto life eternal.'

43   **it** Death (which is the gateway to 'Life'). This sentence echoes *Hamlet*, V.ii.231–37, and *King Lear*, V.ii.9–11.

48   **Business** Isabella's phrasing proves to be revealing. She uses 'business' terminology in her opening remarks to Claudio in an effort to prevent him from focusing on the 'Business' Angelo has proposed, or on the fears the 'Friar' has just counselled Claudio to set aside. Compare I.v.9, 71–72.

52–53 **Bring . . . Conceal'd** either (a) bring them, so that I may hear them, to speak where I may secretly eavesdrop, or (b) bring them to a place where [after they have spoken] they may hear me speak to them privately. Most editions emend the first part of this passage to read 'Bring me to hear them speak'.

53   **the Comfort** the comfort you bring me. Claudio's question recalls the assurance Isabella gave Lucio in I.v.89–90.

55   **Affairs to Heaven** business to conduct with Heaven. Subsequent events will render Isabella's words true in ways she little intends here.

56   **Intends . . . Ambassador** plans to send you right away as his agent.

57   **Leiger** legate, ambassador (here a resident one).

58   **Appointment** preparation, arrangement of affairs.

59   **to Morrow** both (a) tomorrow, and (b) with 'Morrow' as your destination. Here *Morrow* is capitalized in the Folio text. See the note to II.ii.7.
       set on set on your way (depart). Isabella's euphemism comes close to the literal truth: Claudio is to set his head on the block. *Remedy* recalls II.i.294–99, II.ii.49–51, 74–76, II.iv.113–15.

64   **implore** beg (perhaps with wordplay on *employ*, use).

To sue to live, I find I seek to die,
And seeking Death, find Life. Let it come on.

Enter Isabella.

ISABELLA   What ho? Peace here; Grace and
   good Company.
PROVOST   Who's there? Come in, the Wish deserves
   a Welcome.   45
DUKE   Dear Sir, ere long I'll visit you again.
CLAUDIO   Most holy Sir, I thank you.
ISABELLA   My Business is a Word or two with
   Claudio.
PROVOST   And very Welcome. – Look, Signior,
   here's your Sister.
DUKE   Provost, a Word with you.   50
PROVOST   As many as you please.
DUKE   Bring them to hear me speak where I may
   be
Conceal'd.   *[Duke and Provost withdraw.]*
CLAUDIO   Now Sister, what's the Comfort?
ISABELLA   Why,
   As all Comforts are: most good, most good
     indeed.
   Lord Angelo, having Affairs to Heaven,   55
   Intends you for his swift Ambassador,
   Where you shall be an everlasting Leiger:
   Therefore your best Appointment make with
     speed,
   To Morrow you set on.
CLAUDIO   Is there no Remedy?
ISABELLA   None but such Remedy as, to save a Head,   60
   To cleave a Heart in twain.
CLAUDIO   But is there any?
ISABELLA   Yes, Brother, you may live;
   There is a divelish Mercy in the Judge,

65   **fetter**   shackle, chain, or bind with some other 'Restraint'.
       Perpetual Durance   unending imprisonment.

66   **just**   precisely.

67–68 **Through . . . Scope**   [that will fetter you] through all the
       vastness of the world allotted you to roam in. Most editions
       emend *Through* to *Though*. *Restraint* recalls I.iii.9–13, I.v.4,
       and II.iv.47–50; *Scope* echoes I.i.63, I.iii.12–13, and I.iv.35.

69   **you . . . to't**   if you gave your assent to it.

70   **bark**   strip bare (like bark removed from a tree trunk).
       Compare *Antony and Cleopatra*, IV.xii.23–24.
       Trunk   body. Isabella's imagery recalls II.iv.101–5.

71   **the Point**   the precise terms. Compare I.i.82, II.i.14–16.

73–74 **Least . . . respect**   for fear that you might prefer instead to
       shiver through six or seven more bone-chilling winters. The
       phrase *feverous Life* parallels the title character's reference to
       'Life's fitful Fever' in *Macbeth*, III.ii.25. Here as in II.iii.29,
       Least means 'lest'. *Entertain* recalls I.iii.36. Compare lines
       73–74 with *The Tempest*, I.ii.294–96, where Prospero,
       speaking like the stern God of the recalcitrant children of
       Israel, tells Ariel: 'If thou more murmur'st, I will rend an Oak
       / And peg thee in his knotty Entrails till / Thou hast howl'd
       away twelve Winters.'

76   **in Apprehension**   in our fearful anticipation of it. See the note
       to line 41.

78   **corporal Sufferance**   physical suffering. Compare II.iv.169.
       Giant (line 78) echoes II.ii.109–11.

80–81 **Think . . . Tenderness?**   Do you think I need to be told in florid
       (figurative) language that death is not really painful in order
       to meet it with manly resolve?

82–83 **I . . . Bride**   Claudio's honeymoon imagery is more to the point
       than he realizes. He echoes Isabella's inadvertently apt
       phrasing in II.iv.101–5. And he uses *encounter* with the same
       copulative implications as in III.vii.32 of *All's Well That Ends
       Well*. See the note to I.ii.110.

84–85 **my . . . Voice**   the grave (strong and dignified) spirit of my
       father spoke through his son as if resurrected from the grave.

If you'll implore it, that will free your Life
But fetter you till Death.

CLAUDIO   Perpetual Durance?   65

ISABELLA   Ay just, perpetual Durance, a Restraint
Through all the World's Vastidity you had
To a determin'd Scope.

CLAUDIO   But in what Nature?

ISABELLA   In such a one as, you consenting to't,
Would bark your Honour from that Trunk you bear   70
And leave you Naked.

CLAUDIO   Let me know the Point.

ISABELLA   Oh, I do fear thee, Claudio, and I quake,
Least thou a feverous Life shouldst entertain,
And six or seven Winters more respect
Than a perpetual Honour. Dar'st thou die?   75
The Sense of Death is most in Apprehension,
And the poor Beetle that we tread upon
In corporal Sufferance finds a Pang as great
As when a Giant dies.

CLAUDIO   Why give you me
This Shame? Think you I can a Resolution
Fetch from flow'ry Tenderness? If I   80
Must die, I will encounter Darkness as
A Bride and hug it in mine Arms.

ISABELLA   There spake
My Brother; there my Father's Grave did utter
Forth a Voice. Yes, thou must die; thou art   85

86–87 **in Base Appliances** through shameful remedies (ignoble
  means). *Base* echoes lines 13–15. The phrase *outward sainted*
  (apparently pious) recalls II.ii.180–81, II.iv.1–17, 93–95,
  163–65.

89 **emmew** entrap (as in a mew or cage), capture. Many editions
  emend to *enew* or *ennew*, 'to drive into the water'. Here
  Follies refers to the ill-advised indiscretions of impetuous,
  'burning Youth' (I.iv.6); compare lines 11–13. The phrase
  Nips Youth i'th Head can refer either to beheading (the
  punishment Claudio faces) or to the sharp peck a falcon uses
  to disable or kill its prey.

91 **cast** (a) calculated (as in casting a horoscope) or measured
  (casting accounts), or (b) analysed for diagnostic purposes (as
  in casting, or examining, urine), or (c) cast out, vomited, or
  evacuated. Compare II.ii.170–75.

92 **Prenzie** This word probably combines (a) 'puritan', (b)
  'entrapping' (from the French verb *prendre*, to seize, grasp, or
  capture), and (c) 'princely'.

94 **damnest** damnedst, most deeply damned.

95 **prenzie Gardes** deceptive trappings (*prendre garde* means
  'beware'), the 'cunning Livery' in which 'Hell' invests (clothes)
  its subtle agents. Lines 93–95 recall I.iv.50–51; *cunning*
  echoes II.ii.180–81, and *Livery* II.iv.140.

102–3 **as frankly . . . Pin** as freely as if it were no more than a pin.
  Compare II.ii.46–47, and see the note to II.i.103.

106 **Affections** feelings, desires. See II.iv.170.

107 **force it** compel it [in a direction contrary to its normal bent].
  Lines 106–7 recall I.iii.39–47, I.iv.19–23.

109 **Seven** The seven deadly (mortal) sins were pride, covetousness,
  lust, wrath, gluttony, envy, and sloth.

111 **momentary Trick** brief, illicit encounter. *Trick* echoes
  II.ii.118–24.

112 **perdurably fin'd** eternally condemned. Compare line 65; *fin'd*
  recalls I.i.34–35, II.ii.40–42.

Too Noble to conserve a Life in Base
Appliances. This outward sainted Deputy,
Whose settled Visage, and deliberate Word,
Nips Youth i'th' Head, and Follies doth emmew
As Falcon doth the Fowl, is yet a Divel: 90
His Filth within being cast, he would appear
A Pond as deep as Hell.
CLAUDIO   The Prenzie, Angelo?
ISABELLA   Oh 'tis the cunning Livery of Hell
The damnest Body to invest and cover
In prenzie Gardes. Dost thou think, Claudio,   95
If I would yield him my Virginity
Thou might'st be freed?
CLAUDIO   Oh Heavens, it cannot be.
ISABELLA   Yes, he would give't thee, from this
     rank Offence
So to offend him still. This Night's the time
That I should do what I abhor to name,   100
Or else thou diest to morrow.
CLAUDIO   Thou shalt not do't.
ISABELLA   O, were it but my Life, I'd throw it down
For your Deliverance as frankly as
A Pin.
CLAUDIO   Thanks, dear Isabel.
ISABELLA   Be ready,
     Claudio, for your Death to morrow.
CLAUDIO   Yes.   105
Has he Affections in him that thus can make
Him bite the Law by th' Nose when he would
     force it?
Sure it is no Sin, or of the Deadly
Seven it is the least.
ISABELLA   Which is the least?
CLAUDIO   If it were Damnable, he being so Wise,   110
Why would he for the momentary Trick
Be perdurably fin'd? Oh Isabel.

116   **in cold Obstruction** in bleak darkness, obstructing the flow of
moisture in the cold ground. Compare *Hamlet*, V.i.214–16,
where the Prince imagines the 'Noble Dust of Alexander . . .
stopping a Bunghole'.

118   **kneaded** compressed.
    the delighted Spirit the soul that now enjoys and inspires such
spritely joy.

119– **recide / In** both (a) recede into, and (b) reside in. Compare line
20   279, and see *Othello*, I.iii.240–42. *Bath* means 'bathe'.

120   **thrilling** piercing, bone-chilling. See *Romeo and Juliet*,
IV.iii.15, where Romeo says, 'I have a faint, cold Fear thrills
through my Veins'.

121   **viewless** both (a) invisible, and (b) blind. In *Macbeth*, I.v.51,
Macbeth's Lady uses *sightless* to convey a similar complex of
meanings.

123   **pendant** suspended, hanging in space.

124   **lawless and incertain** ungoverned (unrestrained in its
'Apprehension', line 76) and uncertain (incapable of knowing
what the future holds).

125   **howling** screaming in tormented agony. Here as in *The
Tempest*, I.ii.294–96 (see the note to lines 73–74),
Shakespeare associates howling with the biting winds of
winter. Compare *Romeo and Juliet*, III.iii.47–48, where
Romeo says that 'the Damned' use the word 'Banish'd' in
Hell, where 'Howling attends it', and see *Hamlet*, V.i.253–55.

129   **To** compared to.

131– **What . . . Virtue** Claudio's words echo what Angelo said in
33   II.iv.64–65. Rather than invoking 'Charity' (Christian love),
however, Claudio appeals to Isabella in the name of 'Nature'
(here the feelings common to all living things).

132   **dispenses with** pardons, grants a dispensation; literally,
'weighs out' or removes from the scales of justice and
distributes. See the note to II.iv.172.

ISABELLA   What says my Brother?
CLAUDIO   Death is a fearful thing.
ISABELLA   And shamed Life a hateful.
CLAUDIO   Ay, but to die and go we know not where;   115
To lie in cold Obstruction, and to rot;
This sensible warm Motion to become
A kneaded Clod; and the delighted Spirit
To bath in fiery Floods, or to recide
In thrilling Region of thick-ribbed Ice;   120
To be imprison'd in the viewless Winds
And blown with restless Violence round about
The pendant World; or to be worse than worst
Of those that lawless and incertain Thought
Imagine howling, 'tis too horrible.   125
The weariest and most loathed worldly Life
That Age, Ache, Perjury, and Imprisonment
Can lay on Nature is a Paradise
To what we fear of Death.
ISABELLA   Alas, alas.
CLAUDIO   Sweet Sister, let me live.   130
What Sin you do to save a Brother's Life,
Nature dispenses with the Deed so far
That it becomes a Virtue.
ISABELLA   Oh you Beast,

[handwritten marginal note: nouns are capitalized have power beyond human control]

134 **faithless** both (a) unfaithful, undependable (as a brother who should protect his sister's virtue even at the cost of his life), and (b) lacking in Christian faith (as a man who should view death not as something to be feared but as the gateway to eternal bliss). *Faithless* can also mean *dishonest*, unchaste, wanton, lacking in sexual fidelity.

135 **be . . . Man** both (a) make your fortune and (b) win a new lease on life. Compare II.ii.78–80, II.iv.126–32. To an audience, of course, *Vice* sounds indistinguishable from the word meaning a clamp; compare *Much Ado About Nothing*, V.ii.18–22, where *Vice* refers to both a clamp (a *vise*, as the word for that sense is spelled in America) and a screw.

138 **Heaven . . . fair** either (a) Heaven forbid that my mother was true to my father (since it would be better to think you a bastard), or (b) Heaven assure that my mother was true to her vows (though your behaviour makes me doubt her). Now that Claudio is wavering in 'Resolution' (line 80), Isabella no longer hears the 'Voice' of her father in his words (lines 83–85).

139 **warped . . . Wilderness** deformed scion from wild, alien stock. *Slip* recalls II.ii.64–66; see the second note to I.iv.20.

140 **Defiance** declaration of open hostility.

141– **Might . . . proceed** Even if all I had to do to win you a reprieve
42 (stay of execution) were to bend down in prayerful pleading, I would still let your sentence be carried out.

146 **Thy . . . Trade** The sin that got you here was not an aberration from your normal virtue, but part of a habitual profession and disposition (as in I.ii.112, II.i.236–38, 269–70).

152 **Might . . . Leisure** if you would bestow on me some of your leisure time. *Dispense* echoes line 132. *Will* (line 151) recalls II.iv.163–69, 177.

Oh faithless Coward, oh dishonest Wretch,
Wilt thou be made a Man out of my Vice? 135
Is't not a kind of Incest to take Life
From thine own Sister's Shame? What should I
   think,
Heaven shield my Mother play'd my Father fair:
For such a warped Slip of Wilderness
Ne'er issu'd from his Blood. Take my Defiance: 140
Die, perish. Might but my bending down
Reprieve thee from thy Fate, it should proceed.
I'll pray a thousand Prayers for thy Death,
No Word to save thee.
CLAUDIO   Nay, hear me, Isabel.
ISABELLA   Oh fie, fie, fie. 145
Thy Sin's not Accidental, but a Trade;
Mercy to thee would prove it self a Bawd.
'Tis best that thou diest quickly.
CLAUDIO   Oh hear me, Isabella.
                    [The Duke steps forward.]
DUKE   Vouchsafe a Word, young Sister, but one
   Word. 150
ISABELLA   What is your Will?
DUKE   Might you dispense with your Leisure, I
   would by and by have some Speech with you:

154– **the ... Benefit** what I request to satisfy myself is at the same
55   time 'your own Benefit' – a phrase that can mean both (a)
      your own advantage, and (b) your own benefaction
      (performing of good deeds, as in lines 204–5). *Satisfaction*
      recalls I.i.80–82; it is a word that frequently relates (a) to
      fulfilling the claims of justice or revenge, as in *The Merchant
      of Venice*, III.i.98–104, and (b) to meeting the demands of
      sexual desire, as in lines 276–78 and in *Romeo and Juliet*,
      II.i.167–68. But it can also refer to the penance imposed by a
      confessor to help a sinner remove a burden of guilt.

156   **superfluous** excess; literally, overflowing (compare *Influences*,
      line 9). Shakespeare probably intends that Isabella's reply
      (lines 156–58) should come across as restrained impatience.
      Though she feels that she can ill afford the time for
      conversation now, she will nevertheless 'attend' the Friar for a
      while because of the authority of his position. *Stay* recalls
      II.ii.27, II.iii.17. *Affairs* echoes line 55.

161   **corrupt her** bribe her to surrender her honour.
      onely only, solely, as in I.iii.32, I.iv.25, 50, II.iv.5, 124, 167,
      and III.i.3. Here as occasionally elsewhere, *onely* hints at a
      sense of 'one-ly' that calls attention to the unruly male 'one'
      (1), the upright 'I', that has led Angelo to 'make an Assay of'
      Isabella's 'Virtue'. See the note to II.i.119.

162   **Assay** experimental trial. Compare II.iv.147–49, and see the
      notes to I.i.34–35, I.iii.64, I.v.77.

162– **practise ... Natures** test his own ability to judge character and
63   prompt people to reveal their true selves.

165   **gracious Denial** pious refusal. See II.iv.78.

166   **Confessor** The Duke's description of his role will prove to be
      an honest one; see V.i.359–67.

168– **satisfy ... Fallible** encourage yourself (and thereby regain a
69   sense of manly resolve) by relying on hopes that will fail you.
      Satisfy echoes lines 154–55 and II.ii.106–7, and *Resolution*
      recalls line 80.

174   **Hold you there** remain in that disposition. Compare II.iii.35.
      While the Duke speaks with the Provost in the lines that
      follow, Claudio probably requests and receives his sister's
      'pardon' (line 171) in a silent reconciliation scene.

the Satisfaction I would require is likewise
your own Benefit.   155
ISABELLA   I have no superfluous Leisure; my Stay
must be stolen out of other Affairs; but I will
attend you a while.   *[She steps aside to wait.]*
DUKE   — Son, I have overheard what hath pass'd
between you and your Sister. Angelo had never   160
the purpose to corrupt her; onely he hath made
an Assay of her Virtue to practise his Judgement
with the Disposition of Natures. She, having
the truth of Honour in her, hath made him that
gracious Denial which he is most glad to receive.   165
I am Confessor to Angelo, and I know this to be
true: therefore prepare your self to Death. Do
not satisfy your Resolution with Hopes that are
Fallible. To morrow you must die: go to your
Knees, and make ready.   170
CLAUDIO   Let me ask my Sister pardon. I am so
out of love with Life that I will sue to be rid
of it.   *[Claudio retires.]*
DUKE   Hold you there: farewell.
— Provost, a Word with you.   *[Provost steps forward.]*   175
PROVOST   What's your Will, Father?
DUKE   That now you are come, you will be gone.
Leave me a while with the Maid; my Mind

179   **promises . . . Habit**   is in accord with my apparel as a man of
       God. Compare I.iv.45–48.

179–   **no . . . Company**   she will suffer no harm from being left alone
80   with me. *Loss* echoes II.iv.90–91.

181   **In good time**   very well; so be it.

183–   **The . . . Fair**   The kind of 'Goodness' that sells its beauty
86   cheaply makes 'Beauty' a thing that is good (virtuous) for only
       a short while; but the spirit of divine 'Grace' that animates
       your disposition shall keep the 'Body' that houses it forever
       'Fair' (beautiful). Compare *Hamlet*, I.iii.119–30, III.i.100–12.
       Complexion (both inner and outer beauty) echoes line 24.

185   **Assault**   attack on the fortress that shields your chastity.
       Compare *Attempt*, line 268.

188   **but**   if it were not.
       Frailty   susceptibility to temptation. Compare II.iv.123–32.

189   **Examples for**   prior instances of.
       wonder a   be amazed, at, be unable to believe.

199   **How . . . content**   what will you do to satisfy. See the notes to
       lines 154–55 and to I.ii.110.

191   **Substitute**   Deputy, serving in the absence of the Duke. The
       Friar's phrasing hints at the nature of the 'Remedy' he is
       about to propose.

192   **resolve him**   dissolve any doubts he may have.

194   **borne**   both (a) borne, carried (see the notes to II.iii.19, 27),
       and (b) born. Compare II.ii.99.

195   **deceiv'd in**   mistaken in his judgement of (confidence in).

197   **discover his Government**   disclose (a) the conduct of his own
       life, and (b) the kind of governor he is for the state. *Vain*
       echoes II.iv.12.

199   **avoid**   both (a) evade, sidestep, and (b) make void, invalidate
       legally (by saying 'he made Trial of you onely', line 200,
       echoing line 161).

202   **Remedy**   solution; literally, a cure (see line 246, and compare
       line 2). The Duke echoes line 60.

208   **peradventure**   by chance. *Business* (line 209) recalls line 48.

promises with my Habit, no Loss shall touch
her by my Company.   180
PROVOST   In good time.
                 Exit. [The Duke rejoins Isabella.]
DUKE   The Hand that hath made you Fair hath made
  you Good. The Goodness that is cheap in Beauty
  makes Beauty brief in Goodness; but Grace,
  being the Soul of your Complexion, shall keep   185
  the Body of it ever Fair. The Assault that
  Angelo hath made to you Fortune hath convey'd
  to my Understanding; and but that Frailty hath
  Examples for his Falling, I should wonder at
  Angelo. How will you do to content this   190
  Substitute, and to save your Brother?
ISABELLA   I am now going to resolve him. I had
  rather my Brother die by the Law than my Son
  should be unlawfully borne. But oh how much is
  the good Duke deceiv'd in Angelo: if ever he   195
  return, and I can speak to him, I will open my
  Lips in vain or discover his Government.
DUKE   That shall not be much amiss. Yet as the
  matter now stands, he will avoid your
  Accusation: he made Trial of you onely.   200
  Therefore fasten your Ear on my Advisings,
  to the love I have in doing good: a Remedy
  presents it self. I do make my self believe
  that you may most uprighteously do a poor
  wronged Lady a merited Benefit, redeem your   205
  Brother from the angry Law, do no Stain to
  your own gracious Person, and much please the
  absent Duke, if peradventure he shall ever
  return to have Hearing of this Business.
ISABELLA   Let me hear you speak farther: I have   210

211   **Fowl**   foul. Compare II.iv.115.

215   **miscarried**   wrecked, perished. Compare line 194.

219–   **was . . . Oath**   [he] was her fiancé by means of a solemn oath
20   ('Contract', line 221) to marry in the near future. Unlike the
       contract between Claudio and Julietta (which was a *sponsalia
       per verba de praesenti*, an oral declaration of commitment
       from the present moment foward), the agreement between
       Angelo and Mariana appears to have been a *sponsalia per
       verba de futuro*, an engagement to marry in due course that
       could be severed either by mutual consent or by one party to
       the betrothal who could prove the other party in default for
       some reason.

220–   **Nuptial appointed**   wedding date set. The phrase *Limit of the
21   Solemnity* (line 222) means 'the time to elapse before the date
       of the ceremony'. *Appointed* recalls line 58.

223   **wrack'd**   shipwrecked.

224   **Dowry**   fortune ('Portion', line 228) to be bestowed on the
       groom as part of the marriage agreement. Compare
       I.iii.29–35.

225   **heavily**   grievously, sadly. *Befell* recalls I.i.57.

229   **Sinew**   strength, sustenance.

230   **combinate**   bound ('combined'), committed. The Folio spelling,
       combynate, is likely to be an indication of how this word was
       to be pronounced here. *Seeming* echoes II.iv.152; compare
       I.iv.53–54.

232–   **so leave her**   forsake her on account of these circumstances.
33

236–   **pretending . . . Dishonour**   claiming to have discovered that she
37   was unchaste. *Comfort* echoes lines 53–54.

237   **in few**   in short (few words). Compare I.v.40.

237–   **bestow'd . . . Lamentation**   gave her over to her own sorrow.
38   Line 238 suggests that Mariana is dressed in mourning.

239   **a Marble . . . Tears**   as impenetrable to being moved or
       dissolved by her tears as if he were a piece of cold marble.
       Compare I.iv.50–53, I.v.58–59, and II.i.39–40.

244   **avail**   be helped, strengthened. *Corruption* (line 242) echoes
       lines 160–61.

Spirit to do any thing that appears not fowl
in the Truth of my Spirit.

DUKE   Virtue is bold, and Goodness never fearful.
Have you not heard speak of Mariana, the Sister
of Frederick the great Soldier, who miscarried   215
at Sea?

ISABELLA   I have heard of the Lady, and Good
Words went with her Name.

DUKE   She should this Angelo have married;
was affianced to her Oath, and the Nuptial   220
appointed; between which Time of the Contract
and Limit of the Solemnity her brother
Frederick was wrack'd at Sea, having in that
perished Vessel the Dowry of his Sister. But
mark how heavily this befell to the poor   225
Gentlewoman: there she lost a noble and
renowned Brother, in his love toward her ever
most kind and natural; with him the Portion and
Sinew of her Fortune, her Marriage Dowry; with
both, her combinate Husband, this well-seeming   230
Angelo.

ISABELLA   Can this be so? Did Angelo so leave
her?

DUKE   Left her in her Tears, and dried not one
of them with his Comfort; swallowed his Vows   235
whole, pretending in her Discoveries of
Dishonour; in few, bestow'd her on her own
Lamentation, which she yet wears for his sake,
and he, a Marble to her Tears, is washed with
them but relents not.   240

ISABELLA   What a Merit were it in Death to take
this poor Maid from the World? What Corruption
in this Life, that it will let this Man live?
But how out of this can she avail?

245 **Rupture** wound, fault; here a breach of contract. *Cure* (line 246) plays on the medicinal sense of *Remedy*, line 202.

250 **Affection** love. Compare line 106. *Continuance* recalls II.i.196–203, 275–76.

253 **it** both (a) 'the Current', and (b) 'her Love', line 252. *Unkindness* (line 251) recalls II.iv.168–69.

255 **plausible** both (a) convincing, and (b) pleasing [to Angelo]. **Demands** 'his Requiring' (line 254, an echo of line 154).

255– **to the Point** in every detail. See the note to II.i.15. And
56 compare II.iv.163 and III.i.71.

256 **refer . . . to** reserve for yourself. *Advantage* recalls II.iv.121–22.

258 **all Shadow** complete darkness and secrecy. Compare Claudio's phrasing in lines 82–83. *Stay* echoes line 156; *long* recalls II.iv.35–37.

259– **answer to Convenience** be fitting in every way. The literal
60 meaning of *Convenience* is 'coming together'; see the note to II.iv.31. See the note to I.ii.110, and see *All's Well That Ends Well*, II.ii.30–35, for a pertinent sense of *answer*. *Place* recalls II.iv.93, 158.

262 **steed . . . Appointment** take your place for the appointment. Here *steed* (a common Shakespearean spelling for *stead*, stand in place, as in I.v.18) echoes the other horse imagery in the play; see I.ii.39–47, I.iv.20. Meanwhile *steed up* (literally, 'uphold', as in *carry* and *holding up* in lines 269, 275), *Appointment* (a word that echoes line 211 and plays on the sexual implications of *point*), and *go in your Place* reinforce the suggestiveness of *Encounter* (see lines 82–83), *fit* (see II.iv.163), *Doubleness*, *Content*, and *grow* (lines 263–73).

264 **compel . . . Recompense** force him to make amends to her. *Recompense* derives from the same Latin roots as *compensate*, which literally means 'to weigh one thing with or against another'. See the note to III.i.132.

267 **scaled** (a) weighed on scales [and recompensed], (b) stripped of his scales like a fish (compare *bark* in line 70), and (c) mounted (taken) with scaling ladders (since 'his Attempt', an echo of I.v.78–80, can refer to an attempt on him as well as an attempt by him). See the note to II.iv.172. *Corrupt* echoes line 242. *Fit* (line 268) recalls II.iv.163, 189.

275 **holding up** maintaining your composure as you play your part in the deception. *Prosperous* echoes I.iii.67–69, where Claudio commends his sister's 'prosperous Art'.

DUKE   It is a Rupture that you may easily heal;   245
and the Cure of it not onely saves your Brother,
but keeps you from Dishonour in doing it.

ISABELLA   Shew me how, good Father.

DUKE   This fore-named Maid hath yet in her the
Continuance of her first Affection; his unjust   250
Unkindness (that in all Reason should have
quenched her Love) hath (like an Impediment in
the Current) made it more violent and unruly.
Go you to Angelo, answer his Requiring with a
plausible Obedience, agree with his Demands   255
to the Point. Onely refer your self to this
Advantage: first, that your Stay with him may
not be long; that the Time may have all Shadow
and Silence in it; and the Place answer to
Convenience. This being granted in course (and   260
now follows all), we shall advise this wronged
Maid to steed up your Appointment, go in your
Place; if the Encounter acknowledge it self
hereafter, it may compel him to her Recompense;
and here by this is your Brother saved, your   265
Honour untainted, the poor Mariana advantaged,
and the corrupt Deputy scaled. The Maid will
I frame and make fit for his Attempt. If you
think well to carry this as you may, the
Doubleness of the Benefit defends the Deceit   270
from Reproof. What think you of it?

ISABELLA   The Image of it gives me Content
already, and I trust it will grow to a most
prosperous Perfection.

DUKE   It lies much in your holding up: haste   275
you speedily to Angelo. If for this Night he
entreat you to his Bed, give him Promise of
Satisfaction. I will presently to Saint Luke's;

279 **moated Grange** moat-surrounded country house. *Satisfaction* (line 278) echoes lines 154–55.
recides both (a) resides, and (b) recedes (withdraws from company). Compare lines 119–20.

280 **dejected** both (a) cast off, rejected, and (b) downcast, forlorn.

285 **Remedy for it** alternative to it. Most editions treat this line as the beginning of a new scene (III.ii). But the Folio does not specify an exit for the Duke or indicate a scene division. *Remedy* recalls line 202; *Comfort* (line 283) echoes line 235.

287– **drink . . . Bastard** both (a) drink dark and light wine (*bastard*
88 was a sweet wine from Spain), and (b) be populated with brown- and white-skinned offspring from illicit liaisons.

290– **of two Usuries** two means of producing issue (children and
91 income from interest-bearing loans), fornication and moneylending. Pompey's phrase *put down* echoes I.ii.99–100, 105–6; it also carries a literal physical sense reminiscent of *The Merry Wives of Windsor*, II.i.29–31, where Mistress Page speaks of introducing 'a Bill in the Parliament for the putting down of Men'. *Usuries* recalls the Duke's financial metaphor in I.i.35–39.

293– **furr'd . . . too** made with fox skins (signifying 'Craft', line 294)
94 on the outside ('Facing') and lamb skins (signifying 'Innocency', line 295) on the inside.

295 **stands . . . Facing** (a) is preferred for display on the outside, (b) signifies deception ('Facing', counterfeiting), and (c) 'stands' upright for 'counter-fitting' (see the notes to I.ii.102, 110, and II.iii.14). Compare the clothing imagery in I.ii.30–40.

297 **Father Friar** literally, Father Brother. The Duke's reply (line 298) parodies the oxymoronic greeting that Elbow has given him.

301 **take him to be** both (a) regard him as, and (b) arrest him as.

302 **Pick-lock** instrument for picking locks. This term was often used to refer to the picking (unlocking) of chastity belts. See the note to I.v.9.

304 **Sirrah** a term of address for a social inferior. Here *Bawd* means 'pimp'. Compare line 347, where it means 'madam' (and perhaps 'whore'), and lines 356–57, where (depending on how *borne* is construed) it can mean either 'madam' or 'pimp'.

there at the moated Grange recides this
dejected Mariana. At that place call upon me;   280
and dispatch with Angelo, that it may be
quickly.

ISABELLA   I thank you for this Comfort. Fare you
well, good Father.   *Exit.*

Enter Elbow, Clown, Officers.

ELBOW   Nay, if there be no Remedy for it, but   285
that you will needs buy and sell Men and Women
like Beasts, we shall have all the World drink
brown and white Bastard.

DUKE   Oh Heavens, what stuff is here.

CLOWN   'Twas never Merry World since of two   290
Usuries the Merriest was put down, and the
Worser allow'd by order of Law; a furr'd Gown
to keep him warm, and furr'd with Fox and Lamb
Skins too, to signify that Craft, being richer
than Innocency, stands for the Facing.   295

ELBOW   Come your way, Sir. – 'Bless you, good
Father Friar.

DUKE   And you, good Brother Father. What Offence
hath this Man made you, Sir?

ELBOW   Marry Sir, he hath offended the Law; and   300
Sir, we take him to be a Thief, too, Sir: for
we have found upon him, Sir, a strange Pick-lock,
which we have sent to the Deputy.

DUKE   Fie, Sirrah, a Bawd, a wicked Bawd.
The Evil that thou causest to be done,   305
That is thy Means to live. Do thou but think

307   **cram a Maw** stuff a gullet. Lines 304–18 recall II.i.214–70; compare III.i.13–15.

309   **Abhominable** 'Beastly' (beast-like). Elizabethans derived this word from *ab* (away from) and *homine* (man); for them it meant 'inhuman' or 'subhuman'. *Touches* recalls I.i.34–35, 82, II.ii.54–56, 71, and III.i.179–80.

310   **eat . . . self** consume my own better self (my humann spirit).

311   **thy . . . Life** the way you earn your living is a real life.

312   **stinkingly depending** dependent on such a 'filthy Vice' (line 308). *Depending* echoes *pendant*, line 123.
      mend reform your ways (literally, repair or cure yourself).

315   **Proofs for Sin** compelling reasons to commit sin.

316   **prove his** prove to be his possession (and go to Hell).

317   **Correction and Instruction** punishment and teaching. *Correction* recalls II.ii.10, *Instruction* II.iii.37.

322–   **he . . . Errand** he might as well get started on his 'journey'
23   (penalty), because he is sure to be treated severely.

324–   **That . . . free** Oh that all of us were as some people would
25   appear to be: as free from the 'Faults' (vices) common to humanity as the faults themselves are from the 'Seeming' of those who appear to have no faults. *Faults* recalls II.ii.163, II.iv.134–35; *Seeming* echoes lines 230–31; *free* harks back to the jests about venereal disease in I.ii.43–46.

326–   **His . . . Sir** Elbow alludes to the cord around the waist of the
27   Friar's habit worn by the Duke; he means that Pompey's neck will soon be tied with a similar rope.

328   **I . . . Bail** I perceive a source of 'Comfort' (release) who will bail me out. Pompey alludes to the game 'I Spy'. *Comfort* echoes line 283.

330–   **What . . . Triumph?** Lucio implies that, like his namesake,
31   Pompey is being led captive by a triumphant 'Caesar' (here representing the magistrate of the state). Compare Escalus' warning in II.i.262–64.

332–   **Pygmalion's . . . Woman** Lucio alludes to the classical sculptor
33   whose passion for one of his statues caused it to come to life. Here such 'Images' symbolize painted women ('made' women, prostitutes). Compare II.ii.78–80, II.iv.126–32.

What 'tis to cram a Maw, or clothe a Back
From such a filthy Vice: say to thy self,
From their Abhominable and Beastly Touches
I drink, I eat away my self, and live.   310
Canst thou believe thy Living is a Life,
So stinkingly depending? Go mend, go mend.

CLOWN   Indeed, it does stink in some sort, Sir;
but yet, Sir, I would prove.

DUKE   Nay, if the Divel have given thee Proofs
for Sin,   315
Thou wilt prove his. – Take him to Prison,
Officer:
Correction and Instruction must both work
Ere this rude Beast will profit.

ELBOW   He must before the Deputy, Sir, he has
given him Warning: the Deputy cannot abide a   320
Whoremaster; if he be a Whoremonger, and comes
before him, he were as good go a Mile on his
Errand.

DUKE   That we were all, as some would seem to be,
From our Faults, as Faults from Seeming, free.   325

Enter Lucio.

ELBOW   His Neck will come to your Waist; a Cord,
Sir.

CLOWN   I spy Comfort, I cry Bail. Here's a
Gentleman, and a Friend of mine.

LUCIO   How now, noble Pompey? What, at the Wheels   330
of Caesar? Art thou led in Triumph? What, is
there none of Pygmalion's Images newly made
Woman to be had now, for putting the Hand in

128

334 **clutch'd** grasping the money to be found there.

335– **What . . . Rain?** What do you have to say about this way of
36 life? Has it not been washed away now [by the new Deputy's
     'Method']? Pompey alludes to Noah's flood, a divine
     visitation to expunge all but a remnant of a human race that
     had become too reprobate to be salvaged (see Genesis 6–8).
     He alludes even more pointedly to the parable about a foolish,
     impudent man who disregarded repeated warnings and built
     his house on a foundation of sand, 'And the rain descended,
     and the floods came, and the winds blew, and beat upon that
     house; and it fell: and great was the fall of it' (Matthew
     7:24–27). Compare II.i.249–70. To a theatre audience *Rain*
     would be indistinguishable from *reign* (with pertinence to
     Angelo's rule) and *rein* (see I.iii.39–47, I.iv.19–20,
     II.iv.161–2, III.i.262). Lines 331–33 echo lines 234–40.

337 **Trot** usually a name for an old female bawd.

339 **The Trick of it?** The way of the world? See line 111.

343– **Troth . . . Tub** In truth, she has gone through all her
44 prostitutes and is herself being treated for venereal disease in
     the powdering tub. See the note to I.ii.86. *Eaten* echoes line
     310.

346– **Ever . . . Bawd** the young whore has always ended up a
47 diseased madam.

347 **an unshunn'd Consequence** an unavoidable result of living by
     such a trade.

351 **thether** thither.

355 **due** just reward.

356 **of Antiquity** of long standing.

356– **Bawd borne** (a) born(e) of a bawd (his mother), (b) born a
57 bawd, or (c) borne by (supported by) a bawd (his 'Mistress',
     line 341, perhaps one doing double duty as a whore).
     Compare line 194 and see the note to line 304.

359 **keep the House** (a) stay indoors (in the 'keep' or prison), as
     opposed to (b) being the husband to a wife, or (c) being the
     'Husband' (managing the daily affairs) of a 'House'. What
     Pompey will not do is 'keep the House' in the sense that refers
     to continued possession of it or to business transactions that
     occur there. See the note to lines 335–36.

the Pocket and extracting clutch'd? What Reply?
Ha? What sayst thou to this Tune, Matter, and   335
Method? Is't not drown'd i'th' last Rain? Ha?
What sayst thou, Trot? Is the World as it was,
Man? Which is the Way? Is it Sad, and few
Words? Or how? The Trick of it?

DUKE   Still thus, and thus: still worse?   340

LUCIO   How doth my dear Morsel, thy Mistress?
Procures she still? Ha?

CLOWN   Troth, Sir, she hath eaten up all her
Beef, and she is her self in the Tub.

LUCIO   Why 'tis good: it is the Right of it; it   345
must be so. Ever your fresh Whore, and your
powder'd Bawd; an unshunn'd Consequence, it
must be so. Art going to Prison, Pompey?

CLOWN   Yes, faith, Sir.

LUCIO   Why 'tis not amiss, Pompey: farewell. Go   350
say I sent thee thether. For Debt, Pompey? Or
how?

ELBOW   For being a Bawd, for being a Bawd.

LUCIO   — Well, then imprison him. If Imprisonment
be the due of a Bawd, why 'tis his Right. Bawd   355
is he doubtless, and of Antiquity too: Bawd
borne. — Farewell, good Pompey. Commend me to
the Prison, Pompey. You will turn good Husband
now, Pompey; you will keep the House.

CLOWN   I hope, Sir, your good Worship will be my   360
Bail?

LUCIO   No indeed will I not, Pompey; it is not the

363   **Wear**   current fashion.

363– **to . . . patiently** to make your punishment even more severe if
64   you do not submit to it willingly [and learn thereby to mend
        your ways]. *Patiently* echoes II.iii.19.

364– **why . . . more** either (a) you'll be the more virtuous if you do,
65   or (b) you'll get more metal (iron shackles) if you don't.
       Mettle recalls I.i.46–49.

368   **paint** wear heavy cosmetics. Bridget is one of Pompey's
       whores. Compare *Hamlet*, III.i.145–49, V.i.203–5.

371   **Then** neither then.

374   **Kennel** here a word for prison (implying that Pompey is a dog).
       Lucio may be comparing Pompey to a puppy.

378   **other some** still others.

382   **mad . . . him** it was a crazy, whimsical quirk on his part.
       Fantastical (wild, undisciplined) recalls II.ii.118–24. *Trick*
       (device) echoes line 339.

383   **steal . . . State** sneak away from Vienna.
       usurp the Beggary assume the livery of a thief (with wordplay
       on the other meaning of *steal*). What Lucio doesn't realize is
       that his jest is an apt description of the 'habit' the Duke has in
       fact usurped (a Friar in a mendicant order dependent on alms
       for the wherewithal to do its holy work).

384   **borne** both (a) born, and (b) borne, conveyed. Compare lines
       356–57.

385   **puts . . . to't** lets sin have it (throws the book at lawbreakers).
       Compare the use of *to't* in II.i.246.

387   **Lenity** leniency, tolerance.

388   **something too crabbed** somewhat too harsh (like the perverse
       crustacean) and bitter (like the crab apple). See *The Tempest*,
       III.i.7–8, for a similar use of *crabbed*. *Cure* (line 390) echoes
       lines 245–47.

392   **in good Sooth** in truth.

393   **well allied** well connected.

394   **extirp it quite** extirpate (eradicate) it completely.

Wear. I will pray, Pompey, to increase your
Bondage if you take it not patiently: why, your
Mettle is the more. Adieu, trusty Pompey.   365
– Bless you, Friar.
DUKE   And you.
LUCIO   – Does Bridget paint still, Pompey? Ha?
ELBOW   – Come your ways, Sir, come.
CLOWN   – You will not bail me then, Sir?   370
LUCIO   Then Pompey, nor now. – What News
  abroad, Friar? What News?
ELBOW   Come your ways, Sir, come.
LUCIO   Go to Kennel, Pompey, go.
            [Exeunt Pompey, Elbow, and Officers.]
  – What News, Friar, of the Duke?   375
DUKE   I know none. Can you tell me of any?
LUCIO   Some say he is with the Emperor of Russia;
  other some, he is in Rome. But where is he,
  think you?
DUKE   I know not where; but wheresoever, I wish   380
  him well.
LUCIO   It was a mad fantastical Trick of him to
  steal from the State, and usurp the Beggary he
  was never borne to. Lord Angelo Dukes it well
  in his Absence: he puts Transgression to't.   385
DUKE   He does well in't.
LUCIO   A little more Lenity to Lechery would do
  no Harm in him: something too crabbed that way,
  Friar.
DUKE   It is too general a Vice, and Severity must   390
  cure it.
LUCIO   Yes, in good sooth, the Vice is of a great
  Kindred; it is well allied; but it is impossible
  to extirp it quite, Friar, till Eating and
  Drinking be put down. They say this Angelo was   395

396– **after . . . Creation**   in the ordinary way of propagating the
97   species (the 'downright' position a man assumes when he
       'under-stands' in the sense explained in *The Two Gentlemen
       of Verona*, II.v.20–36). See the note to II.ii.10, and compare
       II.i.170.

400   **Stock-fishes**   dried cod or haddock. Lucio alludes to the fishes'
       stiffness; his implication is that they are frigid and lifeless.

403   **a Motion Generative**   *Motion* means 'puppet', and Lucio
       probably means either (a) generated (conceived) by a puppet,
       or (b) like a puppet in his ability to reproduce.

407   **Codpiece**   a baggy pouch in the crotch of a man's breeches;
       here a metaphor for the male member whose 'Rebellion'
       (uprising) needs to be 'put down' (line 395, echoing line 291).

410   **getting**   begetting, conceiving.

412   **feeling . . . Sport**   appreciation for the 'game'.

412– **the Service**   the 'Trade' (as defined in I.ii.111–16).
13

413   **instructed . . . Mercy**   taught him to be lenient. *Instructed*
       echoes line 317.

414– **detected for**   publicly accused of indulging in the company of.
15   Compare II.i.172–88. *Inclin'd* (disposed) can refer to a man's
       genital posture; see *Pericles*, IV.iii.153–55.

419– **his . . . Clack-dish**   his habit was to deposit a ducat in the dish
20   the 'Beggar' (old whore) would clack to attract attention.
       Lucio's innuendo recalls the dish imagery in II.i.97–100; it
       also echoes the imagery of lines 333–34. *Use* recalls lines
       290–91.

420   **Crotchets**   caprices (with wordplay on *crotch* and perhaps on
       itch and *scratch*, as in *The Tempest*, II.ii.56–57).

423   **Inward**   intimate friend, confidant.

424– **Cause of his Withdrawing**   reason for his stealing away. *Cause*
25   can mean 'case' (see the note to II.i.126), and *Withdrawing*
       can relate to the kind of 'Crotchets' the Duke's 'Inward' was
       alluding to in his previous speech. See the note to I.ii.116.

427– **be . . . Lips**   never be spoken.
28

not made by Man and Woman, after this downright
way of Creation. Is it true, think you?

DUKE   How should he be made then?

LUCIO   Some report a Seamaid spawn'd him; some
that he was begot between two Stock-fishes. But   400
it is certain that when he makes Water, his
Urine is congeal'd Ice: that I know to be true.
And he is a Motion Generative, that's
infallible.

DUKE   You are pleasant, Sir, and speak apace.   405

LUCIO   Why, what a Ruthless thing is this in
him, for the Rebellion of a Codpiece to take
away the Life of a Man? Would the Duke that is
absent have done this? Ere he would have hang'd
a Man for the getting a hundred Bastards, he   410
would have paid for the Nursing a thousand. He
had some feeling of the Sport, he knew the
Service, and that instructed him to Mercy.

DUKE   I never heard the absent Duke much detected
for Women, he was not inclin'd that way.   415

LUCIO   Oh Sir, you are deceiv'd.

DUKE   'Tis not possible.

LUCIO   Who, not the Duke? Yes, your Beggar of
fifty; and his use was to put a Ducket in her
Clack-dish. The Duke had Crotchets in him. He   420
would be Drunk too, that let me inform you.

DUKE   You do him wrong, surely.

LUCIO   Sir, I was an Inward of his: a Shy Fellow
was the Duke, and I believe I know the Cause
of his Withdrawing.   425

DUKE   What, I prethee, might be the Cause?

LUCIO   No, pardon: 'tis a Secret must be lock'd
within the Teeth and the Lips. But this I can let

429 **greater ... Subject** majority of Vienna's citizens. A *File* is a
body of troops.

432 **Unweighing** (a) lacking in judgement (not given to weighing
matters in his mind), (b) light, frivolous (deficient in gravity,
solemnity), and (c) counterfeit (like a coin whose lightness
gives it away). Like *scaled* (line 267), this adjective relates to
the imagery of measuring so prominent elsewhere; see the
note to II.iv.172.

434 **Envy** malice.

436 **Business ... helmed** serious affairs he has steered [the ship of
state through successfully]. The Duke's phrasing is a reminder
of the 'Business' he is now helming. See the note to line 208.

436– **must ... Proclamation** if he needed anyone to vouch for him,
37 yield him a better reputation than this. *Proclamation* recalls
I.ii.82–83, 95–100, II.iv.153.

438– **testimonied ... Bringings-forth** given credit for his
39 accomplishments. Again, the phrasing is suggestive:
Bringings-forth hints at the 'downright way of Creation' (lines
396–97).

439 **the Envious** those who wish him ill.

441 **unskilfully** ignorantly.

441– **if ... Malice** if you know more about the Duke than you
42 appear to, what you know is sullied by your malicious intent.
Dark'ned echoes lines 81–83, 256–60, and anticipates lines
472–73.

445 **dear** true, conscientious.

450 **make ... him** tell him to his face what you have told me.

460 **unhurtful an Opposite** harmless an opponent. *Opposite* echoes
Hamlet, V.ii.60–62.

462 **forswear this again** deny this when asked to say it again.

you understand: the greater File of the Subject
held the Duke to be Wise. 430
DUKE   Wise? Why no Question but he was.
LUCIO   A very Superficial, Ignorant, Unweighing
  Fellow.
DUKE   Either this is Envy in you, Folly, or
  Mistaking: the very Stream of his Life, and 435
  the Business he hath helmed, must upon a
  warranted Need give him a better Proclamation.
  Let him be but testimonied in his own Bringings-
  forth, and he shall appear to the Envious a
  Scholar, a Statesman, and a Soldier. Therefore 440
  you speak unskilfully; or, if your Knowledge
  be more, it is much dark'ned in your Malice.
LUCIO   Sir, I know him, and I love him.
DUKE   Love talks with better Knowledge, and
  Knowledge with dear Love. 445
LUCIO   Come, Sir, I know what I know.
DUKE   I can hardly believe that, since you know
  not what you speak. But if ever the Duke return
  (as our Prayers are he may), let me desire you
  to make your Answer before him; if it be Honest 450
  you have spoke, you have Courage to maintain
  it. I am bound to call upon you, and I pray you
  your Name?
LUCIO   Sir, my name is Lucio, well known to the
  Duke. 455
DUKE   He shall know you better, Sir, if I may live
  to report you.
LUCIO   I fear you not.
DUKE   O, you hope the Duke will return no more;
  or you imagine me too unhurtful an Opposite. 460
  But indeed I can do you little Harm: you'll
  forswear this again?
LUCIO   I'll be hang'd first. Thou art deceiv'd
  in me, Friar. But no more of this. Canst thou

467   **Tun-dish** a type of funnel. Compare lines 419–20.

469   **ungenitur'd Agent** deputy (literally, actor or doer) without a 'Tun-dish'. See the notes to *King Lear*, I.iv.201, 207.

470   **Continency** restraint (literally, 'containment', varying the Tun-dish and Bottle imagery), a trait not associated with sparrows. Compare lines 470–72 with *King Lear*, IV.vi.111–22.

472– **The Duke . . . answered** The aforementioned Duke, by
73   contrast, would handle the deeds of darkness (compare lines 81–83) in a way that 'answered' to them (fit them, by being in kind with them). What Lucio doesn't realize is that he is speaking the truth (in view of the 'answer' the Duke has just arranged for Angelo); see lines 258–60.

473– **bring . . . Light** expose and prosecute them. The name *Lucio*
74   means 'light' (from the Latin *lucere*, to shine), and eventually this wag will be an unwitting agent in the Duke's scheme to bring a number of 'Dark Deeds . . . to Light'. Lucio's role in the action will prove analogous to that of another emblem of darkened light, the Lucifer of Isaiah 14:12–17, particularly in the part he plays as Satan in the Book of Job (see chapter 1, verses 6–12). Lucio questions the Duke's character and tries his patience, and he does so in a way that parodies the testing the Duke imposes on Angelo (see I.i.46–49, I.iv.48–54); see the note to I.v.45.

474   **Marry** indeed. See the note to I.ii.67.

475   **Untrussing** undressing (untying the laces of his hose and doublet).

477   **eat . . . Fridays** disregard the religious restrictions on one's Friday diet. What Lucio means by this phrase is synonymous with 'mouth with a Beggar' (make love to a whore with bad breath). *Mutton*, a term for 'wench' as well as for sheep meat, appears with similar import in *The Two Gentlemen of Verona*, I.i.72–112, *Love's Labour's Lost*, I.i.305–8, and *2 Henry IV*, II.iv.373–79.

482   **Greatness** majesty. Compare lines 392–93, and see the note to II.iv.95. *Censure* (slander or 'calumny', an echo of II.iv.161) recalls II.i.15.

tell if Claudio die to morrow or no? 465
DUKE Why should he die, Sir?
LUCIO Why? For filling a Bottle with a Tun-dish.
I would the Duke we talk of were return'd
again. This ungenitur'd Agent will unpeople the
Province with Continency. Sparrows must not 470
build in his House-eaves, because they are
Lecherous. The Duke yet would have Dark Deeds
darkly answered, he would never bring them to
Light: would he were return'd. Marry, this
Claudio is condemned for Untrussing. Farewell, 475
good Friar: I prethee pray for me. The Duke, I
say to thee again, would eat Mutton on Fridays.
He's now past it, yet (and I say to thee) he
would mouth with a Beggar, though she smelt
Brown-bread and Garlic. Say that I said so. 480
Farewell.   *Exit.*
DUKE No Might nor Greatness in Mortality
Can Censure scape: Back-wounding Calumny
The whitest Virtue strikes. What King so strong
Can tie the Gall up in the slanderous Tongue? 485
But who comes here?

Enter Escalus, Provost, and Bawd.

ESCALUS Go, away with her to Prison.
BAWD Good my Lord, be good to me; your Honour
is accounted a Merciful Man; good my Lord.

490–
91   **Double . . . kind?**   Twice and thrice warned, and still guilty of the same offence? See the note to lines 335–36. *Forfeit* recalls II.ii.74–76.

491–
92   **would . . . Tyrant**   is enough to make even Mercy herself curse and become unjustly cruel. Compare II.i.297–99, II.ii.92–101. *Tyrant* echoes II.iv.169–71.

493   **Continuance**   duration. Compare I.ii.110–12 and II.i.198–203, and see lines 249–50, 354–56.

495   **Information**   accusation, as an informer. See the note on Lucio at lines 473–74, and compare lines 350–52, which suggest that Lucio also volunteered incriminating evidence against Pompey.

496   **Keep-down**   Like Mistress Over-done (the Bawd), Kate has a surname that fits her professional position. Compare lines 275, 395–97.

497   **in . . . time**   when the Duke himself ruled.

499   **come . . . Jacob**   when the Feast of Saint Philip and Saint James arrives on 1 May. As the word *come* reminds us (see the notes to II.i.125, II.iv.31), May Day was a time of release and revelry.

503   **Go to**   enough, be gone.

504–5   **will . . . alter'd**   Escalus means 'will not change his mind'. The word *alter'd* can also mean 'metamorphosed' (changed in nature), however. And when spoken in the theatre, it is indistinguishable from *altar'd* (taken to or placed on the altar). Since Mistress Over-done has just spoken about another man who has promised a woman marriage, we are reminded that Angelo too has refused to be altared (see lines 214–71).

506   **Charitable**   in keeping with *caritas* (the Latin word for the Christian love and grace to be administered by Claudio's 'Divines', priests). Compare II.iv.61–69.

507   **If . . . Pity**   if my fellow justice worked with my kind of compassion.

510   **Entertainment of**   reception of, hospitality to. Compare lines 72–75.

ESCALUS   Double and treble Admonition, and still   490
Forfeit in the same kind? This would make Mercy
swear and play the Tyrant.

PROVOST   A Bawd of eleven years' Continuance,
may it please your Honour.

BAWD   My Lord, this is one Lucio's Information   495
against me. Mistress Kate Keep-down was with
Child by him in the Duke's time; he promis'd
her Marriage. His Child is a Year and a quarter
old come Philip and Jacob. I have kept it my
self, and see how he goes about to abuse me.   500

ESCALUS   That Fellow is a Fellow of much Licence.
Let him be call'd before us. Away with her to
Prison. – Go to, no more Words.
          [Exeunt Officers with Mistress Over-done.]
– Provost, my brother Angelo will not be
alter'd: Claudio must die to morrow. Let him be   505
furnish'd with Divines, and have all Charitable
Preparation. If my Brother wrought by my Pity,
it should not be so with him.

PROVOST   So please you, this Friar hath been with
him, and advis'd him for th' Entertainment of   510
Death.

ESCALUS   Good even, good Father.

DUKE   Bliss and Goodness on you.

ESCALUS   Of whence are you?

515– **though . . . Time** though circumstances call on me to spend
16   time in this country during my present mission.

517   **Of . . . Order** of an order of Friars dedicated to gracious
      undertakings. *Gracious* recalls lines 165, 207.
      the Sea Even if the 'Friar' has come by sea, his words also
      convey that he has come from the Holy See in Rome. *Business*
      (line 518) echoes line 436.

521   **on** afflicting (with 'Goodness' depicted as a patient).

521– **the Dissolution . . . cure it** the death of goodness is the only
22   way to 'cure' (kill) the fever. *Fever* recalls lines 72–75.

522   **Novelty . . . Request** the only thing anyone asks for (is
      interested in) is the latest novelty (new fashion). *Onely* echoes
      lines 161, 246, 256.

523   **Aged** of long continuance, 'Constant' (line 524). Compare line
      493.

524   **as it is** as it is normally or actually.

525   **Truth** honesty, fidelity, honour.

526   **Security** unwarranted self-assurance. See the notes to II.ii.120,
      III.i.335–36. The Duke may be referring specifically to the
      financial 'Security' (pledged capital) required to organize
      'Societies' or 'Fellowships' for corporate ventures; the 'Riddle'
      involved in such 'Security' is that it both masks and
      exacerbates the insecurity of the foundations for such
      speculative undertakings.

527   **Fellowships accurs'd** associations (friendships) scorned.
      Compare *King Lear*, I.ii.116–29.

528   **upon** along the lines of.

530   **Disposition** temperament, inclination. Compare I.iii.3.

532   **Strifes** efforts. Compare *Romeo and Juliet*, II.i.194. Lines
      532–33 invite comparison with *King Lear*, I.i.298–99.

537   **of all Temperance** in complete control of his appetites and
      passions. See the note to II.ii.185.

538   **to his Events** to the outcome of his ventures. *Prosperous* (line
      539) echoes lines 272–74.

DUKE   Not of this Country, though my Chance is
    now   515
  To use it for my Time: I am a Brother
  Of gracious Order, late come from the Sea
  In special Business from his Holiness.
ESCALUS   What News abroad i'th' World?
DUKE   None, but that there is so great a Fever   520
  on Goodness that the Dissolution of it must
  cure it. Novelty is onely in Request, and as it
  is as Dangerous to be Aged in any kind of
  Course as it is Virtuous to be Constant in
  any Undertaking, there is scarce Truth enough   525
  alive to make Societies secure, but Security
  enough to make Fellowships accurs'd. Much
  upon this Riddle runs the Wisdom of the World.
  This News is old enough, yet it is every Day's
  News. I pray you, Sir, of what Disposition   530
  was the Duke?
ESCALUS   One that above all other Strifes
  contended especially to know himself.
DUKE   What Pleasure was he given to?
ESCALUS   Rather rejoicing to see another Merry   535
  than Merry at any thing which profess'd to make
  him rejoice. A Gentleman of all Temperance. But
  leave we him to his Events, with a Prayer they
  may prove Prosperous, and let me desire to know
  how you find Claudio prepar'd? I am made to   540
  understand that you have lent him Visitation.

542– **sinister Measure**   unjust (literally, left-handed) treatment. The
43   word *Measure* echoes line 432, and anticipates lines 567–68.
      Visitation (line 541) recalls I.iv.44–45, II.iii.4–5, III.i.46;
      compare line 560.

544   **Determination**   decision, execution, in this case one that will
      terminate the life of the man who 'humbles' (submits) himself
      by bowing his neck to the block. See the second note to line
      59.

545   **framed to himself**   constructed in his mind and imagination (a
      building metaphor continued in *Instruction*, line 546, echoing
      line 413). Compare II.iv.95. *Framed* echoes lines 267–68.

546   **Instruction**   teaching (literally, erecting, building up). *Frailty*
      recalls lines 188–90.

548   **discredited to him**   disabused him of (by showing him that such
      'Promises' should not be credited, believed).

550   **paid . . . Function**   compensated 'the Heavens' for the privilege
      and benefits of your 'Calling', line 551. See the notes to
      I.i.34–35, 37–38, II.ii.113.

553   **extremest . . . Modesty**   farthest reach of my ability within the
      bounds of what is proper for a person in my subordinate
      position. *Sword* recalls II.ii.60–61, II.iv.163.

555   **indeed Justice**   the very personification of absolute Justice. See
      the note to I.ii.108.

556– **answer . . . Proceeding**   equal (measure up to) the strictness of
57   his adjudication. This phrase is pregnant with reminders of
      the 'straightness' of Angelo's 'answer'. See the notes to I.iii.44,
      66, 67, I.v.86, II.ii.95, III.i.259–60.

565   **Pattern . . . know**   knowing herself to be an example of 'Holy'
      behaviour. Compare lines 532–33.

566   **Grace . . . go**   trust in divine grace to withstand the temptations
      our frailty prompts us to, and inner virtue to 'go forth' in 'fine
      Issues' (I.i.33, 35). The root meaning of *Virtue* is 'manliness'
      (from the Latin *vir*, man, and *virtus*, strength); compare II.i.9,
      38, II.ii.162, 181–83, II.iv.147, III.i.130–33, 161–63, 213,
      483–84. *Stand* recalls I.ii.102, I.v.5, II.iv.58–59, III.i.295.

567– **More . . . weighing**   meting out neither more nor less to others
68   for 'offences' than he weighs out to himself. *Weighing* echoes
      line 432; compare I.iii.5–7, II.ii.127, IV.ii.29–32.

DUKE   He professes to have received no sinister
Measure from his Judge, but most willingly
humbles himself to the Determination of
Justice. Yet had he framed to himself (by the   545
Instruction of his Frailty) many deceiving
Promises of Life, which I (by my good Leisure)
have discredited to him, and now is he resolv'd
to die.

ESCALUS   You have paid the Heavens your Function,   550
and the Prisoner the very Debt of your Calling.
I have labour'd for the poor Gentleman to the
extremest Shore of my Modesty, but my brother-
Justice have I found so Severe that he hath
forc'd me to tell him he is indeed Justice.   555

DUKE   If his own Life answer the Straitness of
his Proceeding, it shall become him well;
wherein if he chance to fail, he hath sentenc'd
himself.

ESCALUS   I am going to visit the Prisoner. Fare   560
you well.

DUKE   Peace be with you.   *[Exit Escalus, with Provost.]*
He who the Sword of Heaven will bear
Should be as Holy as Severe;
Pattern in himself to know,   565
Grace to stand, and Virtue go;
More nor Less to others paying
Than by Self-offences weighing.
Shame to him whose cruel Striking

570 **Faults** sins, failings. But see the note to II.i.39–40 for another relevant sense; compare lines 324–25.

572 **grow** both (a) survive, and (b) expand. See the notes to I.i.10, 34–35, II.i.23, II.iv.6–7, 95, III.i.482, and compare III.i.272–74. *Weed* recalls I.iv.20.

574 **Though . . . Side?** The Duke alludes to the same doctrine Angelo has invoked in II.iv.16–17.

575– **How . . . things?** How easily may magistrates whose crimes are
78 like those of their victims trick 'the Times' by snaring with seemingly playful spiders' webs the most weighty and substantial matters and people. *Likeness* can mean (a) genuine image (identity), (b) real similarity, and (c) seeming similarity (false likeness). It also echoes *Liking* (desiring, inclining) in line 570. The phrase *Likeness made in Crimes* applies to Angelo's falling victim to the same frailty that undid Claudio; in time, however, Angelo's similarity to Claudio will be made even more precise. Once that happens, Angelo will have purchased himself a new 'Likeness made in Crimes'. See the notes to II.i.55–56, II.ii.80, and compare lines 556–59. Most editors assume that at least two lines have been omitted between *Times* (line 576) and *To* (line 577).

579 **Craft** trickery, deception, 'Practice' (the Duke's own 'Strings').

582 **Disguise** both (a) false Angelo and, (b) the 'Craft' Angelo is using to hide and perpetrate his 'Vice'. See lines 573–74.
th' Disguis'd (a) the Duke in his habit as a Friar, (b) the disguised 'old Betrothed', and (c) Isabella, in her role as one who is 'holding up' (line 275), maintaining, the deception.

583 **Pay with Falsehood** both (a) pay out with false currency (by committing a vice that proves him to be living a lie), and (b) be made to pay for his own 'Falsehood'. *Pay* echoes lines 409–11, 550–51, 567–68; compare I.iii.5–7.
false exacting both (a) exacting (requiring) an unjust and fraudulent price from the woman he thinks is exchanging herself for his falsehood, and (b) exacting (receiving) what will turn out to be 'false' merchandise.

584 **perform . . . Contracting** [in the process] make good on an old contract he thought he'd managed to evade. See lines 214–31.

Kills for Faults of his own Liking.   570
Twice treble Shame on Angelo,
To weed my Vice and let his grow.
Oh what may Man within him hide,
Though Angel on the Outward Side?
How may Likeness made in Crimes,   575
Making Practice on the Times,
To draw with idle Spiders' Strings
Most ponderous and substantial things?
Craft against Vice I must apply.
With Angelo to night shall lie   580
His old Betrothed, but despised:
So Disguise shall by th' Disguised
Pay with Falsehood, false exacting,
And perform an old Contracting.   *Exit.*

IV.i   This scene takes place at 'the moated Grange' referred to in III.i.279.

2   **were forsworn** became perjurers (by forswearing, or unswearing, the vows they made to be faithful). In this line *sweetly* probably refers to the swearing of the original vows. If so, the phrase *sweetly were forsworn* means 'told me what turned out to be sweet lies'. *Forsworn* echoes III.i.461–62.

3   **the break of Day** as fresh and beautiful as the dawn. The comma after *Day* does not appear in the Folio printing; it is thus possible to read *Day / Lights* as 'daylights'.

4   **Lights . . . Morn** lights lovely enough to deceive the morning air into thinking that they are the first rays of sunlight.

5   **bring again** return to me.

6   **seal'd in vain** ratified (concluded, brought together, as in the expression 'sealed with a kiss') to no avail. This lament, a maiden's song to the man who has sworn to love her and then forsaken her, is a fitting introduction to the Mariana the Duke has described in the previous scene as having been misled by Angelo. *Vain* recalls I.v.48–49, II.ii.71 (where it means 'vein'), II.iv.9–12, and III.i.195–97.

9   **still'd** quieted, calmed; comforted. *Comfort* echoes III.i.328.
       brawling clamorous, contentious (warring against a patient acceptance of the suffering Providence has given me to bear). Compare the Duke's phrasing in III.i.249–53.

11   **found me** discovered me, come upon me unawares. *Found* recalls I.iii.56–58, II.ii.75–76, III.i.301–3, 552–55.

12   **excuse me** justify myself.
       believe me so please believe that what I tell you is the truth.

13   **My . . . Woe** It did nothing to promote 'Mirth' (happiness), but it did give expression to my 'Woe' (sorrow). In the theatre of Shakespeare's time *displeas'd* would have sounded much like *displac'd*; compare *Macbeth*, III.iv.107, where Macbeth's Lady tells him he has 'displac'd the Mirth'.

14–15 **though . . . Harm** though it is frequently within the power of music to make what is bad seem good, and call forth the good to harm. *Provoke* recalls III.i.17–19; *Harm* echoes II.i.163–69, III.i.387–89, 461–62.

ACT IV

Scene 1

Enter Mariana, and Boy singing.

SONG

Take, oh take those Lips away
    That so sweetly were forsworn,
And those Eyes, the break of Day,
    Lights that do mislead the Morn;
    But my Kisses bring again,
        bring again,   5
    Seals of Love, but seal'd in vain,
        seal'd in vain.

Enter Duke.

MARIANA   Break off thy Song, and haste thee quick
    away:
Here comes a Man of Comfort, whose Advice
Hath often still'd my brawling Discontent.
                                        [Exit Boy.]
— I cry you Mercy, Sir, and well could wish   10
You had not found me here so Musical.
Let me excuse me, and believe me so:
My Mirth it much displeas'd, but pleas'd my
    Woe.
DUKE   'Tis good: though Music oft hath such a
    Charm
To make Bad Good, and Good provoke to Harm.   15

17   **much . . . Time**   at very near this time.

21   **constantly**   firmly, unwaveringly; confidently. Compare
        III.i.520–27.

22–23 **I . . . little**   please pardon my asking you to leave for a short
        while.

23   **anon**   shortly. *Advantage* (line 24) recalls III.i.256–57.

25   **bound to you**   in your debt. Compare I.iv.24, II.iii.3,
        III.i.452–53.

26   **well come**   it is good that you have come.

28   **circummur'd**   walled around.

30   **planched**   planked (made with planks). A *planchet* is a metal
        disc to be imprinted; if that word was already current in
        1603, this adjective is probably another variation on the
        play's coining imagery (see II.iv.46–47).

31   **That . . . Key**   The suggestiveness of this phrasing is reinforced
        by its echo of I.v.9 and III.i.302.

32   **command**   control, provide access to. Isabella's phrasing is a
        reminder of Angelo's importunate command to be admitted to
        another enclosed 'Garden' with his 'bigger Key' (line 31); see
        II.iv.89–99, 163. The word *Middle* in line 35 reinforces those
        suggestions (compare *Hamlet*, II.ii.242–46).

36   **on your Knowledge**   on the basis of what he told you. Compare
        I.v.9, III.i.440–45.

37   **I . . . upon't**   I have noted it down with due (appropriate) care.
        Due recalls III.i.354–55.

39   **In . . . Precept**   with gestures to illustrate his instructions.

40   **Tokens**   distinguishing features; here, pledges, requirements,
        conditions.

41   **concerning her Observance**   that pertain to what she must do.

I pray you tell me, hath any body enquir'd for
me here to day; much upon this Time have I
promis'd here to meet.

MARIANA   You have not been enquir'd after: I
have sat here all Day.   20

Enter Isabel.

DUKE   I do constantly believe you: the Time is
come even now. I crave your Forbearance a
little: may be I will call upon you anon for
some Advantage to your self.

MARIANA   I am always bound to you.   *Exit.*   25

DUKE   — Very well met, and well come.
What is the News from this good Deputy?

ISABELLA   He hath a Garden circummur'd with
   Brick,
Whose Western Side is with a Vineyard back'd;
And to that Vineyard is a planched Gate   30
That makes his Opening with this bigger Key.
This other doth command a little Door
Which from the Vineyard to the Garden leads.
There have I made my Promise, upon the heavy
Middle of the Night to call upon him.   35

DUKE   But shall you on your Knowledge find this
   Way?

ISABELLA   I have ta'en a due and wary Note
   upon't:
With Whispering and most guilty Diligence,
In Action all of Precept, he did show me
The Way twice o'er.

DUKE   Are there no other Tokens   40
Between you 'greed, concerning her Observance?

42   **Repair**   location, meeting place. It may be significant that one sense of *Repair* derives from the Latin *re* (back) + *patria* (one's native country). Like Bertram in *All's Well That Ends Well*, Angelo will be unwittingly repairing (returning) to a 'home' he had run away from (not unlike the Prodigal·Son whose story is told in Luke 15). The result will be another kind of 'Repair' (remedy) 'i'th' Dark'. Compare III.i.245–47. *Dark* echoes III.i.256–60, 441–42, 472–74; *onely* (see the second note to III.i.161) recalls III.i.522.

43   **possess'd . . . Stay**   informed him my longest stay. *Stay* can mean 'support', a sense reinforced by 'borne up' in line 47; see the notes to III.i.258, 262, II.iv.7. Angelo is about to be 'possess'd' in more ways than one.

46   **whose Persuasion is**   who has been led to believe.

47   **I . . . Brother**   I come on behalf of my brother. See the note to line 50.

50   **be acquainted**   be introduced to. See the note to II.i.215–16. The relation between Isabella and Mariana hints at a partnership with analogies to the 'kind of Incest' described in III.i.130–37. Mariana will commit what appears to be a 'Sin' to 'save a Brother's Life'; in the process she will seal a bond with a 'Sister', and she will assure that Angelo is 'made a Man' out of her 'Vice'. *Comes* (line 51, echoing lines 8, 22, 26, 49) keeps us mindful of the kind of 'Repair' the Duke deems necessary to heal the 'Rupture' Angelo's past actions have caused (III.i.245–47); see the notes to II.i.125, II.ii.1, 126, II.iv.31.

53   **found it**   proved it by experience (that you 'respect' me, bear me in your thoughts and seek my welfare). *Found* echoes line 11.

56   **attend your Leisure**   wait for you. Compare III.i.152–53.

57   **vaporous**   infected and unhealthful vapours. See *Julius Caesar*, II.i.233–34, 259–65.

59   **Place and Greatness**   high position. Compare II.iv.12–15, 93–95, III.i.482–84.
      False Eyes   eyes that either (a) fail to see you accurately, or (b) fail to report truthfully what they see.

60   **stuck upon thee**   fastened Upon you (watching you). Compare the image of Rumour in the Induction to *2 Henry IV*.

ISABELLA   No: none but onely a Repair i'th' Dark,
And that I have possess'd him my most Stay
Can be but brief: for I have made him know
I have a Servant comes with me along   45
That stays upon me, whose Persuasion is
I come about my Brother.

DUKE   'Tis well borne up.
I have not yet made known to Mariana
A Word of this. – What ho, within; come forth.

Enter Mariana.

I pray you be acquainted with this Maid: 50
She comes to do you good.

ISABELLA   I do desire the like.

DUKE   Do you persuade your self that I respect
you?

MARIANA   Good Friar, I know you do, and have
found it.

DUKE   Take then this your Companion by the Hand,
Who hath a Story ready for your Ear.   55
I shall attend your Leisure, but make Haste:
The vaporous Night approaches.

MARIANA   Will't please you walk aside?

Exit [with Isabella].

DUKE   – Oh Place and Greatness, millions of False
Eyes
Are stuck upon thee; volumes of Report   60

61   **Run . . . false**   accompany these false eyes.
       most contrarious   in a most hostile manner.

61–62 **quest / Upon**   either (a) raise questions about, or (b) pursue
       (like hunting dogs chasing a quarry).

62   **Escapes**   (a) escapades, transgressions, (b) sallies, ventures. *Wit*
       recalls II.i.283, II.ii.127–29.

63–64 **Make . . . Fancies**   treat you as the occasion of their
       unrestrained imaginings and collect and torture you in their
       foolish notions of you. *Dream* recalls II.ii.179, III.i.32–34.
       Rack can mean both (a) inventory, put on a rack or shelf (as
       in *The Merchant of Venice*, I.i.181), and (b) stretch on a rack
       (instrument of torture); here it also hints at *wrack*, 'wreck'
       (see *King Lear*, V.iii.311), and thus echoes III.i.223.

65   **Enterprise**   undertaking. *Enterprise* derives from the French
       entre- (in, between) + *prendre* (to take). In this context its
       implications are reinforced by *Consent* (Latin *com-*, with, +
       sentire, to feel), a word that echoes II.iv.162–3, and *Entreaty*
       (French *en-*, in, + *traiter*, treat, entertain) in lines 66–67.

71   **Pre-contract**   a promise to marry in the future. See the notes to
       I.iii.27, III.i.219–20.

73   **Sith**   Since.

74   **flourish the Deceit**   both (a) make the 'Deceit' flower and bear
       fruit (a harvest image reinforced by 'Our Corn's to reap' in
       line 75), and (b) embellish or beautify what might otherwise
       appear to be nothing more than a 'Sin'. The word *flourish*
       (which often means 'brandish', as in *Romeo and Juliet*,
       I.i.80–81) also suggests 'the Sword of Heaven' (III.i.563).

75   **Our . . . sow**   Our grain remains to be harvested, for we have
       yet to sow (plant) the seed that will produce our 'Tithe' (the
       tenth of a farmer's proceeds to be given back to the Lord in
       thanksgiving for His bounty). The Duke's harvest imagery
       recalls I.i.31–39, I.ii.102, and I.v.40–45. It also hints at a
       New Testament teaching that will prove pertinent:
       'whatsoever a man soweth, that shall he also reap. For he that
       soweth to his flesh shall reap corruption; but he that soweth
       to the Spirit shall of the Spirit reap life everlasting. And let us
       not be weary in well doing: for in due season we shall reap, if
       we faint not' (Galatians 6:7–9).

Run with these false, and most contrarious
   quest
Upon thy Doings; thousand Escapes of Wit
Make thee the Father of their idle Dream,
And rack thee in their Fancies.

Enter Isabella and Mariana.

              – Welcome: how agreed?
ISABELLA   She'll take the Enterprise upon her,
    Father,   65
    If you advise it.
DUKE   It is not my Consent,
    But my Entreaty too.
ISABELLA   Little have you to say
    When you depart from him, but, soft and low,
    'Remember now my Brother.'
MARIANA   Fear me not.
DUKE   Nor, gentle Daughter, fear you not at all: 70
    He is your Husband on a Pre-contract:
    To bring you thus together 'tis no Sin,
    Sith that the Justice of your Title to him
    Doth flourish the Deceit. Come let us go:
    Our Corn's to reap, for yet our Tithe's to sow.   75
                             Exeunt.

IV.ii. This scene takes place in the prison.

1   **Sirrha**   a title for a social inferior, here a new jailer's assistant. Compare III.i.304. *Sirrha* and *Sirrah* are alternate spellings (perhaps to indicate alternate pronunciations) for the same word. The Everyman edition preserves the form that appears in the control text in each instance.

4   **his Wive's Head**   his wife's master (an allusion to Ephesians 5:23, where the Apostle Paul says that 'the husband is the head of the wife, even as Christ is the head of the church').

5   **cut . . . Head**   take a woman's maidenhead. For similar wordplay see *Romeo and Juliet*, I.i.23–28.

6   **Snatches**   both (a) punning jests, and (b) references to maidenheads. *Snatch* was also a term for a quick encounter; see *Titus Andronicus*, II.i.95–96.

7   **direct Answer**   The Provost's phrasing subverts his intended meaning. See the notes to II.ii.10 (regarding *direct*) and III.i.259–60, 556–57 (regarding *Answer*).

9   **Office**   job, function.

12   **Gyves**   fetters. *Redeem* recalls II.iv.114–15.
      your full Time   the entire term of your sentence.

13   **Deliverance**   release.

16–17 **Time . . . Mind**   for longer than I can remember. *Content* recalls II.ii.80, 107, III.i.190–91, 272.

19   **Instruction**   training. Compare III.i.546.

24   **to morrow**   tomorrow. But here *to morrow* can also mean (a) to arrive at morrow, and (b) to bring about morrow (the afterlife) for your victims. See the note to II.ii.7.

25   **meet**   suitable.
      compound   agree to terms.

26   **abide**   remain, reside.

27–28 **plead . . . you**   claim to be above the kind of work you do. *Estimation* means 'social standing', 'esteem'.

30   **Mystery**   the name commonly applied to a skilled trade.

Scene 2

Enter Provost and Clown.

PROVOST Come hither, Sirrha. Can you cut off a
Man's Head?

CLOWN If the Man be a Bachelor, Sir, I can; but
if he be a Married Man, he's his Wive's Head,
and I can never cut off a Woman's Head. 5

PROVOST Come, Sir, leave me your Snatches, and
yield me a direct Answer. To morrow morning are
to die Claudio and Barnardine. Here is in our
Prison a common Executioner, who in his Office
lacks a Helper. If you will take it on you to 10
assist him, it shall redeem you from your
Gyves; if not, you shall have your full Time
of Imprisonment, and your Deliverance with
an unpitied Whipping; for you have been a
notorious Bawd. 15

CLOWN Sir, I have been an unlawful Bawd, Time
out of Mind, but yet I will be content to be a
lawful Hangman. I would be glad to receive some
Instruction from my fellow Partner.

PROVOST — What ho, Abhorson: where's Abhorson 20
there?

Enter Abhorson.

ABHORSON Do you call, Sir?

PROVOST Sirrha, here's a Fellow will help you
to morrow in your Execution. If you think it
meet, compound with him by the Year, and let 25
him abide here with you; if not, use him for
the Present, and dismiss him. He cannot plead
his Estimation with you: he hath been a Bawd.

ABHORSON A Bawd, Sir? Fie upon him, he will
discredit our Mystery. 30

31 **waigh equally** are of equal 'Estimation' (weight) in society. The Provost's phrasing links this episode with the others in the play that involve the weighing and comparing of characters. Compare I.iii.6 and III.i.567–68.

32 **turn the Scale** tip the balance. The Provost's phrasing echoes III.i.267. Compare *All's Well That Ends Well*, II.iii.160–62.

33 **Favour** Pompey plays on at least three senses: (a) kind disposition, (b) face, and (c) expression.

35 **Hanging Look** both (a) the look of a hangman, and (b) downcast demeanour. Compare II.i.157–61.

37 **I** both (a) I [do], and (b) Ay. See II.ii.148.

40 **Painting** not (a) the painting of objects or of pictures, as implied in line 38, but (b) the applying of cosmetics, as in III.i.368.

40–41 **prove . . . Mystery** As a bawd (pimp), Pompey supervises painters, and is thus a man whose 'Occupation' is just as much a 'Mystery' as the Hangman's. Since *Occupation* was a term for the activity Pompey sponsors (compare *2 Henry IV*, II.iv.161), Pompey wittily implies that his own type of 'Hanging' (see II.i.250) has a better claim to legitimacy than that of the 'lawful Hangman' (line 18).

46 **True Man** law-abiding, honest man. Abhorson's implication seems to be that since as executioner he inherits the clothes of the thieves he hangs, he has a full range of 'Apparel' to sell to people like the 'true men' from whom the thief has stolen the clothes in the first place. This makes the Hangman, like the Thief, a man who 'fits' clothes (that is, a Tailor with a true 'Mystery' for his occupation). *Fits* recalls III.i.268.

48–51 **If . . . enough** Pompey extends the Hangman's argument by noting that if the Thief sells what he has stolen from one 'True Man' to another 'True Man', it doesn't matter whether it fits the Thief's own frame. It 'fits [suits] your Thief' so long as it fits his customer. In line 48 *too little* may mean 'too small a take to bother with'; if so, *big enough* (line 49) means 'just fine'. Most editions reassign lines 48–52 to Abhorson.

53 **Are . . . agreed?** This question echoes IV.i.64.

PROVOST   Go to, Sir, you waigh equally: a Feather
will turn the Scale.   *Exit.*

CLOWN   Pray Sir, by your good Favour (for surely,
Sir, a good Favour you have, but that you have a
Hanging Look), do you call, Sir, your Occupation   35
a Mystery?

ABHORSON   I, Sir, a Mystery.

CLOWN   Painting, Sir, I have heard say, is a
Mystery; and your Whores, Sir, being Members
of my Occupation, using Painting, do prove my   40
Occupation a Mystery. But what Mystery there
should be in Hanging, if I should be hang'd, I
cannot imagine.

ABHORSON   Sir, it is a Mystery.

CLOWN   Proof.   45

ABHORSON   Every True Man's Apparel fits your
Thief.

CLOWN   If it be too little for your Thief, your
True Man thinks it big enough. If it be too
big for your Thief, your Thief thinks it little   50
enough. So every True Man's Apparel fits your
Thief.

Enter Provost.

PROVOST   Are you agreed?

CLOWN   Sir, I will serve him: for I do find your

55 **Penitent** spiritually humble (an echo of Lucio's mocking counsel to Pompey in III.i.362–64). Pompey is punning on *pendant* (hanging) and *pins*, proverbially associated with both tailors and bawds (see the notes to I.iii.48, II.i.103, III.1.312).

56 **ask Forgiveness** The executioner customarily asked his victim for forgiveness before he carried out his duty. See *As You Like It*, III.v.3–7, and *Richard II*, V.iii.108–33.

62 **to . . . Turn** to make use of my professional services for your own needs. *Turn* has the same connotations as *Trick* (see III.i.111), as illustrated by *Titus Andronicus*, II.i.95–96, and *Othello*, IV.i.254–58. Compare I.v.9, II.ii.144–46. Pompey is also playing on the term 'turning off' (a euphemism for the kind of hanging Abhorson claims as his 'Mystery').

63 **yare** adroit and brisk on your behalf, willing to serve you.

66 **iot** jot (from the Greek letter *iota*).

70 **made Immortal** sent into eternal life (a euphemism for 'delivered a mortal blow' by the executioner). Isabella has spoken with similar indirectness in III.i.55–59.

71 **guiltless Labour** the weariness of a person who has been engaged in honest effort and whose repose is disturbed by no guilt.

72 **Traveller's** This word relates to *travail* ('Labour', hardship) as well as to *travel*. The spellings for the two concepts were interchangeable, as illustrated by I.iv.14.

73 **Who . . . him?** Who can help a soul so slothful as his? Compare I.iii.25, I.v.75–76, 78–80, III.i.201–2.

Hangman is a more Penitent Trade than your   55
Bawd: he doth oft'ner ask Forgiveness.
PROVOST – You Sirrah, provide your Block and
your Axe to morrow, four a' clock.
ABHORSON – Come on, Bawd, I will instruct thee
in my Trade: follow.   60
CLOWN I do desire to learn, Sir; and I hope, if
you have Occasion to use me for your own Turn,
you shall find me yare. For truly, Sir, for your
Kindness, I owe you a Good Turn.
PROVOST Call hether Barnardine and Claudio.   65
                    Exit Abhorson [with Pompey].
– Th' one has my Pity, not a iot the other.
Being a Murtherer, though he were my Brother.

                    Enter Claudio.

– Look, here's the Warrant, Claudio, for thy
   Death.
'Tis now dead Midnight, and by eight to morrow
Thou must be made Immortal. Where's
   Barnardine?   70
CLAUDIO As fast lock'd up in Sleep as guiltless
   Labour,
When it lies starkly in the Traveller's Bones:
He will not wake.
PROVOST   Who can do good on him?
Well, go prepare your self.   *[A Knocking within.]*
                    But hark, what Noise?
Heaven give your Spirits comfort.   *[Exit Claudio.]*
          [Knocking.]   – By and by.   75
– I hope it is some Pardon, or Reprieve
For the most gentle Claudio.

                    Enter Duke.

80   **Curfew** the evening bell (originally, a signal for people to cover their fires – the literal meaning of *Curfew* – and retire for the night).

82–83 **There's . . . Hope** What the Duke implies to the Provost is that Claudio's only 'Comfort' (line 82, echoing IV.i.8–9) is in his 'Hope' of salvation (in the sense implied in line 70). But what he means privately is that 'there's some reason to be hopeful'.

84–85 **his . . . Justice** his own life is just as straight and strict as the justice he renders. Compare I.v.56–62, III.i.556–57. One meaning of great is 'engorged, swollen' (see the notes to II.i.230, IV.i.59, and compare *Twelfth Night*, III.iv.49). *Stroke and Line* can refer to the striking of the executioner's axe and to the rope of the hangman. But a *Stroke* can also be (a) a line, such as one drawn by a pen (see the note to I.iii.48), (b) a caress, or (c) a thrust by 'the Sword of Heaven' (III.i.563).

87   **spurs . . . Powre** incites his power, authority. The Duke knows that while Angelo appears to be subduing his own passions, he is actually spurring them forward at full tilt. Compare I.iii.41–44 and II.iv.161–65. *Powre* is a common Shakespearean spelling for 'pour' (see *Macbeth*, I.iii.98, I.v.28, IV.i.18), and here it reinforces our awareness that at this moment Angelo is sowing 'Seed' (I.ii.102). Compare I.i.78, I.v.77, IV.iii.137.

88   **qualify** control, subdue. Compare I.i.64.
       meal'd with mixed with, touched or spotted by.

89   **corrects** disciplines. Compare II.ii.10, III.i.317. *Corrects* recalls II.ii.10 and echoes *direct Answer*, line 7.

91   **sildom when** it is seldom (rare) that.

92   **steeled Gaoler** hardened jailer.

93   **Hast** haste. The Folio spelling, a common one for this word in Shakespeare, serves here as a reminder that Angelo now 'has't' as he 'spurs on his Powre'.

— Welcome, Father.

DUKE   The best and wholesom'st Spirits of the Night
Envelop you, good Provost. Who call'd here of
  late?

PROVOST   None since the Curfew rung.   80

DUKE   Not Isabel?

PROVOST   No.

DUKE   They will then ere't be long.

PROVOST   What Comfort is for Claudio?

DUKE   There's some
In Hope.

PROVOST   It is a bitter Deputy.

DUKE   Not so, not so: his Life is parallel'd
Even with the Stroke and Line of his great
  Justice.   85
He doth with holy Abstinence subdue
That in himself which he spurs on his Powre
To qualify in others. Were he meal'd with that
Which he corrects, then were he Tyrannous;
But this being so, he's Just.   *[Knocking within.]*
                  Now are they come.   90
— This is a gentle Provost: sildom when
The steeled Gaoler is the Friend of Men.   *[Knocking.]*
— How now? What Noise? That Spirit's possess'd
  with Hast

94   **unsisting**   a Shakespearean coinage that plays on *assisting* and
      sister (recalling Isabella and Mariana) and on such Latin
      senses as (a) *sistere*, to cause to stand, (b) *vadimonium sistere*,
      to answer bail, to stand firm, to endure, and (c) *sis* (*si vis*),
      please, if you please. The *Postern* ('little Door', IV.i.32) that is
      being struck is 'holding up' (see the note to III.i.262), but the
      Duke's phrasing suggests that it will not be able to delay the
      complete invasion of its importunate assailant for long.
      Postern reminds us of the 'Garden' in which Mariana is now
      being 'possess'd' (line 93, echoing IV.i.43). This implication is
      reinforced by 'Just' (upright), 'Now are they come' (line 90,
      recalling IV.i.49–50, and anticipating lines 101–2), and the
      suggestive phrases in lines 95–96. Compare *All's Well That
      Ends Well*, IV.iii.1–87, and *Romeo and Juliet*, III.iv.1–35,
      where Shakespeare uses similar techniques to keep the
      audience aware of a conjugal encounter that is taking place at
      the same time in another setting.

95   **stay**   remain, stand. See the note to IV.i.43.

97   **Countermand**   reversal of the command for execution. See the
      note to I.ii.110, and compare the evocative phrasing in lines
      101–2.

100   **Happely**   haply (perhaps); here to be pronounced
      trisyllabically.

102   **Example**   prior instance, precedent.

103   **Siege**   seat. *Siege* is also a military term, of course, and here it
      reminds us that 'Justice' is being besieged by a magistrate who
      not only 'leans upon' it (II.i.48) but perverts it. Compare the
      siege imagery in *All's Well That Ends Well*, I.i.120–44.

113   **Pardon**   the 'Countermand' the Duke was asking about in line
      97. While the Duke is speaking, the Provost opens and reads
      the 'Note' from Angelo. Based on what the Provost has said in
      lines 100–5, most editors reassign line 106 to the Duke; but
      see lines 76–77.

114   **in**   implicated in (the same crime as that of the man whose
      'Pardon' has just been transacted). *In* echoes the wording in
      lines 95–96; see the note to line 94.

That wounds th' unsisting Postern with these
  Strokes.
PROVOST   There he must stay until the Officer   95
  Arise to let him in: he is call'd up.
DUKE   Have you no Countermand for Claudio yet,
  But he must die to morrow?
PROVOST   None, Sir, none.
DUKE   As near the Dawning, Provost, as it is,
  You shall hear more ere Morning.
PROVOST   Happely   100
  You something know: yet I believe there comes
  No Countermand. No such Example have we;
  Besides, upon the very Siege of Justice
  Lord Angelo hath to the Public Ear
  Profess'd the Contrary.

Enter a Messenger.

DUKE   This is his Lord's Man.   105
PROVOST   And here comes Claudio's Pardon.
MESSENGER   My Lord hath sent you this Note, and
  by me this further Charge: that you swerve not
  from the smallest Article of it, neither in
  Time, Matter, or other Circumstance. Good   110
  morrow: for as I take it, it is almost Day.
PROVOST   I shall obey him.   *[Exit Messenger.]*
DUKE   This is his Pardon, purchas'd by such Sin
  For which the Pardoner himself is in.

115 **his quick Celerity** both (a) its quick expedience (probably referring to the speed with which the 'Offence', once embraced, is pardoned), and (b) his [Angelo's] lively haste (see line 93). One meaning of *quick* is 'alive' (as in 1 Peter 4:5, 'Who shall give account to him that is ready to judge the quick and the dead'); another is 'fleshly'; a third is 'pregnant'. Compare I.i.52, II.iv.52, III.i.280–82. The suggestiveness of the Duke's phrasing is reinforced by such words as *borne*, *high*, *extended*, *Fault's*, *Putting on*, *us'd it*, and *Satisfaction* in the lines that follow.

116 **When . . . Authority** when the same burden is carried by the judge himself. *Vice* recalls III.i.135; compare II.ii.5, 30, 137, II.iv.116–18, III.i.308, 390–93, 571–72, 579.

117 **so extended** (a) held out in such a way, and (b) so willingly offered. See the note on *prone*, I.iii.66.

118 **for . . . Love** out of a love of the 'Vice'. Compare II.ii.38–42. *Fault's* recalls III.i.569–70.

120 **belike** in all likelihood. See lines 202–3.

122 **unwonted putting on** unaccustomed pressure [to do my job]. Compare II.i.280, II.ii.134, II.iii.21–22, II.iv.138–40.

128 **For . . . Satisfaction** the more to assure me. *Satisfaction* recalls I.i.80–82, III.i.154–55, 278.

132– **as . . . Peril** since you will be at great risk [if you fail]. *Answer*
33 echoes lines 6–7.

137 **Bohemian borne** carried, born, and reared in Bohemia.

140 **deliver'd . . . Liberty** set him free.

143 **still wrought** continually obtained.

144 **Fact** crime, deed.

144– **in . . . Angelo** since Angelo has been serving as Deputy.
45 *Government* recalls I.i.2, III.i.195–97.

147 **apparant** apparent, clear beyond all doubt.

Hence hath Offence his quick Celerity,   115
When it is borne in high Authority.
When Vice makes Mercy, Mercy's so extended
That for the Fault's Love is th' Offender
   friended.
— Now Sir, what News?

PROVOST   I told you: Lord Angelo, belike thinking   120
me Remiss in mine Office, awakens me with this
unwonted putting on, methinks strangely, for he
hath not us'd it before.

DUKE   Pray you let's hear.

[PROVOST *reading*] *the Letter.*   'Whatsoever you may   125
   hear to the contrary, let Claudio be executed
   by four of the Clock, and in the Afternoon
   Barnardine. For my better Satisfaction, let
   me have Claudio's Head sent me by five. Let
   this be duly performed, with a Thought that   130
   more depends on it than we must yet deliver.
   Thus fail not to do your Office, as you will
   answer it at your Peril.'
What say you to this, Sir?

DUKE   What is that Barnardine, who is to be   135
executed in th' Afternoon?

PROVOST   A Bohemian borne, but here nurs'd up
and bred: one that is a Prisoner nine Years old.

DUKE   How came it that the absent Duke had not
either deliver'd him to his Liberty or executed   140
him? I have heard it was ever his manner to do
so.

PROVOST   His Friends still wrought Reprieves
for him: and indeed his Fact till now, in the
Government of Lord Angelo, came not to an   145
undoubtful Proof.

DUKE   It is now apparant?

PROVOST   Most manifest, and not denied by himself.

150   **touch'd**   affected by his situation. Compare I.i.34–35,
      II.ii.54–56. *Penitently* echoes lines 54–56.

151   **apprehends**   contemplates, anticipates. Compare III.i.76.

152   **dreadfully**   with fear.

153   **wreakless**   reck-less, without care or concern.

154   **insensible of Mortality**   with no sense of his impending death.
      Compare line 70.

155   **desperately Mortal**   so completely given over to mortal sin that
      he is in a well nigh hopeless spiritual condition.

156   **wants Advice**   lacks counsel. *Advice* recalls I.i.4–6, IV.i.8–9;
      compare II.i.259–61, III.i.260–63, IV.i.65–66.

158   **Liberty . . . Prison**   freedom to move about the prison.
      leave   permission, opportunity.

164   **anon**   shortly; so also in line 213.

165   **Constancy**   reliability, conscientiousness. Compare
      III.i.522–27.

166   **ancient Skill beguiles**   time-honoured ability [to read character]
      misleads. *Ancient* recalls III.i.355–56.

167   **Cunning**   skill, knowledge. But the 'Friar' is also displaying
      cunning in the usual modern sense. Once again, his phrasing
      reminds us of what that cunning entails in Claudio's case; see
      the note to I.ii.110.

168   **lay . . . Hazard**   put myself at risk.

169– **Forfeit to the Law**   subject to condemnation and punishment.
70   *Forfeit* recalls I.v.65–67, II.ii.72–76, III.i.490–91.

171– **in a manifested Effect**   in a demonstration that will make it
72   clear beyond doubt. *Manifested* echoes line 148.

172   **Respite**   wait, delay.

178   **limited**   defined, fixed. Compare III.i.219–24.

179 . **in . . . Angelo**   to Angelo's presence.

179– **I . . . smallest**   I run the risk of putting myself in the same
81   situation as Claudio if I go counter to this in the slightest
      detail.

185   **borne**   carried.

DUKE   Hath he borne himself penitently in Prison?
How seems he to be touch'd?   150
PROVOST   A man that apprehends Death no more
dreadfully but as a drunken Sleep: careless,
wreakless, and fearless of what's past,
present, or to come; insensible of Mortality,
and desperately Mortal.   155
DUKE   He wants Advice.
PROVOST   He will hear none. He hath evermore
had the Liberty of the Prison: give him leave to
escape hence, he would not. Drunk many times
a Day, if not many Days entirely Drunk. We have   160
very oft awak'd him, as if to carry him to
Execution, and shew'd him a seeming Warrant
for it; it hath not moved him at all.
DUKE   More of him anon. There is written in your
Brow, Provost, Honesty and Constancy. If I   165
read it not truly, my ancient Skill beguiles
me; but in the Boldness of my Cunning, I will
lay my self in Hazard. Claudio, whom here you
have Warrant to execute, is no greater Forfeit
to the Law than Angelo who hath sentenc'd him.   170
To make you understand this in a manifested
Effect, I crave but four days' Respite: for
the which you are to do me both a present and
a dangerous Courtesy.
PROVOST   Pray Sir, in what?   175
DUKE   In the delaying Death.
PROVOST   Alack, how may I do it? Having the Hour
limited, and an express Command, under Penalty,
to deliver his Head in the view of Angelo? I
may make my Case as Claudio's to cross this in   180
the smallest.
DUKE   By the Vow of mine Order I warrant you,
if my Instructions may be your Guide, let this
Barnardine be this Morning executed, and his
Head borne to Angelo.   185

187 **discover the Favour** recognize the face [as other than Claudio's]. *Favour* recalls lines 33–34.

191 **bar'd** barbered; made bare of hair. The Folio spelling hints at wordplay on Barnardine's name. *Penitent* (line 190) echoes line 149.

192 **fall to you** befall you, happen to you. See I.i.54–57.
   upon this because of this ruse.

196 **against** in violation of.

199 **him** the Duke.

201 **avouch** vouch for, sanction, acknowledge, maintain.

204 **Coat** cloak, Friar's habit. Lines 202–3 echo III.i.569–70, 575–78.

205–6 **attempt you** tempt you (mislead you). Compare III.i.267–68. *Pluck* recalls II.iv.147–49.

208 **Hand and Seal** handwriting ('Character') and insignia ('Signet'), line 209. The Duke is also showing the Provost his physical hand. *Character* (line 209) recalls I.i.25–28, I.iii.35–38.

212 **this** the sealed document bearing the Duke's handwriting.

213 **anon** shortly.

217 **of Strange Tenor** with misleading implications. Here *Strange* means 'estranging', creating a gap between the truth and what Angelo is told.

219– **by . . . writ** in any event, nothing of what is written here.
20

220– **Look . . . Shepherd** Observe, the newly emerging morning star
21 tells the shepherd that it is time for him to unfold (release from their fold or pen) the sheep in his care. The Duke's phrasing tells us that it is 'almost clear Dawn' (near the time when light will reappear), line 228; it also reminds us that 'Shepherd' (*pastor* in Latin) was a term for both priests (such as the 'Friar') and rulers, two senses deriving from Jesus' reference to himself as the 'good Shepherd' in John 10:14.

PROVOST   Angelo hath seen them both, and will
discover the Favour.

DUKE   Oh Death's a great Disguiser, and you may
add to it: shave the Head, and tie the Beard
and say it was the desire of the Penitent to   190
be bar'd before his Death. You know the Course
is common. If any thing fall to you upon this
more than Thanks and Good Fortune, by the Saint
whom I profess I will plead against it with my
Life.   195

PROVOST   Pardon me, good Father, it is against
my Oath.

DUKE   Were you sworn to the Duke or to the Deputy?

PROVOST   To him and to his Substitutes.

DUKE   You will think you have made no Offence if   200
the Duke avouch the Justice of your Dealing?

PROVOST   But what Likelihood is in that?

DUKE   Not a Resemblance, but a Certainty. Yet
since I see you Fearful, that neither my Coat,
Integrity, nor Persuasion can with Ease attempt   205
you, I will go further than I meant, to pluck
all Fears out of you. Look you, Sir, here is
the Hand and Seal of the Duke. You know the
Character, I doubt not, and the Signet is not
strange to you?   210

PROVOST   I know them both.

DUKE   The Contents of this is the Return of the
Duke; you shall anon over-read it at your
Pleasure, where you shall find within these
two Days he will be here. This is a thing that   215
Angelo knows not, for he this very Day receives
Letters of Strange Tenor, perchance of the
Duke's Death, perchance entering into some
Monastery, but by chance nothing of what is
writ. Look th' unfolding Star calls up the   220
Shepherd. Put not your self into Amazement,

222 **Difficulties** imponderables, enigmas.

225 **a present Shrift** an immediate confession. *Advise* echoes line 156.

227 **this . . . you** this letter will completely dispel your doubts. The reference to *Dawn* (line 228) echoes lines 99–100, 110–11, 220–21.

IV.iii This scene takes place somewhat later in the prison. Here, as elsewhere, *Clown* refers to Pompey.

5–8 **he's . . . Money** Master Rash (the name means 'hasty' or 'reckless', and here it also alludes to a smooth silk or worsted fabric) has borrowed himself into debtors' prison, taking a loan in 'Commodity' (material goods) rather than in cash, and finding out too late that what he had been assured was worth 197 pounds would actually yield only a bit more than 3 pounds in income (a mark being 13 shillings, 4 pence, or two-thirds of a pound). *Acquainted* (line 1) recalls II.i.215–16, IV.i.50.

8 **Ginger** a spice much favoured by 'old Women'.

11 **Three-Pile the Mercer** The Mercer has sued a prancing gallant who failed to pay for his fashionable suits. Compare I.ii.30–38.

12–13 **which . . . Beggar** which now leaves him impeached (accused) and in beggary (imprisoned as a debtor).

14 **Dizzy** a name that connotes a dimwitted, impulsive gallant. **Deep-Vow** a gallant prone to oaths and rash challenges.

15 **Copper-Spur** a gallant who gives the spur to his passions. **Starve-Lackey** This gallant's name may refer to his use of a sword and dagger in duels that deprive lackeys (servants) of their masters, and thus of their livelihoods; but his name probably refers primarily to his stinginess to his own serving men (compare *The Two Gentlemen of Verona*, II.iv.40–45, where Master Thurio is derided for the 'bare Liveries' of his followers). *Drop-Heir* (line 16) is Starve-Lackey's counterpart.

18 **Forth-Light** a tilter who either rides forth lightly or alights unhurt. Like those of his fellow 'great Doers' (line 21), Forth-Light's name suggests the kind of 'tilting' that has landed him in jail.

how these things should be: all Difficulties are
but Easy when they are known. Call your
Executioner, and off with Barnardine's Head.
I will give him a present Shrift, and advise   225
him for a Better Place. Yet you are amaz'd:
but this shall absolutely resolve you. Come
away, it is almost clear Dawn.   *Exeunt.*

Scene 3

Enter Clown.

CLOWN   I am as well acquainted here as I was in
our House of Profession. One would think it
were Mistress Over-done's own House, for here
be many of her old Customers. First, here's
young Master Rash: he's in for a Commodity of   5
Brown Paper, and old Ginger, nine Score and
seventeen Pounds, of which he made five Marks
ready Money. Marry then, Ginger was not much
in Request, for the old Women were all dead.
Then is there here one Master Caper, at the   10
Suit of Master Three-Pile the Mercer, for some
four Suits of Peach-colour'd Satin, which now
peaches him a Beggar. Then have we here young
Dizzy, and young Master Deep-Vow, and Master
Copper-Spur, and Master Starve-Lackey, the   15
Rapier and Dagger Man, and young Drop-Heir,
that kill'd lusty Pudding, and Master
Forth-Light the Tilter, and brave Master

19   **Shoo-Tie**   shoe-trimming, an affected fashion imported from
      the Continent. The Folio spelling, *Shootie*, may involve a pun
      on 'shoo' as a word a 'great Traveller' speaks to his horse.
      Compare *The Merchant of Venice*, I.ii.44–47, for a parallel
      use of *shoo*.

20   **that stabb'd Pots**   who 'nicked' ale-pots to make them appear
      to hold more.

21–22 **now . . . sake**   now reduced to begging help with the words 'for
      the Lord's sake' from all who pass by their barred windows.

27   **A Pox . . . Throats**   May your throats (voices) be afflicted with
      syphilis to punish you for disturbing my rest.

28   **What**   who (here used to identify the speaker in terms of his
      function).

29–30 **Your . . . Death**   Pompey's phrasing echoes the discussion of
      various types of hanging in IV.ii.33–56. *Rise* recalls II.i.38.

35   **sleep afterwards**   Pompey alludes to the commonplace that
      death is a form of sleep. The Prince refers to this notion in
      Hamlet, III.i.60–66. Compare III.i.32–43.

44   **clap . . . Prayers**   fall to your prayers (to prepare your soul for
      death).

47   **fitted for't**   prepared for death. Compare II.iii.14, II.iv.41, 163,
      189, III.i.268, and IV.ii.46, 51.

Shoo-Tie, the great Traveller, and wild Half-Can,
that stabb'd Pots, and I think forty more, all   20
great Doers in our Trade, and are now for the
Lord's sake.

Enter Abhorson.

ABHORSON Sirrah, bring Barnardine hither.
CLOWN Master Barnardine, you must rise and be
hang'd, Master Barnardine.   25
ABHORSON What ho, Barnardine.
BARNARDINE *within* A Pox o' your Throats. Who
makes that Noise there? What are you?
CLOWN Your Friends, Sir, the Hangman. You must
be so good, Sir, to rise and be put to Death.   30
BARNARDINE Away, you Rogue, away, I am Sleepy.
ABHORSON Tell him he must awake, and that
quickly too.
CLOWN Pray Master Barnardine, awake till you are
executed, and sleep afterwards.   35
ABHORSON Go in to him, and fetch him out.
CLOWN He is coming, Sir, he is coming: I hear
his Straw rustle.

Enter Barnardine.

ABHORSON Is the Axe upon the Block, Sirrah?
CLOWN Very ready, Sir.   40
BARNARDINE How now, Abhorson? What's the
News with you?
ABHORSON Truly, Sir, I would desire you to
clap into your Prayers: for look you, the
Warrant's come.   45
BARNARDINE You Rogue, I have been drinking all
Night: I am not fitted for't.
CLOWN Oh the better, Sir: for he that drinks all

49   **betimes**   early.

51   **ghostly**   spiritual, holy.

54   **depart**   part this life for eternity. *Charity* (line 53) recalls II.iii.3
        and II.iv.64–69.

57   **will have**   insist upon having.

59   **Billets**   blocks of wood.

63–64 **for . . . Persuasion**   no matter who tries to persuade me.
        Journey (line 62) recalls III.i.27; compare III.i.320–22.

67   **Ward**   guarded cell.
        thence   from there.

69   **Gravel Heart**   heart as hard as gravel.

72   **unpre-par'd**   unprepared. The Folio spelling, reproduced here,
        may involve wordplay on *par'd*: (a) 'bar'd before his Death'
        (IV.ii.191), with his head shaved, and (b) bereft of the guilt he
        would carry to his Judgement Day if he died unconfessed and
        unabsolved (see IV.ii.225–26, and compare *Hamlet*
        I.v.73–79, III.iii.80–86).
        unmeet   unfit. See II.ii.84–86, where Isabella argues that
        Claudio is 'unmeat' for execution.

73   **transport him**   send him into eternity.
        in . . . is   in his unregenerate frame of mind.

74   **Were damnable**   would be to risk one's own damnation (for
        knowingly sending a man to Hell, without making every
        effort to persuade him to repent and die in a state of grace).
        The Duke's remarks provide an interesting perspective on the
        Prince of Denmark's spiritual condition at the point when he
        decides to spare Claudius at prayer because he fears that his
        father's murderer might die and go to Heaven (*Hamlet*,
        III.iii.73–98).

Night, and is hanged betimes in the Morning, may
sleep the sounder all the next Day.   50

Enter Duke.

ABHORSON Look you, Sir, here comes your ghostly
  Father: do we jest now, think you?
DUKE Sir, induced by my Charity, and hearing how
  hastily you are to depart, I am come to advise
  you, comfort you, and pray with you.   55
BARNARDINE Friar, not I. I have been drinking
  hard all Night, and I will have more time to
  prepare me, or they shall beat out my Brains
  with Billets. I will not consent to die this
  Day, that's certain.   60
DUKE Oh Sir, you must: and therefore I beseech you
  Look forward on the Journey you shall go.
BARNARDINE I swear I will not die to day for any
  man's Persuasion.
DUKE But hear you —   65
BARNARDINE Not a Word: if you have any thing
  to say to me, come to my Ward, for thence
  will not I to day.   *Exit.*

Enter Provost.

DUKE Unfit to live or die: oh Gravel Heart.
  — After him, Fellows, bring him to the Block.   70
                          [Exeunt Abhorson and Pompey.]
PROVOST Now Sir, how do you find the Prisoner?
DUKE A Creature unpre-par'd, unmeet for Death,
  And to transport him in the Mind he is
  Were damnable.
PROVOST   Here in the Prison, Father,
  There died this Morning of a cruel Fever   75
  One Ragozine, a most notorious Pirate:

77　**Years**　age.

78　**omit**　neglect, disregard, pass over.

79　**were well inclin'd**　should be prepared for death. *Inclin'd*
　　echoes III.i.414–15.

82　**Accident**　seemingly chance occurrence.

83　**Dispatch it presently**　do what you propose immediately.
　　Dispatch recalls III.i.280–82; *Prefix'd* (line 84) echoes line 47.

85　**according to Command**　in keeping with Angelo's orders.
　　Elizabethans would probably have been reminded of Herod's
　　command to have the head of John the Baptist brought to him
　　(see Matthew 14:1–13). Compare IV.ii.97–102.

89　**continue Claudio**　keep Claudio alive in prison. Compare
　　II.i.196–203. *Continue* recalls II.i.196–203, III.i.249–50, 493.

93–94　**Ere . . . Generation**　before the sun has twice made its daily
　　(*journal*) appearance to those who live yonder (either those
　　outside the prison, or those on the far side of the Earth).

96　**free Dependant**　willing assistant. *Dependant* echoes
　　IV.ii.54–56, 130–31, 190, and recalls III.i.311–12.

100　**witness**　bear witness.

101　**Injunctions**　enjoinings (biddings or urgings). The Duke's
　　phrasing in lines 101–2 is deliberately couched in ambiguity,
　　and one of its purposes is to remind us that the returning
　　magistrate's business will have at least something to do with
　　the 'great Injunctions' by which Angelo is now 'bound' to the
　　woman he has just entered privately. *Bound* echoes IV.i.25.

103　**consecrated Fount**　holy fountain or spring. The Duke's
　　phrasing hints at the baptismal font.

104　**A League**　three miles.

105　**By cold Gradation**　by cool (deliberate) steps up to the city.
　　Weal-balanc'd Form　stately, dignified movements. *Weal* is
　　probably meant to combine two senses: (a) state (as in
　　'commonweal'), and (b) well.

A Man of Claudio's Years, his Beard and Head
Just of his Colour. What if we do omit
This Reprobate till he were well inclin'd.
And satisfy the Deputy with the Visage   80
Of Ragozine, more like to Claudio?
DUKE   Oh, 'tis an Accident that Heaven provides:
Dispatch it presently, the Hour draws on
Prefix'd by Angelo. See this be done,
And sent according to Command, whiles I   85
Persuade this rude Wretch willingly to die.
PROVOST   This shall be done, good Father,
      presently;
But Barnardine must die this Afternoon,
And how shall we continue Claudio,
To save me from the Danger that might come   90
If he were known alive?
DUKE   Let this be done,
Put them in secret Holds, both Barnardine
      and Claudio;
Ere twice the Sun hath made his journal
      Greeting
To yond Generation, you shall find
Your Safety manifested.   95
PROVOST   I am your free Dependant.
DUKE   Quick, dispatch, and send the Head to
      Angelo.   *Exit [Provost].*
– Now will I write Letters to Angelo
(The Provost he shall bear them), whose
      Contents
Shall witness to him I am near at Home,   100
And that by great Injunctions I am bound
To enter publicly. Him I'll desire
To meet me at the consecrated Fount,
A League below the City, and from thence,
By cold Gradation and Weal-balanc'd Form,   105

106   **proceed** The Duke's implied meaning is 'walk forward together', in a formal procession. But because of the way Angelo has proceeded (gone forward), the Duke is also planning to 'proceed' in a legal sense. See III.i.556–59 and the second note to I.iii.67.

108   **Convenient** fitting, opportune (literally, coming together). See the note to I.ii.110.

109   **commune** communicate; here accented on the first syllable.

110   **want ... yours** are for your ears only.

114   **Ignorant ... Good** unaware of her good fortune. The Duke's phrasing can also be interpreted to mean ignorant of (a) what is good for her, (b) what goodness resides within her, and (c) what good lies in store for her. See III.i.154–55. *Tongue* (line 112) recalls I.i.43–44, I.v.34, II.ii.46–47, 139–42, II.iv.2–4, 141, 174–76, III.i.484–85. *Comforts* (line 115) echoes line 55 and recalls IV.ii.75, 82.

120   **He ... World** These words echo III.i.6–8, 42–43.

123   **close Patience** tightly reined, silent bearing of affliction. Compare II.iii.19, III.i.363–65.

125   **to his Sight** to his presence. The Duke's phrasing picks up on Isabella's threat to Angelo's eyes. And it echoes Lucio's request to be admitted 'to the sight of Isabella' in I.v.19.

127   **Injurious** both (a) unjust, and (b) harmful. Compare II.iii.38–40.

128   **nor ... nor** neither ... nor. *Profits* (benefits) recalls I.v.61–62. **iot** jot, iota.

We shall proceed with Angelo.

Enter Provost.

PROVOST   Here is the Head, I'll carry it my self.
DUKE   Convenient is it: make a swift Return,
For I would commune with you of such things
That want no Ear but yours.
PROVOST   I'll make all Speed.   *Exit.*   110
ISABEL *within*   Peace ho, be here.
DUKE   The Tongue of Isabel. She's come to know
If yet her Brother's Pardon be come hither;
But I will keep her Ignorant of her Good
To make her heavenly Comforts of Despair   115
When it is least expected.

Enter Isabella.

ISABELLA   Ho, by your leave.
DUKE   Good morning to you, fair and gracious
     Daughter.
ISABELLA   The better given me by so Holy a Man;
Hath yet the Deputy sent my Brother's Pardon?
DUKE   He hath releas'd him, Isabel, from the
     World.   120
His Head is off, and sent to Angelo.
ISABELLA   Nay, but it is not so.
DUKE   It is no other:
Shew your Wisdom, Daughter, in your close
     Patience.
ISABELLA   Oh, I will to him, and pluck out his Eyes.
DUKE   You shall not be admitted to his Sight.   125
ISABELLA   Unhappy Claudio, wretched Isabel,
Injurious World, most damned Angelo.
DUKE   This nor hurts him, nor profits you a iot:

129 **Forbear it** give it over, cease it.
Cause both (a) complaint, grievance, and (b) case, situation.
See the note to II.i.126, and compare II.i.145–46, II.ii.1,
III.i.424–26.

131 **Verity** truth.

133 **Covent** religious house, convent or monastery.

134 **Instance** evidence.

137 **pace** guide, like a rider leading his horse. Lines 137–38 mean
'If you can lead your wisdom properly [direct it], along the
path I commend to you'. *Powre* (power) recalls IV.ii.87.

139 **have your Bosom** have an opportunity to unleash all the wrath
in your heart. The Duke's phrasing is a reminder of the
intimacy Angelo believes he has just had with Isabella.

141 **directed by you** subject to your will. See the note to IV.ii.7.

143 **sent me of** sent to me about.

144 **this Token** this evidence of my wishes. Compare IV.i.40–41.

146 **perfect him withal** acquaint him with. *Cause* (line 145) echoes
line 129.

148 **home and home** to the fullest extent of your grievances.
Compare *Hamlet*, III.iv.1.

149 **combined** bound, committed. Compare the phrase *combinate
Husband* in III.i.230.

150 **Wend** go.

151 **fretting Waters** trench-making tears.
from out of, away from. *Command* echoes line 85.

153 **pervert your Course** lead you astray. Compare III.i.178–80.
Lucio's greeting, *Good even* ('Good evening', as in III.i.512),
appear to contradict the Duke's *Good morning* in line 117,
but sometimes Shakespeare contrives to make time move very
quickly; compare *Romeo and Juliet*, IV.iii, where a single
scene covers the period from bedtime to midday.

Forbear it therefore, give your Cause to
  Heaven,
Mark what I say, which you shall find   130
By every Syllable a faithful Verity.
The Duke comes home to morrow; nay dry your Eyes;
One of our Covent, and his Confessor,
Gives me this Instance. Already he hath carried
Notice to Escalus and Angelo,   135
Who do prepare to meet him at the Gates,
There to give up their Powre. If you can pace
  your Wisdom,
In that good Path that I would wish it go,
And you shall have your Bosom on this Wretch,
Grace of the Duke, Revenges to your Heart,   140
And general Honour.
ISABELLA   I am directed by you.
DUKE   This Letter then to Friar Peter give,
'Tis that he sent me of the Duke's Return:
Say, by this Token, I desire his company
At Mariana's House to night. Her Cause and yours   145
I'll perfect him withal, and he shall bring you
Before the Duke; and to the Head of Angelo
Accuse him home and home. For my poor self,
I am combined by a sacred Vow,
And shall be absent. Wend you with this Letter: 150
Command these fretting Waters from your Eyes
With a light Heart. Trust not my Holy Order
If I pervert your Course. Who's here?

Enter Lucio.

LUCIO   Good even.
Friar, where's the Provost?
FRIAR   Not within, Sir.
LUCIO   Oh pretty Isabella, I am pale at mine Heart   155
to see thine Eyes so red: thou must be Patient.

157 **fain** pleased (here meaning 'compelled'). *Patient* (line 156)
echoes line 123.
dine and sup take my midday and evening meals.
Bran coarse brown bread.

158 **for my Head** for fear of losing my head (in lust or anger, and
as a result in literal fact). Compare II.i.250–53.

159 **set me to't** cause me to do something that would get me in
trouble. Lines 157–59 could also refer to grief-induced
nausea. Compare *to't* in II.i.246, III.i.385.

162 **fantastical . . . Corners** whimsical Duke who engaged in
activities that he had to keep secret. Lucio has spoken
similarly of the Duke in III.i.382–85, 420–21, and 472–74.
Once again, Lucio is more accurate than he realizes. *Dark*
echoes IV.i.42.

164 **beholding** indebted.

168 **Woodman** forester or hunter, here one who pursues women.
Compare *The Merry Wives of Windsor*, V.v.27–34, where the
lust-crazed Falstaff refers to himself as a woodman. The term
may derive, at least in part, from *wood* (usually *wodde* in
Shakespeare) as a word meaning 'mad'; see *A Midsummer
Night's Dream*, II.i.192, and *King Lear*, II.ii.184, 199.
Woodman may also relate to tillage (See I.v.40–45), the
sowing of seeds to produce trees.

173 **pretty** entertaining.

175 **were** would be.

177 **before him** brought before him for trial.

180 **fain** obliged. Compare line 157. Here *marry* means 'indeed'
(see the note to I.ii.67), but before long Lucio will find that he
speaks more than he recognizes; see V.i.501–11, where he
receives a comeuppance that parodies the fates of Claudio and
Angelo.
forswear deny. Compare III.i.461–62; compare III.i.321–23.

182 **rotten Medler** spoiled piece of fruit. Medlars are apple-like
fruit that become edible only after they have begun to rot. The
term was often used to refer to wantons ('meddlers') and to
the genitalia. Compare *Romeo and Juliet*, II.i.34–36, and *As
You Like It*, III.ii.124–28 (where the word is applied to a
diseased whoremonger). Lines 177–82 confirm what Mistress
Over-done has said in III.i.495–500.

I am fain to dine and sup with Water and Bran;
I dare not for my Head fill my Belly. One
fruitful Meal would set me to't. But they say
the Duke will be here to Morrow. By my troth,   160
Isabel, I lov'd thy Brother; if the old
fantastical Duke of Dark Corners had been
at Home, he had lived.

DUKE   Sir, the Duke is marvellous little beholding
to your Reports; but the best is, he lives not   165
in them.

LUCIO   Friar, thou knowest not the Duke so well
as I do: he's a better Woodman than thou tak'st
him for.

DUKE   Well; you'll answer this one Day. Fare ye   170
well.

LUCIO   Nay tarry, I'll go along with thee. I can
tell thee pretty Tales of the Duke.

DUKE   You have told me too many of him already,
Sir, if they be true; if not true, none were   175
enough.

LUCIO   I was once before him for getting a Wench
with Child.

DUKE   Did you such a thing?

LUCIO   Yes marry did I; but I was fain to forswear   180
it. They would else have married me to the
rotten Medler.

183   **Fairer** more pleasant (amusing).

185–   **I'll . . . End** This promise echoes IV.iii.61–62; compare
86   III.i.321–23.

188   **Bur** prickly seedcase. Pandarus alludes to the same proverb in
      Troilus and Cressida, III.ii.120–22. Lucio enjoys irritating the
      Friar, and in the final scene his resolve to 'stick' him (prick his
      dignity) and stick to him will prove comically catastrophic.

IV.iv. This scene returns us to the palace where Angelo presides over
      the affairs of Vienna.

1–2   **disvouch'd other** disavowed or nullified the preceding one.
      Evidently one letter has told Angelo to meet the Duke 'A
      League before the City' (see IV.iii.102–6); now Angelo is
      instructed to be at the 'Gates' to the city instead (see lines
      5–6). *Disvouch'd* echoes IV.ii.201.

3   **uneven** irregular, inconsistent.
      distracted distraught, 'much like to Madness' (bordering on
      insanity), line 4.

5   **tainted** impaired. See I.ii.45–46, and compare *rotten* in
      IV.iii.182.

6   **reliver** redeliver, be relieved (delivered, lightened) of. The Folio
      word probably relates to the Latin *relevare* (to lighten; to lift
      up or raise again; to relieve or alleviate), perhaps by way of
      the French *relever* (to raise, lift, or rebuild).

9   **Redress** correction. *Proclaim* (line 8) echoes II.iv.153–56.

10   **exhibit** hold forth, display.

13   **a Dispatch** a rapid and complete disposal. Compare IV.iii.83.

14   **Devices hereafter** later attempts to contrive against us. *Stand*
      (line 15) recalls III.i.556–57.

17   **betimes** early. Compare IV.iii.49.

18   **such . . . Suit** men of such rank or position.

21   **unshapes me** disconcerts me (bends me out of shape). Compare
      II.i.1–4, II.ii.181–86, II.iv.1–17.
      Unpregnant unprepared, unapt (not ready to give birth). This
      word recalls I.i.8–12, II.i.23–25.

DUKE   Sir, your Company is Fairer than Honest,
rest you well.

LUCIO   By my troth, I'll go with thee to the   185
Lane's End. If Bawdy Talk offend you, we'll
have very little of it. Nay Friar, I am a kind
of Bur, I shall stick.   *Exeunt.*

Scene 4

Enter Angelo and Escalus.

ESCALUS   Every Letter he hath writ hath disvouch'd
other.

ANGELO   In most uneven and distracted manner, his
Actions show much like to Madness: pray Heaven
his Wisdom be not tainted. And why meet him at   5
the Gates and reliver our Authorities there?

ESCALUS   I guess not.

ANGELO   And why should we proclaim it in an Hour
before his Ent'ring that if any crave Redress
of Injustice they should exhibit their Petitions   10
in the Street?

ESCALUS   He shows his Reason for that: to have
a Dispatch of Complaints, and to deliver us
from Devices hereafter, which shall then have
no power to stand against us.   15

ANGELO   Well: I beseech you let it be proclaim'd
Betimes i'th' Morn. I'll call you at your House.
Give Notice to such Men of Sort and Suit
As are to meet him.

ESCALUS   I shall, Sir: fare you well.

ANGELO   Good night.   *Exit [Escalus].*   20
— This Deed unshapes me quite, makes me
unpregnant

22   **dull . . . Proceedings** inattentive to everything else. Compare
III.i.556–59 and IV.iii.106.

23   **eminent Body** eminent (high-placed) official. Compare
I.iii.45–47. Here *Body* is an apt reminder of II.iv.89–99; *Loss*
(line 25) echoes the same passage, as well as III.i.178–80.

27   **bears . . . Bulk** carries such an overawing weight. *Credent*
means 'credible, believable'; compare II.iv.156–61. *Tongue*
(line 26) echoes IV.iii.112.

28   **particular Scandal** charge against my private behaviour. See
Troilus and Cressida, II.ii.9, where *particular* hints at
'part-tickler'. Compare the phrasing in II.i.31 and in *All's
Well That Ends Well*, II.v.65–67. And see I.i.39–40,
II.i.219–21, and II.iv.19–30 for previous uses of the word
part. *Touch* recalls I.i.34–35, 81–82, II.ii.54–56, 71,
III.i.178–80, 308–10, IV.ii.150.

29   **confounds the Breather** boomerangs on and demolishes the
person who breathes the charge.

29–30 **He . . . Sense** he would have been permitted to live except that
his unruly youthful spirit and dangerous sense [of having been
treated unjustly]. *Sense* recalls I.v.56–67, II.i.228–30,
II.ii.142–44, 168–70, II.iv.75, III.i.76. And the phrase *times
to come* echoes IV.ii.151–55.

32–33 **By . . . Shame** for having to be a party to such a shameful
ransom. Compare II.iv.113–15, 179–85, III.i.133–37.

34   **our . . . forgot** we have disregarded the principles of our faith
and neglected to act in accordance with the promptings of
'Grace' (the Holy Spirit).

35   **we would . . . not** Angelo's words echo those with which
Isabella began her appeal to the Deputy in II.ii.30–34. And
even more urgently than Isabella's, they evoke the Apostle
Paul's description of the fruitless strivings of the flesh in
Romans 7:15–25.

IV.v   This scene probably takes place at or near the 'Friar's' cell before
he departs for the 'consecrated Fount' (IV.iii.103).

1   **at fit time** at the appropriate time. See the note to IV.iii.47.
Deliver me (deliver for me) echoes IV.iii.6, 13.

3   **a foot** on foot, underway. *Instruction* recalls IV.ii.19.
    keep both (a) adhere to, and (b) keep secret.

And dull to all Proceedings. A deflow'red Maid,
And by an eminent Body, that enforc'd
The Law against it? But that her tender Shame
Will not proclaim against her Maiden Loss,   25
How might she tongue me? Yet Reason dares her
   no,
For my Authority bears of a credent Bulk,
That no particular Scandal once can touch
But it confounds the Breather. He should have
   liv'd,
Save that his riotous Youth with dangerous
   Sense   30
Might in the times to come have ta'en Revenge
By so receiving a dishonour'd Life
With Ransom of such Shame. Would yet he had lived.
Alack, when once our Grace we have forgot,
Nothing goes right: we would, and we would not.   35

                                                    Exit.

Scene 5

Enter Duke and Friar Peter.

DUKE   These Letters at fit time deliver me.
   The Provost knows our Purpose and our Plot:
   The Matter being a foot, keep your Instruction

4 **special Drift** private plan.

5 **blench** deviate, swerve. Compare *Hamlet*, II.ii.635–36.

6 **As . . . minister** as occasion requires. *Cause* echoes IV.iii.129.
  Minister recalls II.ii.85–88, II.iii.5–8.

10 **speeded** both (a) performed, and (b) done quickly. Compare
  III.i.58.

11 **Haste** Here, as in IV.ii.93, the Folio spelling is *hast*.

IV.vi This scene takes place near the City Gate.

1 **Indirectly** far from the straightforward truth. Compare
  Hamlet, II.i.63, where Polonius says, 'By Indirections find
  Directions out'.
  loath reluctant.

2 **so** by speaking 'the Truth' directly.

3 **Part** role (here in the theatrical sense). Isabella and Mariana
  are discussing the parts that the 'Friar' has assigned to them.
  Isabella's phrasing is a reminder of other senses of *Part* that
  relate to Mariana's role in the plot; see the note to IV.iv.28.
  advis'd . . . it wise to do as the Friar says. *Advis'd* echoes
  IV.ii.156.

4 **vail** both (a) veil, hide, and (b) lower, humble.
  full Purpose an open disclosure of our strategy. *Purpose* recalls
  I.i.72, I.ii.80–81, I.iv.3–6, 53–54, II.i.11–13, 158,
  II.iv.150–52, III.i.160–61, IV.v.2.

5 **peradventure** perhaps. Compare III.i.208.

6 **Adverse** opposed (adversary's).

7 **Physic** medical treatment.

And hold you ever to our special Drift,
Though sometimes you do blench from this to
   that   5
As Cause doth minister. Go call at Flavius'
   House,
And tell him where I stay. Give the like Notice
To Valencius, Rowland, and to Crassus,
And bid them bring the Trumpets to the Gate.
But send me Flavius first.
PETER   It shall be speeded well.   10

[Exit.]

Enter Varrius.

DUKE   I thank thee, Varrius, thou hast made good
   Haste;
Come, we will walk. There's other of our
   Friends
Will greet us here anon; my gentle Varrius.

Exeunt.

Scene 6

Enter Isabella and Mariana.

ISABELLA   To speak so Indirectly I am loath;
I would say the Truth, but to accuse him so
That is your Part; yet I am advis'd to do it,
He says, to vail full Purpose.
MARIANA   Be rul'd by him.
ISABELLA   Besides he tells me that if peradventure   5
He speak against me on the Adverse Side,
I should not think it strange, for 'tis a
   Physic

8   **Bitter . . . End**   bitter-tasting now, but only to bring about an outcome that will be sweet. Lines 7–8 moralize much of the action of the play; compare the medical imagery in I.ii.38–62, I.iii.9–15, II.i.118–21, 297–99, II.ii.49, 74–76, 135–37, II.iii.20–22, II.iv.19–30, III.i.2–3, 28–39, 126–29, 202–3, 245–47, 519–22, IV.i.57. Meanwhile, they provide an implicit elaboration on the title and action of *All's Well That Ends Well*. *End* recalls I.iv.3–6, II.ii.95–101.

        I . . . Peter   either (a) I wish Friar Peter would come, or (b) I hope the arrival I hear is that of Friar Peter.

10   **Stand**   place to stand (with analogies to the stand used by hunters to remain unseen while their pray unwittingly drifts into range).

        fit   suitable. In context with *Stand*, this word reverberates with other senses relevant to the situation in which Isabella and Mariana now find themselves. See the notes to I.ii.102, IV.iv.14, and IV.v.1.

11   **Vantage on**   favourable position for viewing and addressing. *Vantage* echoes II.ii.74–76, IV.i.23.

13   **generous**   most noble (from Latin *generosus*, high-born). Compare *Hamlet*, I.iii.74.

        gravest   most dignified.

14   **hent**   taken hold of, occupied. Compare *Hamlet*, III.iii.88, and *The Winter's Tale*, IV.iii.131–32.

        near upon   near this time, soon.

That's Bitter to Sweet End.

Enter Peter.

MARIANA   I would Friar Peter.
ISABELLA   Oh Peace, the Friar is come.
PETER   Come, I have found you out a Stand most
    fit,   10
    Where you may have such Vantage on the Duke
    He shall not pass you. Twice have the Trumpets
        sounded;
    The generous and gravest Citizens
    Have hent the Gates; and very near upon
    The Duke is ent'ring. Therefore hence away.   *Exeunt.*   15

V.i   This scene takes place at the City Gate. For the first time since the beginning of I.iii, we see the Duke apparelled in his own person as Vienna's head of state.

1   **Cousin**   Angelo. The word *Cousin* was not limited to blood relatives. A head of state often used it to address another high-ranking nobleman.

2   **Friend**   Escalus.

4   **Thankings**   thanks.

5   **made . . . you**   asked about you while we were away.

8   **Forerunning more Requital**   in anticipation of greater rewards. What the Duke knows, of course, is that the 'Requital' to be delivered in due course will be somewhat different from the 'Public Thanks' here proclaimed.
     my Bonds   my sense of obligation (indebtedness) to you. Compare IV.i.25, IV.iii.101–2.

9   **your . . . loud**   your deservings proclaim themselves. Again, the Duke's words carry verbal irony; he knows that in a short while those who can speak in more detail about Angelo's 'Desert' will be doing so even more loudly. Compare II.iv.153–56, IV.iii.124–27.

10   **Wards**   cells. Compare IV.iii.67.
     covert Bosom   a hidden heart. The Duke has used similar imagery in I.i.28–35 and in I.iv.1–3; compare IV.iii.139. His phrasing is a variation on the derogatory terms that Lucio has applied to him; see the note to IV.iii.162.

11   **Characters of Brass**   engraved inscriptions in brass. Compare I.i.26–28, I.iii.35–37, IV.ii.208–10.

12   **forted Residence**   fortified refuge.

13   **Razure of Oblivion**   the erasure brought about by forgetfulness (the obliteration of all memory). Compare I.ii.11, and see Sonnets 55 (lines 1–8) and 107 (lines 13–14) and *Love's Labour's Lost*, I.i.1–7.

14   **Subject**   subjects (subject people). Compare III.i.429–30.

ACT V

Scene 1

Enter Duke, Varrius, Lords, Angelo, Escalus, Lucio,
Citizens at several Doors.

DUKE   My very worthy Cousin, fairly met.
  – Our old and faithful Friend, we are glad to
    see you.
ANGELO, ESCALUS   Happy Return be to your royal
  Grace.
DUKE   Many and hearty Thankings to you both:
  We have made Enquiry of you, and we hear   5
  Such Goodness of your Justice that our Soul
  Cannot but yield you forth to public Thanks
  Forerunning more Requital.
ANGELO   You make my Bonds still greater.
DUKE   Oh your Desert speaks loud, and I should
      wrong it
  To lock it in the Wards of Covert Bosom   10
  When it deserves with Characters of Brass
  A forted Residence 'gainst the Tooth of Time
  And Razure of Oblivion. Give we your Hand
  And let the Subject see, to make them know

15 **outward Curtesies** external manifestations of courtly manners. See *The Merchant of Venice*, I.iii.129, where *Curtesies* (courtesies) plays on *Cur*; compare *Julius Caesar*, III.i.35–43.

would fain are eager to. The Duke's phasing is a reminder that he is only feigning these 'outward Curtesies'. *Fain* echoes IV.iii.157, 180, and anticipates line 21. *Proclaim* recalls IV.iv.8.

16 **Favours . . . within** good wishes that reside within the heart. What the Duke would 'fain proclaim' in reality he must 'keep within' for now. *Keep* echoes IV.v.3.

18 **Supporters** The Duke is probably alluding to the heraldic figures (called 'supporters') on the two sides of a shield in a coat of arms.

20 **Vail your Regard** lower your sights. *Vail* echoes IV.vi.4.

21 **fain** preferably. Isabella, too, is feigning when she implies she is no longer a 'Maid'. Compare IV.iv.22–26.

24 **Complaint** accusation.

27 **shall** who shall.

28 **Reveal . . . him** The Duke is speaking with the aptness of private irony, knowing the nature of the charge soon to be levelled against Angelo. Compare II.iv.52–56, 101–5, 163.

29 **of** from, at the hands of. *Redemption* recalls II.iv.113–15.

32 **Redress** correction of an injustice, compensation.

33 **Firm** stable, reliable. *Firm* anticipates *Infirmity* (weakness, illness) in line 48; it recalls I.iv.12.

36 **strange** strangely, preposterously.

38 **Forsworn** an oath-breaker. Compare IV.i.2, IV.iii.180–81.

That outward Curtesies would fain proclaim   15
Favours that keep within. – Come, Escalus,
You must walk by us, on our other Hand:
And good Supporters are you.

Enter Peter and Isabella.

PETER   Now is your Time: speak loud, and kneel
   before him.
ISABELLA   Justice, O royal Duke, vail your Regard   20
   Upon a wrong'd – I would fain have said a Maid.
   Oh worthy Prince, dishonour not your Eye
   By throwing it on any other Object
   Till you have heard me in my true Complaint
   And given me Justice, Justice, Justice,
   Justice.   25
DUKE   Relate your Wrongs: in what, by whom? Be
   brief:
   Here is Lord Angelo shall give you Justice,
   Reveal your self to him.
ISABELLA   Oh worthy Duke,
   You bid me seek Redemption of the Divel,
   Hear me your self: for that which I must speak   30
   Must either punish me, not being believ'd,
   Or wring Redress from you. Hear me, oh hear me,
   here.
ANGELO   My Lord, her Wits I fear me are not
   Firm.
   She hath been a Suitor to me, for her Brother
   Cut off by Course of Justice.
JUSTICE   By Course of Justice.   35
ANGELO   And she will speak most bitterly, and
   strange.
ISABELLA   Most Strange: but yet most Truly will
   I speak.
   That Angelo's Forsworn, is it not Strange?

45   **all**   both (a) just, and (b) every bit.

47   **To . . . Reck'ning**   till all accounting is completed. See the note to IV.vi.8. Isabella's phrasing echoes Sonnet 116.

48   **in . . . Sense**   as a person whose common sense (use of her 'Wits', line 33) is imprinted. The Duke's phrasing derives much of its irony from the play's earlier references to *Sense*, among them that in IV.iv.29–33.

49   **conjure**   solemnly appeal to [in the name of Heaven]. *Comfort* echoes IV.iii.114–16.

51   **neglect**   disregard (literally, fail to gather).

52   **touch'd with Madness**   afflicted with insanity. Isabella's phrasing echoes previous variations on *touch* in such passages as IV.iv.28.

53   **Unlike**   unlikely, improbable. Compare III.i.575–78 and IV.ii.202–3. Isabella's phrasing in lines 52–53 recalls what Helena says in I.i.241–43 of *All's Well That Ends Well*.

54   **But one**   that one who is.
      Caitiff   villain (literally, captive).

55   **Shy**   bashful, reserved. Lucio has applied the same adjective to the Duke in III.i.423.
      Grave   dignified, upright, strict ('Absolute'). *Just* recalls IV.ii.88–90; see the note to IV.ii.94.

57   **Dressings**   both (a) apparel of office, and (b) outward appearance.
      Caracts   signifying marks, seals ('characters'), and carats. Compare line 11.

59   **less**   other than what I tell you he is (less than an 'Arch-Villain').

62   **oddest . . . Sense**   most peculiar structure of logic (odd in the sense that it seems so unlike madness). Polonius speaks similarly about the 'Method' in the Prince of Denmark's 'Madness' (*Hamlet*, II.ii.212–13). *Frame* recalls III.i.267–68, 545–47.

63   **Dependency**   literally, hanging; logical connection. See the notes to IV.ii.35, 40–41, 55, and compare III.i.311–12.

That Angelo's a Murtherer, is't not Strange?
That Angelo is an Adulterous Thief,   40
An Hypocrite, a Virgin Violator,
Is it not Strange, and Strange?
DUKE   Nay it is ten times Strange!
ISABELLA   It is not Truer he is Angelo
Than this is all as True as it is Strange;   45
Nay, it is ten times True, for Truth is Truth
To th' End of Reck'ning.
DUKE   — Away with her: Poor Soul,
She speaks this in th' Infirmity of Sense.
ISABELLA   Oh Prince, I conjure thee, as thou
    believ'st
There is another Comfort than this World,   50
That thou neglect me not with that Opinion
That I am touch'd with Madness. Make not
    Impossible
That which but seems Unlike: 'tis not
    Impossible
But one the wicked'st Caitiff on the Ground
May seem as Shy, as Grave, as Just, as Absolute   55
As Angelo; even so may Angelo,
In all his Dressings, Caracts, Titles, Forms,
Be an Arch-Villain. Believe it, royal Prince,
If he be less, he's nothing; but he's more,
Had I more name for Badness.
DUKE   By mine Honesty,   60
If she be mad, as I believe no other,
Her Madness hath the oddest Frame of Sense,
Such a Dependency of Thing on Thing,
As ere I heard in Madness.
ISABELLA   Oh gracious Duke,

65   **banish Reason**   both (a) rule out the possibility that I am fully possessed of my reason, and (b) refuse to apply your own reasoning powers to the adjudication of my case. See the second note to line 108.

66   **For Inequality**   both (a) because of the inequality of Angelo's position and mine, and (b) because of the disparity between Angelo's reputation and what I tell you he is in reality.

68   **seems**   that seems.

69   **sure**   assuredly.

72   **loose**   both (a) loose, release, and (b) lose. Compare I.v.78–80, III.i.7–8 and V.i.421.

73   **in . . . Sisterhood**   in the probationary period prior to my being admitted to an order of nuns for the rest of my life.

75   **As then**   serving on that occasion as.
     and't like   if it please.

76   **desir'd**   urged. Compare I.i.75, II.ii.46–47, III.i.449–50, IV.iii.43, 102, 144.

79   **bid**   requested.

80   **wish**   The Duke echoes Lucio's verb; *wish* is a mild way of saying 'command'. Compare *desir'd*, line 76.

82   **Business**   matter of business. See the notes to I.v.9, III.i.436, 517.

83   **Perfect**   both (a) prepared (like an actor who knows his lines), and (b) free of guilt. Compare IV.iii.145–46.
     warrant   assure.

84   **Warrant**   warning, assurance. The Duke advises Lucio to hold his peace by alluding to the kind of 'Warrant' (I.v.74) that relates to the 'Business' under discussion.

85   **somewhat**   something.

89   **madly**   intemperately. *Pernicious* (line 88) means both 'malicious' and 'deadly'. *Caitiff* (villainous) recalls II.i.184, 195.

Harp not on that; nor do not banish Reason 65
For Inequality, but let your Reason serve
To make the Truth appear where it seems hid,
And hide the False seems True.

DUKE   Many that are
Not Mad have sure more lack of Reason. What
    would
You say?

ISABELLA I am the Sister of one Claudio, 70
Condemn'd upon the Act of Fornication
To loose his Head, condemn'd by Angelo.
I, in probation of a Sisterhood,
Was sent to by my Brother, one Lucio
As then the Messenger.

LUCIO   That's I, and't like your Grace. 75
I came to her from Claudio, and desir'd her
To try her gracious Fortune with Lord Angelo
For her poor Brother's Pardon.

ISABELLA   That's he indeed.

DUKE   — You were not bid to speak.

LUCIO   No, my good Lord,
Nor wish'd to hold my Peace.

DUKE   I wish you now then, 80
Pray you take Note of it: and when you have
A Business for your self, pray Heaven you then
Be Perfect.

LUCIO   I warrant your Honour.

DUKE   That Warrant's for your self: take heed to't.

ISABELLA   This Gentleman told somewhat of my Tale. 85

LUCIO   Right.

DUKE   It may be Right, but you are i'th' Wrong
To speak before your Time. — Proceed.

ISABELLA   I went
To this pernicious Caitiff Deputy.

DUKE   That's somewhat madly spoken.

ISABELLA   Pardon it,

90 **to the Matter** appropriate to the subject and occasion.
    Mended again The madness appears to be repaired again.

92 **to . . . by** to make a long story short (by omitting all
    unnecessary details in the narrative).

93 **persuaded** pleaded, sought to convince.

94 **refell'd me** put me down (rejected my suit).

95 **vild** vile, foul.

98 **concupiscible** passionate (literally, eagerly wishing to come
    together).

99 **Debatement** internal debate, rumination.

100 **Remorse confutes** pity strikes down, out-argues. Compare this
    account of Isabella's 'Sisterly Remorse' with her earlier
    remarks in II.iv.186–87.

101 **betimes** early. Compare IV.iii.49.

102 **His Purpose sufeiting** having overindulged his 'Purpose' (here
    synonymous with 'appetite', as in II.iv.163). *Purpose* echoes
    IV.vi.4.

105 **fond** foolish, deranged. Lines 103–4 echo lines 52–53.

106 **suborn'd** instigated by someone in an underhanded fashion.

107 **Practice** trickery, intrigue. So also in line 123. *Integrity*
    ('one-ness') plays on the phallic sense of 'one' noted in
    II.i.119.

108 **Stands** maintains itself. See the notes to I.ii.102, IV.vi.10.
    imports no Reason is contrary to reason. Here *imports*
    (introduces) plays on its literal sense in Latin: 'bears in'. See
    the note to I.i.55. Meanwhile *Reason*, which was often
    pronounced like *raisin* in Shakespeare's time, reinforces the
    suggestion of tumescence in *Stands*. See the note to I.iii.68.

109 **Vehemency** eagerness, insistence. *Vehemency* derives from the
    Latin verb *vehere*, to carry.

109– **pursue . . . himself** prosecute crimes of which he himself was
10   guilty. The word *Faults* reverberates with the implications of
    such earlier passages as I.iii.40, I.iv.35, II.i.28, 40, II.ii.35–42,
    139, 163, II.iv.135, III.i.325, 570, and IV.ii.118. Here *proper*
    means 'personal'; see the notes to I.i.29, I.iii.14, 66, 67.

The Phrase is to the Matter.

DUKE   Mended again.   90
The Matter: proceed.

ISABELLA   In brief, to set the needless Process
    by –
How I persuaded, how I pray'd, and kneel'd,
How he refell'd me, and how I replied
(For this was of much Length) – the vild
    Conclusion   95
I now begin with Grief and Shame to utter.
He would not, but by Gift of my chaste Body
To his concupiscible intemperate Lust,
Release my Brother; and after much Debatement,
My Sisterly Remorse confutes mine Honour,   100
And I did yield to him. But the next Morn
    betimes,
His Purpose surfeiting, he sends a Warrant
For my poor Brother's Head.

DUKE   This is most likely.

ISABELLA   Oh that it were as Like as it is True.

DUKE   By Heaven, fond Wretch, thou know'st not
    what thou speak'st,   105
Or else thou art suborn'd against his Honour
In hateful Practice. First, his Integrity
Stands without Blemish. Next, it imports no
    Reason
That with such Vehemency he should pursue
Faults proper to himself: if he had so offended,   110

111 **waigh'd . . . himself** weighed (treated) your brother as a fellow sinner. This line echoes II.ii.127–29, II.iv.186–87, and III.i.567–68.

118 **Countenance** both (a) Angelo's 'facing' (hypocrisy), and (b) the Duke's countenancing it (disinclination to expose and punish it). See the note to I.ii.110.

120 **fain** gladly. Compare line 21.

122 **blasting** blighting, withering.

126 **ghostly** both (a) spiritual (spoken sarcastically), and (b) moving about under cover of darkness, like a ghost. Compare III.i.472–74, IV.iii.162. *Ghostly* echoes IV.iii.51–52.

127 **meddling** both (a) intriguing, and (b) 'mingling' sexually (as in *Troilus and Cressida*, I.i.87–88). For wordplay on *Meddler* and *medlar*, see IV.iii.182, and compare line 144.

128 **Lay** not a number of the clergy.

130 **swing'd** beaten (from *swinge*, a verb that rhymes with *hinge*).

131 **'a** is a.

133 **found** located and brought here. In due course, the Friar will be 'found' (discovered) in another sense. The word *found* is also significant in *All's Well That Ends Well*; see V.iii.307–8 of that play.

135 **saucy** impudent, sassy.

136 **scurvy** base, villainous.

He would have waigh'd thy Brother by himself
And not have cut him off. Some one hath set
   you on:
Confess the Truth, and say by whose Advice
Thou cam'st here to complain.
ISABELLA   And is this all?
  – Then oh you blessed Ministers above,   115
Keep me in Patience, and with ripened Time
Unfold the Evil which is here wrapp'd up
In Countenance. – Heaven shield your Grace
   from Woe,
As I, thus wrong'd, hence unbelieved go.
DUKE   I know you'd fain be gone. – An Officer: 120
To Prison with her. Shall we thus permit
A blasting and a scandalous Breath to fall
On him so near us? This needs must be a
   Practice.
– Who knew of your Intent and Coming hither?
ISABELLA   One that I would were here, Friar
   Lodowick.   *[Exit, guarded.]* 125
DUKE   A ghostly Father, belike. – Who knows that
   Lodowick?
LUCIO   My Lord, I know him, 'tis a meddling Friar,
I do not like the Man: had he been Lay, my
   Lord,
For certain Words he spake against your Grace
In your Retirement, I had swing'd him soundly. 130
DUKE   Words against me? This 'a good Friar belike.
And to set on this wretched Woman here
Against our Substitute. Let this Friar be
   found.
LUCIO   But yesternight, my Lord, she and that
   Friar
I saw them at the Prison: a saucy Friar,   135
A very scurvy Fellow.
PETER   Blessed be your Royal Grace:

138   **abus'd**   both (a) deceived, and (b) misused.

140   **Touch ... her**   having had any blemishing physical contact with her. See the note to line 52.

141   **ungot**   unbegotten (and hence unborn).

144   **temporary Medler**   meddler in temporal matters (see the note to II.ii.155). What Peter and Lucio don't know is that this 'Man Divine and Holy' *has* been a 'temporary Medler', inserting himself into affairs of a sexual nature for a period of time. See the note to line 127.

147   **vouches**   avows, testifies. Compare IV.iv.1.
      mis-report   bear false witness about.

151   **strange**   mysterious, undiagnosed.
      Upon ... Request   moved solely by his request. *Mere* recalls III.i.11, 30.

153   **hether**   hither.

156   **Probation**   proof. But *Probation* can also refer to 'probing', and that describes what the 'meddling Friar' (line 127) has done to 'come to Knowledge that there was Complaint ... 'gainst Lord Angelo' (lines 152–53).
      Clear   This word echoes the 'Friar's' observation that 'it is almost clear Dawn' (IV.ii.228). Compare line 149.

157   **convented**   summoned here to testify. Friar Peter's phrasing echoes IV.iii.133.
      for   as for.

160   **disproved**   refuted, discredited (proven to be a liar).

163   **Vanity**   foolish, empty pride.

165   **Impartial**   a non-participant. The Duke implies that his withdrawal from the case will enable justice to be served without bias. But what he is also noting privately is that Angelo himself cannot really be 'Impartial', because his 'part' has been involved in the same kind of case as that of the brother condemned to death. See the note to II.i.31, and compare IV.iv.28.

166   **Cause**   case. What the Duke says here plays on his advice to Isabella in IV.iii.129. Compare IV.v.5–6.

I have stood by, my Lord, and I have heard
Your Royal Ear abus'd. First hath this Woman
Most wrongfully accus'd your Substitute,
Who is as free from Touch or Soil with her   140
As she from one ungot.
DUKE   We did believe no less.
  Know you that Friar Lodowick that she speaks
    of?
PETER I know him for a Man Divine and Holy,
  Nor Scurvy, nor a temporary Medler
  As he's reported by this Gentleman;   145
  And on my Trust, a Man that never yet
  Did (as he vouches) mis-report your Grace.
LUCIO My Lord, most villainously, believe it.
PETER Well: he in time may come to clear himself;
  But at this instant he is Sick, my Lord,   150
  Of a strange Fever. Upon his mere Request,
  Being come to Knowledge that there was
    Complaint
  Intended 'gainst Lord Angelo, came I hether
  To speak, as from his Mouth, what he doth know
  Is True and False, and what he with his Oath   155
  And all Probation will make up full Clear
  Whensoever he's convented. First, for this
    Woman,
  To justify this worthy Noble Man,
  So vulgarly and personally accus'd,
  Her shall you hear disproved to her Eyes   160
  Till she her self confess it.
DUKE   Good Friar, let's hear it.
  — Do you not smile at this, Lord Angelo?
  Oh Heaven, the Vanity of wretched Fools.
  — Give us some Seats. — Come, cousin Angelo,
  In this I'll be Impartial: be you Judge   165
  Of your own Cause.

168 **shew your Face** Most editions emend to 'show her face'. But the Folio reading (here retained) may well be correct, with *your* to be heard by Angelo as a contraction for 'you her'. The face Mariana shows will turn out to be Angelo's face, since, without recognizing it, he has claimed it in a consummation of his spousal vows; he and Mariana are now 'one flesh' (Genesis 2:24), and thus her face is his and vice versa. Meanwhile, here as elsewhere (see *Macbeth*, I.ii.14–15, I.iii.52) *shew* can function as an aphetic form of *eschew*, and Mariana is now discountenancing the 'Face' (appearance, guise) Angelo has tried to put on his previous behaviour; see III.i.232–40, V.i.52–60, 115–18.

169 **bid me** asks me to do so.

170 **Maid** virgin. Compare line 21, and see the note to I.ii.95.

173 **Punk** prostitute.

175 **Cause** reason. But the Duke is privately thinking of the same kind of 'Cause' that pertains to Angelo (line 166): a legal case. In this instance it relates to the 'case' of Lucio's own mistreated 'Punk'. See the notes to II.i.126.

176 **To . . . himself** to be forced to defend himself from accusation with his idle chatter.

179 **known** engaged in intimate relations with.

187 **In self-same manner** by the same token.

Enter Mariana.

— Is this the Witness, Friar?
First, let her shew your Face, and after, speak.

MARIANA Pardon, my Lord, I will not shew my Face
Until my Husband bid me.

DUKE   What, are you married?

MARIANA No, my Lord.

DUKE   Are you a Maid?

MARIANA   No,   170
My Lord.

DUKE   A Widow then?

MARIANA   Neither, my Lord.

DUKE Why you are nothing then: neither Maid,
Widow, nor Wife?

LUCIO My Lord, she may be a Punk: for many of
them are neither Maid, Widow, nor Wife.

DUKE — Silence that Fellow: I would he had some
Cause   175
To prattle for himself.

LUCIO   Well, my Lord.

MARIANA My Lord, I do confess I ne'er was
married,
And I confess, besides, I am no Maid;
I have known my Husband, yet my Husband
Knows not that ever he knew me.   180

LUCIO He was Drunk then, my Lord, it can be no
better.

DUKE For the benefit of Silence, would thou wert
so too.

LUCIO Well, my Lord.

DUKE   This is no Witness for
Lord Angelo.

MARIANA   Now I come to't, my Lord.   185
She that accuses him of Fornication
In self-same manner doth accuse my Husband,

189   **depose** swear under oath. The word *depose* derives from the Latin *deponer*, to lay down, put down, or set down; to put aside or get rid of; or to wager. Mariana's phrasing reminds us that at least two senses of *depose* apply to what Angelo has done to her; meanwhile her testimony is designed to depose (remove) him from his position as judge of his own case. See the note to II.iv.52.

190   **effect** both (a) working, manifestation, and (b) consequences.

191   **moe** more (a larger number).
       know know carnally (in the sense of lines 179, 194–5).

193   **just** even so. The riddling in lines 191–93 is quite similar to that in V.iii.287–91 of *All's Well That Ends Well*.

196   **Abuse** (a) deception, (b) misuse of language, and (c) waste of our time and affront to our dignity. Compare line 138.

198   **This is that Face** See the note to line 168. The Clown (Lavatch) has employed comparable phrasing in I.iii.74 of *All's Well That Ends Well*.

201   **belock'd** locked, clasped (as explained in III.i.219–40). Compare III.i.301–2, 427–28, IV.ii.71–72.

202   **the Match** both (a) the appointed 'Encounter' (III.i.263), and (b) the marriage bonding that resulted from the consummation of the earlier 'vow'd Contract' (line 200).

203   **supply thee** meet your requirements. The verb *supply* derives from Latin *sub-* (under) + *plere* (to fill). Compare I.i.17 and I.iv.46.

210   **for that** because.
       Proportions dowry (the portion to be supplied to the bridegroom as part of the marriage contract). Compare I.ii.24. Many editors emend the Folio's *promis'd* to *promised* to yield an extra syllable. But if *promis'd* is pronounced 'prom's'd' and treated as a single syllable metrically, *Proportions* can be extended to four full syllables ('pro-por-shi-ons') and yields a metrically regular line.

211   **Composition** what had been agreed to in the compact that would put our two fortunes together. *Compose* means 'place with'. *Composition* recalls I.ii.1–3.

And charges him, my Lord, with such a Time
When I'll depose I had him in mine Arms
With all th' effect of Love.   190
ANGELO   – Charges she moe than me?
MARIANA   Not that I know.
DUKE   No? You say your Husband.
MARIANA   Why just, my Lord, and that is Angelo,
Who thinks he knows that he ne'er knew my Body,
But knows, he thinks, that he knows Isabel's.   195
ANGELO   This is a strange Abuse: let's see thy
   Face.
MARIANA   My Husband bids me, now I will unmask.
                              [She unveils.]
   This is that Face, thou cruel Angelo,
   Which once thou swor'st was worth the looking
      on;
   This is the Hand which with a vow'd Contract   200
   Was fast belock'd in thine; this is the Body
   That took away the Match from Isabel
   And did supply thee at thy Garden-house
   In her imagin'd Person.
DUKE   Know you this Woman?
LUCIO   Carnally, she says.
DUKE   Sirrha, no more.   205
LUCIO   Enough, my Lord.
ANGELO   My Lord, I must confess I know this
   Woman,
   And five Years since there was some Speech of
      Marriage
   Betwixt my self and her; which was broke off
   Partly for that her promis'd Proportions   210
   Came short of Composition, but in chief

212– **dis-valued / In Levity** cheapened because of her light (wanton)
13   behaviour. Angelo implies that it came to his attention that
      his would-be bride was not a virgin. See III.i.234–40.

218 **affianced** pledged, vowed.

223 **confixed** attached (fixed together). See the note to I.ii.110, and
      compare IV.iii.47.

224 **Marble Monument** *Marble* recalls III.i.239 and Lucio's
      reference to 'Pygmalion's Images' (III.i.331–34).

225– **give . . . Justice** give me full authority to bring justice to bear
26   upon this case. What Angelo doesn't realize is that he will
      soon be given 'the Scope of Justice' in a sense he little
      anticipates. Compare I.i.63 and I.iii.12–13.

226 **My . . . touch'd** my ability to forbear this patiently is now
      affected. See the note to line 52. *Patience* recalls IV.iii.123,
      V.i.116.

227 **informal** distracted, mentally infirm. Compare line 48, and see
      I.iv.47.

228 **Member** person, member of the populace. Angelo's phrasing is
      a reminder of the 'Member' whose lawlessness was ultimately
      responsible for setting on these 'informal Women'. See the
      note to II.iv.95, and compare *The Merchant of Venice*,
      III.v.35–42, and *Love's Labour's Lost*, IV.i.41, IV.ii.82–83.
      way full liberty.

231 **your . . . Pleasure** The Duke's phrasing is ironically apt. See the
      note to II.iv.31. *Practice* echoes lines 107, 123.

233 **Compact** in league, conspiring; literally, fastened together.

234 **particular** individual. See the note to IV.iv.28. *Saint* echoes
      II.ii.180–81.

235 **Were** would serve as.

236 **seal'd in Approbation** confirmed in approval (proven worthy).
      See the note to line 156.

237 **Pains** efforts.

238 **find . . . Abuse** discover the source of this deception. *Abuse*
      echoes line 196.

For that her Reputation was dis-valued
In Levity; since which time of five Years
I never spake with her, saw her, nor heard
   from her,
Upon my Faith and Honour.
MARIANA   Noble Prince,   215
  As there comes Light from Heaven, and Words
    from Breath,
  As there is Sense in Truth, and Truth in Virtue,
  I am affianced this Man's Wife, as strongly
  As Words could make up Vows. And my good
    Lord,
  But Tuesday Night last gone, in's Garden-house   220
  He knew me as a Wife. As this is true,
  Let me in Safety raise me from my Knees,
  Or else for ever be confixed here
  A Marble Monument.
ANGELO   I did but smile till now.
  Now, good my Lord, give me the Scope of Justice.   225
  My Patience here is touch'd: I do perceive
  These poor informal Women are no more
  But Instruments of some more mightier Member
  That sets them on. Let me have way, my Lord,
  To find this Practice out.
DUKE   Ay, with my Heart;   230
  And punish them to your Height of Pleasure.
  – Thou foolish Friar, and thou pernicious Woman
  Compact with her that's gone: think'st thou thy
    Oaths,
  Though they would swear down each particular
    Saint,
  Were Testimonies against his Worth and Credit   235
  That's seal'd in Approbation? – You, Lord
    Escalus,
  Sit with my Cousin; lend him your kind Pains
  To find out this Abuse, whence 'tis deriv'd.

243 **abides** resides.

245 **warranted** guaranteed, approved (proven trustworthy).

246 **forth** till every piece of evidence has been brought forward.

247 **Do ... Injuries** handle the injustices against you [the ones that will be demonstrated in the trial that follows]. Compare IV.iii.127.

248 **In any Chastisement** using whatever punishment seems advisable to you.

250 **determin'd** concluded (arrived at a final judgement). Compare II.i.267–68, III.i.66–68.

251 **throughly** thoroughly.

254 **Cucullus ... Monachum** a Latin phrase meaning 'the cowl does not make the monk'. Lucio again speaks more truly than he realizes; the same is true of Escalus in line 259.

256 **of** about, concerning.

257 **abide** remain.

258 **enforce ... him** accuse him of his crimes to his face.

259 **Notable** noteworthy (here meaning 'notorious'). What Escalus doesn't know is that 'this Friar' is also 'Notable' in the notice he has taken of what has transpired in his supposed absence. Compare II.ii.92–101, IV.i.37, V.i.81, 308–14. *Find* echoes line 133.

263 **leave** permission, liberty. Here *give* means 'if you will give'.

264 **handle her** deal with her. Lucio gives the phrase a literal sense in line 265.

268 **privately** both (a) in private, and (b) in reference to her privates. Compare I.i.66–67, and see the note to II.i.96–100.
confess disclose her secrets, speak out. For similar innuendo on *confession*, see *1 Henry VI*, I.ii.119–20, *3 Henry VI*, III.ii.106–7, and *Troilus and Cressida*, I.iii.268.

S.D. **Enter Duke** Once again the Duke enters in the guise of a Friar.

There is another Friar that set them on,
Let him be sent for.   240
PETER   Would he were here, my Lord, for he indeed
Hath set the Women on to this Complaint;
Your Provost knows the place where he abides,
And he may fetch him.
DUKE   — Go, do it instantly.
                                        [Exit Provost.]
— And you, my noble and well-warranted Cousin,   245
Whom it concerns to hear this matter forth,
Do with your Injuries as seems you best
In any Chastisement. I for a while
Will leave you; but stir not you till you have
Well determin'd upon these Slanderers.   250
ESCALUS   My Lord, we'll do it throughly.   *Exit [Duke].*
— Signior Lucio, did not you say you knew that
Friar Lodowick to be a Dishonest Person?
LUCIO   *Cucullus non facit Monachum,* honest in
nothing but in his Clothes, and one that hath   255
spoke most villainous Speeches of the Duke.
ESCALUS   We shall entreat you to abide here till
he come, and enforce them against him.
We shall find this Friar a Notable Fellow.
LUCIO   As any in Vienna, on my Word.   260
ESCALUS   — Call that same Isabel here once again:
I would speak with her.   *[Exit an Attendant.]*
— Pray you, my Lord, give me leave to question,
you shall see how I'll handle her.
LUCIO   Not better than he, by her own Report.   265
ESCALUS   Say you?
LUCIO   Marry Sir, I think if you handled her
privately she would sooner confess; perchance
publicly she'll be asham'd.

       Enter Duke, Provost, Isabella.

270 **darkly** Escalus means 'cunningly' (indirectly, without letting her know his drift). Lucio (line 271) means 'in the dark' (as in IV.iii.162).

271 **Light** wanton (with wordplay on the more usual senses of *Light*: 'illuminated' and 'not heavy'). See lines 212–13. Lines 270–72 echo III.i.472–4.

274 **denies** who denies.

283 **'Tis false** Pretending to be 'saucy' (line 135), the 'Friar' denies the accusation. As the audience knows, he speaks the truth; he did 'set these Women on', but not to 'slander Lord Angelo' (who only appears to have been subjected to false accusations). *Slander* recalls II.i.191–2.

285 **Respect . . . Place** with all due respect for your eminent position. As the rest of the 'Friar's' speech makes clear, he is being sardonic, suggesting that Angelo's 'great Place' (an echo of II.iv.93) is just as deserving of honour as the Devil's 'burning Throne' in Hell. See the note to II.iv.95.
Divel The Duke's imagery recalls Angelo's reflections about his 'burning Throne' in II.iv.15–17. The Duke alludes to 1 Corinthians 7:7–9, where the Apostle Paul says, 'to the unmarried and widows, it is good for them if they abide even as I do. But if they cannot abstain, let them marry: for it is better to marry than to burn.' The Prince refers to this passage in *Hamlet*, III.i.150–53.

287 **should** who should.

288 **in us** represented in me (deputized as his 'Substitute', line 137).

290 **of** from (by enquiring of).

291 **Good . . . Redress** if so, you may as well bid goodnight to any hope of having your injustices remedied. *Redress* recalls line 32.

293 **retort** turn back, respond to (refusing to give a personal reply). *Cause* (line 292) echoes line 175.
manifest open, public.

297 **unhallowed** unholy, impious, lacking in reverence.

298 **suborn'd** incited to insubordination. See line 106.

300 **proper** own. See the note to lines 109–10.

ESCALUS   I will go darkly to work with her.   270
LUCIO   That's the way: for Women are Light at
    Midnight.
ESCALUS   Come on, Mistress, here's a Gentlewoman,
    denies all that you have said.
LUCIO   My Lord, here comes the Rascal I spoke of: 275
    here, with the Provost.
ESCALUS   In very good time: speak not you to him
    till we call upon you.
LUCIO   Mum.
ESCALUS   Come, Sir, did you set these Women on   280
    to slander Lord Angelo? They have confess'd you
    did.
DUKE   'Tis false.
ESCALUS   How? Know you where you are?
DUKE   Respect to your great Place; and let the
    Divel   285
    Be sometime honour'd for his burning Throne.
    Where is the Duke? 'Tis he should hear me
    speak.
ESCALUS   The Duke's in us, and we will hear you
    speak:
    Look you speak justly.
DUKE   Boldly, at least. – But oh Poor Souls,
    Come you to seek the Lamb here of the Fox;   290
    Good night to your Redress. Is the Duke gone?
    Then is your Cause gone too. The Duke's unjust
    Thus to retort your manifest Appeal,
    And put your Trial in the Villain's Mouth
    Which here you come to accuse.   295
LUCIO   This is the Rascal: this is he I spoke of.
ESCALUS   Why, thou unreverend and unhallowed
    Friar,
    Is't not enough thou hast suborn'd these Women
    To accuse this Worthy Man? But in Foul Mouth,
    And in the Witness of his proper Ear,   300

301 **glance** divert your charge, ricochet.

302 **tax him with** attack him for, accuse him of.

303 **Rack** an instrument of torture on which a person was stretched unmercifully until he either confessed or died. See the note to IV.i.63–64.
towze tear. *Purpose* (line 304) echoes line 102.

307–8 **His . . . Provincial** I am not subject to his authority, nor am I subject to the religious authorities of this province. The 'Friar' appears to be speaking saucily again, as a freely wandering brother of a religious order subject to no territorial limitations (in other words, a 'temporary Medler', line 144). But of course everything he says is also true of the Duke who is actually uttering these seemingly impudent words.

309 **Looker-on** observer. The 'Friar' is proving to be a 'Notable Fellow' (line 259) indeed.

311 **Stew** The Duke's culinary metaphor is particularly apt with reference to the kind of 'Corruption' that is boiling over in Vienna. One meaning of *Stew* was 'brothel'. See the note to II.i.95.

312 **countenance'd** tolerated. This word echoes line 118.

313 **Forfeits . . . Shop** lists of penalties for bad behaviour that were hung up in the shops of barbers (who performed surgery as well as the functions now associated with members of the tonsorial profession). *Forfeits* recalls IV.ii.169–70.

314 **As . . . Mark** as much in jest as to be 'marked' (noted). The punishments listed or illustrated in barbers' shops may well have been jesting ones to 'Mock' (satirize) the penalties meted out by the state for real crimes. Compare I.iv.19–31.

315 **vouch** testify. Compare line 147.

318 **Goodman Baldpate** Master Baldhead. 'Goodman' was a designation for a man below the rank of gentleman; here it is meant to be an insult.

324 **notedly** accurately (having noted it down). See lines 259, 309.

325– **Flesh-monger** whoremonger.
26

328 **change** exchange, switch.

To call him Villain, and then to glance from him
To th' Duke himself, to tax him with Injustice?
— Take him hence: to th' Rack with him. — We'll
   towze you
Joint by Joint. But we will know his Purpose:
What? Unjust?

DUKE   Be not so hot: the Duke   305
Dare no more stretch this Finger of mine than
   he
Dare rack his own. His Subject am I not,
Nor here Provincial: my Business in this State
Made me a Looker-on here in Vienna,
Where I have seen Corruption boil and bubble   310
Till it o'er-run the Stew. Laws for all Faults,
But Faults so countenanc'd that the strong
   Statutes
Stand like the Forfeits in a Barber's Shop,
As much in Mock as Mark.

ESCALUS   Slander to th' State:
Away with him to Prison.

ANGELO   What can you vouch   315
Against him, Signior Lucio? Is this the Man
That you did tell us of?

LUCIO   'Tis he, my Lord.
— Come hither, Goodman Baldpate, do you
   know me?

DUKE   I remember you, Sir, by the Sound of your
Voice. I met you at the Prison in the absence   320
of the Duke.

LUCIO   Oh did you so? And do you remember what
you said of the Duke.

DUKE   Most notedly, Sir.

LUCIO   Do you so, Sir: and was the Duke a Flesh-   325
monger, a Fool, and a Coward, as you then
reported him to be?

DUKE   You must, Sir, change Persons with me ere

333   **I protest ... self**   Once again the Duke speaks with private
       irony. His phrasing echoes Luke 10:27.

334   **close**   come to an agreeement, resolve his differences with me.
       The 'Friar' is actually 'closing' (and closing in) in an even
       more fundamental sense, not by speaking favourably of the
       Duke but by speaking as the Duke. *Abuses* (line 335) echoes
       line 238.

336   **withal**   with.

338   **Bolts**   shackles (iron fetters).

340   **Giglets**   wanton women.

341   **confederate Companion**   Friar Peter. Compare *Fedary*
       (II.iv.124), and see the note to II.iv.124–25.

347   **Sheep-biting Face**   Lucio implies that beneath the Friar's hood
       is a wolf rather than a shepherd. Lucio alludes to Matthew
       7:15, where Jesus warns his disciples to 'Beware of false
       prophets, which come to you in sheep's clothing, but inwardly
       they are ravening wolves'. Lucio's imagery recalls the
       shepherd reference in IV.ii.220–21. Compare line 290.

348   **hang'd an Hour**   Dogs who bit sheep (instead of protecting
       their flocks from wolves) were executed by hanging. *Hang'd*
       recalls IV.ii.33–64, IV.iii.29–50.

349   **ere**   e'er. But the other sense, 'before', is also applicable. So also
       in line 368.
       mad'st a Duke   This phrase would normally mean 'rose all the
       way up to the rank of Duke'. Here, however, it has an
       unexpected literal sense that gives ironic point to the scene's
       previous references to 'finding' the saucy Friar (lines 133,
       227–30, and 238–40). It also echoes the allusions to making
       men in such passages as II.ii.80 and III.i.135.

350   **bail**   stand bail for (and thus liberate). Compare III.i.328,
       360–71.

354   **you**   The Duke addresses Escalus.

355   **We'll ... him**   I'll take the seat now occupied by Angelo. *Place*
       recalls such previous passages as I.i.76–77, I.ii.111–12,
       I.iii.45–47, I.iv.11–13, I.v.56–62, II.i.8–16, II.iv.12–15,
       89–99, 156–61, III.i.256–63, IV.i.59–60, V.i.285.

356   **or Word**   either Word. *Impudence* means 'shamelessness'.

you make that my Report. You indeed spoke so of
him, and much more, much worse.   330
LUCIO   Oh thou damnable Fellow, did not I pluck
thee by the Nose for thy Speeches?
DUKE   I protest, I love the Duke as I love my self.
ANGELO   Hark how the Villain would close now,
after his treasonable Abuses.   335
ESCALUS   Such a Fellow is not to be talk'd withal.
Away with him to Prison. Where is the
Provost? Away with him to Prison. Lay Bolts
enough upon him: let him speak no more. Away
with those Giglets too, and with the other   340
confederate Companion.
        [The Provost attempts to execute Escalus' order.]
DUKE   Stay Sir, stay a while.
ANGELO   What, resists he? Help him, Lucio.
LUCIO   Come, Sir; come, Sir; come, Sir. Foh, Sir,
why you Bald-pated lying Rascal. You must be   345
hooded, must you? Show your Knave's Visage
with a Pox to you; show your Sheep-biting Face,
and be hang'd an Hour. Will't not off?
        [Lucio pulls off the Friar's Hood.]
DUKE   Thou art the first Knave that ere mad'st a
    Duke.
 — First, Provost, let me bail these gentle
    three.   350
 — Sneak not away, Sir, for the Friar and you
Must have a Word anon. — Lay hold on him.
LUCIO   This may prove worse than Hanging.
DUKE   — What you have spoke, I pardon. Sit you
    down:
We'll borrow place of him. — Sir, by your
    leave: 355
Hast thou or Word, or Wit, or Impudence

357   **That ... Office**   that can serve you now.

359   **hold ... out**   stand silently no longer. The Duke's phrasing is
       another sardonic reminder of the nature of Angelo's
       'Impudence'. See the notes to II.iv.35, 101, 168, III.i.424–25,
       556–57, IV.ii.84–85, 94.
       dread   revered (here 'feared' in a greater than usual sense, as in
       I.iv.19–34).

361   **Undiscernible**   undetected, unperceived for what I am.

362   **like Powre Divine**   with an unseen omniscience like that of God
       himself. Angelo thinks of himself as the irresponsible, unjust
       steward of Luke 12:42–48, the servant whose master has
       come back unexpectedly and caught him and is now prepared
       to 'cut him off'. See the note to I.i.28, and compare *King*
       Lear, I.v.54–55. *Powre* (power) recalls IV.iii.137.

363   **Passes**   trespasses, sins. *Passes* can also mean 'thrusts' (from
       passado, a fencing term, as in *Hamlet*, V.ii.311); see the note
       to IV.ii.84–85. Compare I.iv.38–39, II.i.22–23.

364   **Session**   formal trial proceedings.

366   **sequent Death**   death to follow forthwith. *Confession* (line 365)
       recalls III.i.166.

371   **Office**   duty, function.
       consummate   once completed. The Duke's phrasing is a
       reminder that the union has already been consummated and
       now lacks only 'the Denunciation' of 'outward Order'
       (I.iii.30–31).

374   **Strangeness of it**   astonishing way it has come about and been
       disclosed.

375   **Prince**   ruler (from the Latin *princeps*, first, chief).

376   **Advertising ... Business**   attentive (giving heed and counsel)
       and consecrated to promoting your welfare. *Business* echoes
       line 82.

377–   **Not ... Service**   I remain, with no less solicitude now that I
78   have exchanged the 'Habit' of a friar for the robes of a duke,
       an agent committed to serving you. *Changing* (which can here
       mean both 'altering' and 'exchanging') echoes line 328.

379   **Vassail**   vassal, servant.

380   **unknown**   unrecognized (because undisclosed).

That yet can do thee Office? If thou hast,
Rely upon it till my Tale be heard,
And hold no longer out.
ANGELO   Oh, my dread Lord,
I should be Guiltier than my Guiltiness   360
To think I can be Undiscernible,
When I perceive your Grace, like Powre Divine,
Hath look'd upon my Passes. Then, good Prince,
No longer Session hold upon my Shame,
But let my Trial be mine own Confession: 365
Immediate Sentence then, and sequent Death,
Is all the Grace I beg.
DUKE   — Come hither Mariana.
— Say: wast thou ere contracted to this Woman?
ANGELO   I was, my Lord.
DUKE   Go take her hence, and marry her instantly.   370
— Do you the Office, Friar: which consummate,
Return him here again. — Go with him, Provost.
    Exit [Angelo, with Friar Peter, Provost, and Mariana].
ESCALUS   My Lord, I am more amaz'd at his Dishonour
Than at the Strangeness of it.
DUKE   — Come hither, Isabel.
Your Friar is now your Prince. As I was then   375
Advertising, and Holy to your Business,
Not changing Heart with Habit, I am still,
Attorney'd at your Service.
ISABELLA   Oh give me Pardon
That I, your Vassail, have employ'd and pain'd
Your unknown Sovereignty.
DUKE   You are pardon'd, Isabel: 380
And now, dear Maid, be you as free to us.
Your Brother's Death I know sits at your Heart,

383   **obscur'd** hid (literally, covered over).

384   **marvaile** marvel. The Folio spelling hints at 'mar-vail' or 'mar-veil'; compare IV.vi.1–4 and V.i.20–21.

385   **rash Remonstrance** hasty display.

386   **let** permit.

387   **Celerity** quickness. Compare IV.ii.115.

388   **Which . . . on** which I had expected to come more slowly.

389   **brain'd** smashed the brains out of.

390– **That . . . fear** The Duke's reference to the blessings of eternal
91   life is one of many allusions to the afterlife in a play that can be read, among other things, as an extended *memento mori* meditation (a reflection on the inevitability of death and the need to be prepared for it). The theological message implicit in such meditations is *contemptus mundi* (contempt for this world), a doctrine most succinctly stated in 1 John 2:15–17: 'Love not the world, neither the things that are in the world.' For 'the world passeth away, and the lust thereof: but he that doeth the will of God abideth for ever'. The Duke's words recall III.i.1–43, 72–83.

394   **salt Imagination** lustful desire for you. Compare *Othello*, II.i.244–48, III.iii.394.

395– **pardon . . . sake** forgive (because although he lusted after you
96   in his heart, he actually committed no fornication with you). See Matthew 5:27–30.

396   **But . . . Brother** but for condemning your brother.

397   **in double Violation** on two counts (for two kinds of offence).

399   **Thereon . . . Life** in his second 'Violation' of excuting your brother despite his vow to you to spare him. *Dependent* echoes line 63.

400   **The . . . out** even the mercy provided for in the law cries out [for justice]. The Duke's phrasing echoes Genesis 4:9–10, quoted in the note to II.iv.187. It also recalls what Isabella said to Claudio in III.i.147, and what Escalus said to Mistress Over-done in III.i.491–92; compare II.i.297–98, II.ii.101–6.

And you may marvaile why I obscur'd my self
Labouring to save his Life, and would not rather
Make rash Remonstrance of my hidden Powre   385
Than let him so be Lost: oh most kind Maid,
It was the swift Celerity of his Death,
Which I did think with slower Foot came on,
That brain'd my Purpose. But Peace be with him:
That Life is better Life past fearing Death,   390
Than that which lives to fear. Make it your
    Comfort,
So happy is your Brother.

Enter Angelo, Mariana, Friar Peter, Provost.

ISABELLA   I do, my Lord.
DUKE For this new-married Man approaching here,
    Whose salt Imagination yet hath wrong'd
    Your well-defended Honour, you must pardon   395
    For Mariana's sake. But as he adjudg'd your
        Brother,
    Being Criminal in double Violation,
    Of sacred Chastity, and of Promise-breach,
    Thereon dependent for your Brother's Life,
    The very Mercy of the Law cries out   400
    Most audible, even from his proper Tongue,
    An Angelo for Claudio, Death for Death;
    Haste still pays Haste, and Leisure answers⎫
        Leisure;   ⎭

404   **quit**   requite, answer. For lines 403–4, see Matthew 7:2, quoted in the note to II.ii.140. *Measure* recalls III.i.542–45. See the notes to IV.ii.31, 32.
    still   both (a) yet, and (b) always.

406   **Vantage**   advantage. This word echoes IV.vi.11.

410   **mock . . . Husband**   deride me by giving me a husband in name only. *Mock* echoes line 314.

412   **Consenting . . . Honour**   acting in such a way as to preserve your chastity (by giving you a 'Marriage fit', with all due ceremony). For *fit*, see the notes to IV.iii.108, IV.vi.10. *Consenting* recalls II.iv.163, IV.i.66–67, IV.iii.59–60.

413   **Imputation**   reproach for dishonour.

414   **knew you**   engaged in carnal embraces with you. Compare lines 179–80, 191–95, 204–5.

415   **choke . . . come**   make it impossible for you to marry with honour in the future (because you can be accused of illicit intercourse).

416–   **Although . . . all**   although, because of the way he has been
17   struck down by the law, they properly belong to the state, I endow you with all his property as his widow.

420   **Definitive**   definite, conclusive (in our decision). *Loose* (lose, line 421) echoes line 72.

423   **take my Part**   plead on my behalf. Mariana's phrasing reminds us that Mariana has earlier taken Isabella's 'Part' (both the role she told Angelo she was willing to play, and the 'part' that Angelo was planning to bestow on her and her own 'part'). See the notes to lines 165, 234.

426   **Against . . . her**   Against all logic and all emotion you endeavour to break her resolve. See the note to line 48.

427   **in . . . this Fact**   to beg mercy for this deed. *Fact* recalls IV.ii.144.

Like doth quit Like, and Measure still for
   Measure.
— Then Angelo, thy Fault's thus manifested,   405
Which, though thou would'st deny, denies thee
   Vantage.
We do condemn thee to the very Block
Where Claudio stoop'd to Death, and with like
   Haste.
— Away with him.
MARIANA   Oh my most gracious Lord,
   I hope you will not mock me with a Husband?   410
DUKE   It is your Husband mock'd you with a
   Husband.
   Consenting to the Safeguard of your Honour,
   I thought your Marriage fit: else Imputation,
   For that he knew you, might reproach your Life,
   And choke your Good to come. For his
     Possessions,   415
   Although by Confutation they are ours,
   We do en-state and widow you with all,
   To buy you a better Husband.
MARIANA   Oh my dear Lord,
   I crave no other, nor no better Man.
DUKE   Never crave him, we are Definitive.   420
MARIANA   Gentle my Liege.   *[She kneels.]*
DUKE   You do but loose your Labour.
— Away with him to Death. — Now Sir, to you.
MARIANA   Oh my good Lord. — Sweet Isabel, take
   my Part;
   Lend me your Knees, and all my Life to come
   I'll lend you all my Life to do you Service.   425
DUKE   Against all Sense you do importune her.
   Should she kneel down in Mercy of this Fact,

428   **paved Bed**   stone-stealed tomb. The Duke's point in lines
427–29 is that a sister's most fundamental urge should be to
be her brother's keeper, in death if no longer in life (see
Genesis 4:9–10, quoted in the note to II.iv.187, and compare
Luke 19:37–40, where the Pharisees tell Jesus to rebuke his
disciples for referring to him as a King and Jesus replies that
'if these should hold their peace, the stones would
immediately cry out'). The Duke's imagery recalls the
promptings of the 'Brother's Ghost' in *Hamlet* and in other
revenge tragedies.

432–   **They ... bad**   Mariana alludes to the traditional Christian
34   teaching that an awareness of one's proclivity to sin is a
necessary precondition of the state of grace available to those
who repent of their faults and ask forgiveness for them.
Compare Escalus' remarks in II.i.8–16, 37–40, and Elbow's in
II.i.54–57, and see the notes to II.i.38, II.ii.80, III.i.55,
V.i.349. *Faults* recalls such previous passages as II.i.39–40,
III.i.570, IV.ii.117–18, and V.i.108–10, 311–14. *Better*
echoes lines 181–82, 265, 390–91, 419; compare II.i.232–33,
II.iv.77–78, 108–10, III.i.444–45, 456–57, IV.ii.225–26,
IV.iii.167–69.

438   **As ... liv'd**   So far as Isabella knows, of course, Claudio is now
dead. The phrase *man condemn'd* echoes II.ii.19.

439   **due**   proper, fitting. Compare IV.i.37.

445   **Subjects**   things subject to prosecution by the law. Lines
443–46 recall II.ii.4; compare II.i.17–31.

446   **Intents ... Thoughts**   and intents (such as Angelo's) are no
more than thoughts.
Merely   only. Compare III.i.11, 30, V.i.151.

447   **unprofitable**   unavailing. This word recalls II.iv.129–30,
III.i.317–18.

448   **bethought me of**   remembered.
Fault   crime.

453   **discharge ... Office**   remove you from your position.

455   **knew it not**   was not certain it was. *Fault* (error) echoes lines
432–34, 448.

456   **more Advice**   further consideration. *Advice* echoes lines
112–14; compare IV.ii.156.

Her Brother's Ghost his paved Bed would break,
And take her hence in horror.
MARIANA   — Isabel,
Sweet Isabel, do yet but kneel by me;   430
Hold up your Hands, say nothing, I'll speak all.
They say best Men are moulded out of Faults,
And for the most, become much more the better
For being a little bad: so may my Husband.
Oh Isabel, will you not lend a Knee?   435
DUKE   He dies for Claudio's Death.
ISABELLA *[kneeling]*   Most bounteous Sir,
Look, if it please you, on this man condemn'd,
As if my Brother liv'd: I partly think
A due Sincerity governed his Deeds
Till he did look on me. Since it is so,   440
Let him not die. My Brother had but Justice,
In that he did the thing for which he died;
For Angelo, his Act did not o'ertake his bad Intent,
And must be buried but as an Intent
That perish'd by the Way. Thoughts are no
    Subjects,   445
Intents but merely Thoughts.
MARIANA   Merely, my Lord.
DUKE   Your Suit's unprofitable. Stand up, I say:
I have bethought me of another Fault.   *[They rise.]*
— Provost, how came it Claudio was beheaded
At an unusual Hour?
PROVOST   It was commanded so.   450
DUKE   Had you a special Warrant for the Deed?
PROVOST   No, my good Lord: it was by private
    Message.
DUKE   For which I do discharge you of your Office:
Give up your Keys.
PROVOST   Pardon me, noble Lord,
I thought it was a Fault, but knew it not,   455
Yet did repent me after more Advice,

457   **For Testimony whereof**   as evidence of which.

458   **else**   otherwise.

462   **him**   Though the context (lines 457–60) implies that *him* refers to Barnardine, the juxtaposition with *Claudio* (line 461) suggests that the Duke is calling for him instead.

464   **still**   always.

465   **slip**   fall. Escalus' phrasing echoes such earlier passages as I.iv.21, II.ii.65, and III.i.139.
      Blood   passion. Compare II.iv.15, 20–23; 180–85, III.i.138–40.

466   **temper'd**   (a) well controlled, governed, (b) well mixed (with Judgement properly aligned with the other parts of one's makeup), and (c) strong and durable (like the tempered steel of a well-made sword). Compare II.ii.185.

467   **procure**   obtain, purchase.

468   **penitent**   See the note to IV.ii.55. *Sticks* recalls I.iv.25–26, IV.i.59–60, IV.iii.187–88. Here as in *Hamlet*, I.v.86–87 and III.iv.33–36, Angelo refers to the 'compunctious Visitings of Nature' (*Macbeth*, I.v.47), the prickings of conscience.

473   **stubborn**   unyielding.

474   **apprehends . . . World**   has no grasp of any realm beyond this life. Compare III.i.76, IV.ii.151–55, IV.iii.72–74.

475   **squar'st . . . according**   [you] use 'this World' as the guide to the conduct of your life (like a carpenter's square for the determination of right angles), not recognizing that temporal life is but a prelude to eternity.

476   **quit**   acquit, forgive. Compare line 404. *Faults* echoes line 455.

478   **advise him**   give him spiritual counsel. Compare line 456. *Better* echoes lines 432–34.

479   **muffled**   hooded in such a way as to mask his identity. See the note to line 462.

For Testimony whereof, one in the Prison
That should by private Order else have died
I have reserv'd alive.
DUKE   What's he?
PROVOST   His name
  Is Barnardine.   460
DUKE   I would thou hadst done so by Claudio.
  Go fetch him hither, let me look upon him.
                                    [Exit Provost.]
ESCALUS   I am sorry one so Learned and so Wise
  As you, Lord Angelo, have still appear'd
  Should slip so grossly, both in the Heat of
    Blood   465
  And lack of temper'd Judgement afterward.
ANGELO   I am sorry that such Sorrow I procure,
  And so deep sticks it in my penitent Heart
  That I crave Death more willingly than Mercy:
  'Tis my Deserving, and I do entreat it.   470

  Enter Barnardine and Provost, Claudio, Julietta.

DUKE   Which is that Barnardine?
PROVOST   This, my Lord.
DUKE   There was a Friar told me of this Man.
  – Sirrha, thou art said to have a stubborn Soul
  That apprehends no further than this World,
  And squar'st thy Life according. Thou'rt
    condemn'd,   475
  But for those earthly Faults, I quit them all,
  And pray thee take this Mercy to provide
  For better times to come. – Friar, advise him,
  I leave him to your Hand. – What muffled
    Fellow's that?
PROVOST   This is another Prisoner that I sav'd,   480
  Who should have died when Claudio lost his
    Head,

485 **Give . . . mine** if you'll give me your hand in marriage. The abruptness of the Duke's proposal to Isabella is one of the most problematic aspects of the play. Why Shakespeare does not give him a 'fitter Time for that' (line 486–87) is unclear. And how Isabella is to respond is left in doubt as well. She has no verbal reply either here or when the proposal is repeated at the end of the play. *Fitter* echoes IV.vi.10, V.i.413.

488 **Quick'ning** life-renewing spark. At a parallel juncture in *All's Well That Ends Well* (V.iii.301) Diana says 'one that's Dead is Quick'. Compare I.i.52, II.iv.52, III.i.281–82, IV.ii.115–16, IV.iii.32–33.

489– **quits / You well** both (a) is well requited (rewarded), and (b)
90 departs from you (thereby acquitting you) in a fortunate fashion. *Quits* echoes line 476.

490– **her . . . yours** both (a) her worth is equal to yours, and (b) all
91 that you are worth you owe to her. There is comparable emphasis on Helena's 'worth' in III.iv.30–32 of *All's Well That Ends Well*.

491 **apt Remission** an aptness (ready disposition) to be forgiving. *Remission* (which literally means 'sending back') is a word with theological resonance. Members of Shakespeare's audience would have associated it with Matthew 26:28, where Jesus says that 'this is my blood of the new testament, which is shed for many for the remission of sins'. Compare Mark 1:4, Luke 24:27, Acts 2:38, 10:43, Hebrews 9:22, 10:18.

493 **knew me for** proclaimed yourself so familiar with me as to declare me.

494 **one . . . Luxury** one completely given over to lechery.

497– **according . . . Trick** jestingly, in keeping with the prevailing
98 fashion. Compare Lucio's use of *Trick* in III.i.339, and see III.i.110–12.

505 **Nuptial** wedding ceremony. Lines 502–5 recall III.i.495–500 and IV.i.177–83.

510 **making . . . Cuckold** turning me into the husband of an unchaste woman. Compare line 349.

512 **therewithal** accordingly, therewith.

And like almost to Claudio as himself.
                              [He unmuffles Claudio.]
DUKE — If he be like your Brother, for his sake
   Is he pardon'd; and for your lovely sake,
   Give me your Hand, and say you will be mine,   485
   He is my Brother too. But fitter Time
   For that. By this Lord Angelo perceives
   He's safe: methinks I see a Quick'ning in
   His Eye. — Well, Angelo, your Evil quits
   You well. Look that you love your Wife: her
      Worth   490
   Worth yours. I find an apt Remission in
   My self: and yet here's one in place I cannot
   Pardon. — You Sirrha, that knew me for
   A Fool, a Coward, one all of Luxury,
   An Ass, a Madman: wherein have I so   495
   Deserv'd of you that you extol me thus?
LUCIO 'Faith, my Lord, I spoke it but according
   to the Trick. If you will hang me for it,
   you may; but I had rather it would please you
   I might be whipp'd.
DUKE Whipp'd first, Sir, and hang'd after.   500
   — Proclaim it, Provost, round about the City,
   If any Woman wrong'd by this lewd Fellow
   (As I have heard him swear himself there's one
   Whom he begot with Child), let her appear,
   And he shall marry her. The Nuptial finish'd,   505
   Let him be whipp'd and hang'd.
LUCIO I beseech your Highness do not marry me
   to a Whore. Your Highness said even now I made
   you a Duke: good my Lord, do not recompense
   me in making me a Cuckold.   510
DUKE Upon mine Honour, thou shalt marry her.
   Thy Slanders I forgive, and therewithal

513 **Remit ... Forfeits** pardon your other penalties (whipping and hanging). *Remit* echoes line 491; *Forfeits* recalls line 313.

515 **is** is equivalent to.

515– **Pressing to Death** Lucio alludes to the torture imposed on an
16 alleged criminal who refused to plead either guilty or not guilty to the charges brought against him. Weights were placed upon him until he either died or relented and entered a plea.

518 **restore** provide for.

520 **confess'd her** heard her confession.

522 **behind** to come.
Gratulate gratifying (rewarding).

524 **Worthier Place** setting more in keeping with your merits. See the note to II.ii.15.

528 **Motion** proposal. Compare Lucio's use of the word *Motions* in I.v.60.
imports your Good signifies your benefit. See the note to line 108. And compare the Duke's remarks in III.i.154–55, IV.iii.114–16.

529 **incline** extend. Compare III.i.414–15, IV.iii.79.

530 **What's mine ... mine** The Duke's phrasing echoes Genesis 2:24 and Ephesians 5:30–32, the biblical teaching that those joined in holy matrimony are to be 'one flesh'. See the note to line 168.

532 **behind** to follow. Compare line 522.

Remit thy other Forfeits. – Take him to Prison,
And see our Pleasure herein executed.

LUCIO   Marrying a Punk, my Lord, is Pressing to   515
Death, Whipping, and Hanging.

DUKE   Slandering a Prince deserves it.

> *[Exeunt Officers with Lucio.]*

– She, Claudio, that you wrong'd, look you
   restore.
– Joy to you, Mariana. – Love her, Angelo;
I have confess'd her, and I know her Virtue.   520
– Thanks, good Friend Escalus, for thy much
   Goodness:
There's more behind that is more Gratulate.
– Thanks, Provost, for thy Care and Secrecy:
We shall employ thee in a Worthier Place.
– Forgive him, Angelo, that brought you home   525
The Head of Ragozine for Claudio's:
Th' Offence pardons it self. – Dear Isabel,
I have a Motion much imports your Good,
Whereto if you'll a willing Ear incline,
What's mine is yours, and what is yours is
   mine.   530
– So bring us to our Palace, where we'll show
What's yet behind that meet you all should
   know.   *[Exeunt omnes.]*

FINIS

PERSPECTIVES ON
Measure for Measure

In what appears to have been the first detailed critical comment on *Measure for Measure*, the neoclassical author Charles Gildon (London, 1710) wrote that

> There are some little under Characters . . . , which are produced naturally enough by the Severity of the new Law, as that of the Bawd and the Pimp; as well as of Lucio, which Character is admirably maintain'd, as Shakespear does every where his Comic Characters, whatever he does his Tragic.
>
> The Unities of Action and Place are pretty well observed in this Play. . . . The Design of the Play carries an excellent Moral, and a just Satire against our present Reformers; who wou'd alter their Course of Nature and bring us to a Perfection, Mankind never knew since the World was half Peopled. . . .
>
> Allowing for some Peccadillos the last Act is wonderful, and moving to such a Degree, that he must have very little Sense of Things, and Nature, who finds himself Calm in the reading it.
>
> The Main Story or Fable of the Play is truly Tragical for it is Adapted to move Terror, and Compassion, and the Action is one. Its having a Fortunate Catastrophe, is nothing to the purpose for that is in many of the Greek Tragedies; tho' Aristotle indeed makes the Unfortunate Ending the most beautiful and perfect.

For a later eighteenth-century critic, Charlotte Lennox, an American-born writer who spent her most productive years in England, *Measure for Measure* was anything but a successful drama. In her 'Observations' on the play (London, 1753), Lennox said that

> As the Character of the Duke is absurd and ridiculous, that of Angelo is inconsistent to the last Degree; his Baseness to Mariana, his wicked Attempts on the Chastity of Isabella, his villainous Breach of Promise,

and Cruelty to Claudio, prove him to be a very bad Man, long practised in Wickedness; yet when he finds himself struck with the Beauty of Isabella, he starts at the Temptation; reasons on his Frailty; asks Assistance from Heaven to overcome it; resolves against it, and seems carried away by the Violence of his Passion, to commit what his better Judgment abhors.

Are these the Manners of a sanctified Hypocrite, such as Angelo is represented to be? Are they not rather those of a good Man, overcome by a powerful Temptation? That Angelo was not a good Man, appears by his base Treatment of Mariana; for certainly nothing can be viler than to break his Contract with a Woman of Merit, because she had accidentally become poor; and, to excuse his own Conduct, load the unfortunate Innocent with base Aspersions, and add Infamy to her other Miseries. Yet this is the Man, who, when attacked by a Temptation, kneels, prays, expostulates with himself, and, while he scarce yields in Thought to do wrong, his Mind feels all the Remorse which attends actual Guilt.

It must be confessed indeed, that Angelo is a very extraordinary Hypocrite, and thinks in a Manner quite contrary from all others of his Order; for they, as it is natural, are more concerned for the Consequences of their Crimes, than the Crimes themselves, whereas he is only troubled about the Crime, and wholly regardless of the Consequences. . . .

I cannot see the Use of all that juggling and Ambiguity at the winding up of the Catastrophe; Isabella comes and demands Justice of the Duke for the Wrongs she had received from his Deputy, declaring she had sacrificed her Innocence to save her Brother's Life, whom Angelo had, notwithstanding his promise to the contrary, caused to be executed.

Upon the Duke's telling her, that he believed her Accusation to be false, she goes away in Discontent, without saying a Word more: Is this natural? Is it probable, that Isabella would thus publicly bring a false Imputation on her Honour, and, though innocent and unstained, suffer the World to believe her violated? . . .

She who rather chose to let her Brother die by the Hands of an Executioner, than sacrifice her Virtue to save his Life, takes undeserved Shame to herself in public, without procuring the Revenge she seeks after.

Mariana's evasive Deposition; Friar Peter's enigmatical Accusation of Isabella; the Duke's winding Behaviour; what does it all serve for? but to perplex and embroil plain Facts, and make up a Riddle without a Solution.

The Play sets out with the Moral in the Title, *Measure for Measure*; but how is this made out? . . . when Angelo was pardoned, and restored to Favour, how then was it *Measure for Measure*? . . .

This Play therefore being absolutely defective in a due Distribution of Rewards and Punishments, *Measure for Measure* ought not to be the Title, since Justice is not the Virtue it inculcates.

Samuel Johnson concurred with many of Lennox's objections to the play. In the notes on *Measure for Measure* that accompanied his edition of Shakespeare's works (London, 1765), Johnson observed that

Shakespeare shows his knowledge of human nature in the conduct of Claudio. When Isabella first tells him of Angelo's proposal he answers with honest indignation, agreeably to his settled principles, 'thou shalt not do't.' But the love of life being permitted to operate, soon furnishes him with sophistical arguments; he believes it cannot be very dangerous to the soul, since Angelo, who is so wise, will venture it. . . .

Angelo's crimes were such, as must sufficiently justify punishment, whether its end be to secure the innocent from wrong, or to deter guilt by example; and I believe every reader feels some indignation when he finds him spared. From what extenuation of his crime can Isabel, who yet supposes her brother dead, form any plea in his favour? 'Since he was good 'till he looked on me, let him not die.' I am afraid our varlet poet intended to inculcate, that women think ill of nothing that raises the credit of their beauty, and are ready, however virtuous, to pardon any act which they think incited by their own charms. . . .

After the pardon of two murderers, Lucio might be treated by the good Duke with less harshness; but perhaps the poet intended to show, what is too often seen, 'that men easily forgive wrongs which are not committed against themselves.'. . .

Of this play the light or comick part is very natural and pleasing, but the grave scenes, if a few passages be excepted, have more labour than elegance. The plot is rather intricate than artful. The time of the action is indefinite; some time, we know not how much, must have elapsed between the recess of the Duke and the imprisonment of Claudio; for he must have learned the story of Mariana in his disguise, or he delegated his power to a man already known to be corrupted.

Early in the nineteenth century the great German scholar August Wilhelm Schlegel anticipated the modern view that *Measure for Measure* is to be classified as a tragicomedy. In his 1808 'Lectures on Dramatic Art and Literature', edited by the Reverend A. J. W. Morrison and translated into English by John Black (London, 1846), Schlegel noted that

> *All's Well that Ends Well, Much Ado about Nothing, Measure for Measure*, and *The Merchant of Venice*, bear . . . a resemblance to each other [in] that, along with the main plot, which turns on important relations decisive of nothing less than the happiness or misery of life, and therefore is calculated to make a powerful impression on the moral feeling, the poet, with the skill of a practised artist, has contrived to combine a number of cheerful accompaniments. . . .
>
> In *Measure for Measure* Shakespeare was compelled, by the nature of the subject, to make his poetry more familiar with criminal justice than is usual with him. All kinds of proceedings connected with the subject, all sorts of active or passive persons, pass in review before us: the hypocritical Lord Deputy, the compassionate Provost, and the hard-hearted Hangman; a young man of quality who is to suffer for the seduction of his mistress before marriage, loose wretches brought in by the police, nay, even a hardened criminal, whom even the preparations for his execution cannot awaken out of his callousness. But yet, notwithstanding this agitating truthfulness, how tender and mild is the pervading tone of the picture! The piece takes improperly its name from punishment; the true significance of the whole is the triumph of mercy over strict justice; no man being himself so free from errors as to be entitled to deal it out to his equals. The most beautiful embellishment of the composition is the character of Isabella, who, on the point of taking the veil, is yet prevailed upon by sisterly affection to tread again the perplexing ways of the world, while, amid the general corruption, the heavenly purity of her mind is not even stained with one unholy thought: in the humble robes of the novice she is a very angel of light. . . . The Duke acts the part of the Monk naturally, even to deception; he unites in his person the wisdom of the priest and the prince. Only in his wisdom he is too fond of round-about ways; his vanity is flattered with acting invisibly like an earthly providence; he

takes more pleasure in overhearing his subjects than governing them in the customary way of princes. As he ultimately extends a free pardon to all the guilty, we do not see how his original purpose, in committing the execution of the laws to other hands, of restoring their strictness, has in any wise been accomplished.

Meanwhile in England, another author immersed in the principles of Romanticism found *Measure for Measure* deeply distressing yet at the same time profoundly sane in its portrayal of common humanity. In his *Characters of Shakespear's Plays* (London, 1817), William Hazlitt described the comedy as

a play as full of genius as it is of wisdom. Yet there is an original sin in the nature of the subject, which prevents us from taking a cordial interest in it. 'The height of moral argument' which the author has maintained in the intervals of passion or blended with the more powerful impulses of nature, is hardly surpassed in any of his plays. But there is in general a want of passion; the affections are at a stand; our sympathies are repulsed and defeated in all directions. The only passion which influences the story is that of Angelo; and yet he seems to have a much greater passion for hypocrisy than for his mistress. Neither are we greatly enamoured of Isabella's rigid chastity, though she could not act otherwise than she did. We do not feel the same confidence in the virtue that is 'sublimely good' at another's expense, as if it had been put to some less disinterested trial. As to the Duke, who makes a very imposing and mysterious stage-character, he is more absorbed in his own plots and gravity than anxious for the welfare of the state; more tenacious of his own character than attentive to the feelings and apprehensions of others. Claudio is the only person who feels naturally; and yet he is placed in circumstances of distress which almost preclude the wish for his deliverance. Mariana is also in love with Angelo, whom we hate. In this respect, there may be said to be a general system of cross-purposes between the feelings of the different characters and the sympathy of the reader or the audience. This principle of repugnance seems to have reached its height in the character of Master Barnardine, who not only sets at defiance the opinions of others, but has even thrown off all self-regard. . . . He is a fine antithesis to the morality and the hypocrisy of the other characters of the play. Barnardine is Caliban transported from Prospero's wizard island to the forests of Bohemia or the prisons of Vienna. He is a creature of bad habits as Caliban is of gross instincts. He has however a strong notion of the natural fitness of things, according to his own sensations, . . . and Shakespear has let him off at last. We do not understand why the philosophical German critic, Schlegel, should be so severe on those pleasant persons, Lucio, Pompey, and Master Froth, as to call them 'wretches'. They appear all mighty comfortable in their occupations, and determined to pursue them, 'as the flesh and fortune should serve'. A very good exposure of the want of self-knowledge and contempt for others, which is so common in the world, is put into the mouth of Abhorson, the jailor, when the Provost proposes to associate Pompey with him in his office – 'A bawd, sir: Fie upon him, he will discredit our mystery.' And the same answer will serve in nine instances out of ten to the same kind of remark. 'Go to, sir, you weigh equally; a feather will turn the scale'. Shakespeare was in one sense the least moral of writers; for morality (commonly so called) is made up of antipathies; and his talent consisted in sympathy with human nature in all its shapes, degrees, depressions, and elevations. The object of the pedantic moralist is to find out the bad in every thing: his was to shew that 'there is some soul of goodness in things evil.' Even Master Barnardine is not left to the mercy of what others think of him; but when he comes in, speaks for himself, and pleads his own cause, as well as if counsel had been assigned him. In one sense, Shakespear was no moralist at all: in another, he was the greatest of all moralists. He was a moralist in the same sense in which nature is one. He taught what he had learnt from her. He shewed the greatest knowledge of humanity with the greatest fellow-feeling for it.

Later in the century, Edward Dowden interpreted *Measure for Measure* and *All's Well That Ends Well* as comedies whose atmospheres reflected the disillusionment of a dramatist whose middle years were supposedly marked by a siege of griefs and doubts. In *Shakspere: A Critical Study of His Mind and Art* (London, 1875), Dowden maintained that

When the former of these plays was written, Shakspere was evidently bidding farewell to mirth. Its significance is grave and earnest; the humorous scenes would be altogether repulsive were it not that they are needed to present, without disguise or extenuation, the world of moral licence and corruption out of and above which rise the virginal strength and severity and beauty of Isabella. At the entrance to the dark and dangerous tragic world into which Shakspere was now about to pass stand the figures of Isabella and of Helena – one the embodiment of conscience, the other the embodiment of will. Isabella is the only one of Shakspere's women whose heart and eyes are fixed upon an impersonal ideal, to whom something abstract is more, in the ardour and energy of her youth, than any human personality. . . . Isabella's saintliness is not of the passive, timorous, or merely meditative kind. It is an active pursuit of holiness through exercise and discipline. She knows nothing of a Manichean hatred of the body; the life runs strongly and gladly in her veins; simply her soul is set upon things belonging to the soul, and uses the body for its own purposes. And that the life of the soul may be invigorated, she would bring every unruly thought into captivity, 'having a readiness to revenge all disobedience.' . . .

The severity of Isabella proceeds from no real turning away, on her part, from the joys and hopes of womanhood; her brother, her schoolfellow Julia, the memory of her father, are precious to her. Her severity is only a portion of the vital energy of her heart. Living actively, she must live purely; and to her the cloister is looked upon as the place where her energy can spend itself in stern efforts towards ideal objects. . . .

[At the end of the action,] putting aside from her the dress of religion, and the strict conventual rule, she accepts her place as Duchess of Vienna. In this there is no dropping-away, through love of pleasure or through supineness, from her ideal; it is entirely meet and right. She has learned that in the world may be found a discipline more strict, more awful, than the discipline of the convent; she has learned that the world has need of her. Her life is still a consecrated life; the vital energy of her heart can exert and augment itself through glad and faithful wifehood, and through noble station, more fully than in seclusion. To preside over this polluted and feculent Vienna is the office and charge of Isabella, 'a thing ensky'd and sainted'.

A little more than a decade after Dowden's remarks, Walter Pater offered his own *Appreciations* (London, 1889) of Shakespeare's works.

In *Measure for Measure*, as in some other of his plays, Shakespeare has remodelled an earlier and somewhat rough composition to 'finer issues', suffering much to remain as it had come from the less skilful hand [of a previous writer], and not raising the whole of his work to an equal degree of intensity. Hence perhaps some of that depth and weightiness which make this play so impressive, as with the true seal of experience, like a fragment of life itself, rough and disjointed indeed, but forced to yield in places its profounder meaning. In *Measure for Measure*, in contrast with the flawless execution of *Romeo and Juliet*, Shakespeare has spent his art in just enough modification of the scheme of the older play to make it exponent of this purpose, adapting its terrible essential incidents, so that Coleridge found it the only painful work among Shakespeare's drama, and leaving for the reader of today more than the usual number of difficult expressions; but infusing a lavish colour and a profound significance into it, so that under his touch certain select portions of it rise far above the level of all but his own best poetry, and working out of it a morality so characteristic that the play might well pass for the central expression of his moral judgements. It remains a comedy, as indeed is congruous with the bland, half-humorous equity which informs the whole composition, sinking from the heights of sorrow and terror into the rough scheme of the earlier piece; yet it is hardly less full of what is really tragic in man's existence than if Claudio had indeed 'stooped to death'. Even the humorous concluding scenes have traits of special grace, retaining in less emphatic passages a stray line or word of power, as it seems, so that we watch to the end for the traces where the nobler hand has glanced along, leaving its vestiges, as if accidentally or wastefully, in the rising of the style.

In what has proven to be one of the most influential twentieth-century essays on the comedy, '*Measure for Measure* and the Gospels', a chapter in his book *The Wheel of Fire* (London, 1930), G. Wilson Knight argued that 'The play tends towards allegory or symbolism.'

The Duke's ethical attitude is exactly correspondent with Jesus': the play must be read in the light of the Gospel teaching, if its full significance is to be apparent. So he, like Jesus, moves among men suffering grief at their sins and deriving joy from an unexpected flower of simple goodness in the deserts of impurity and hardness . . .

The Duke's plot pivots on the testing of Angelo. Angelo is a man of spotless reputation, generally respected. . . . [He] is not a conscious hypocrite: rather a man whose chief faults are self-deception and pride in his own righteousness – an unused and delicate instrument quite useless under the test of actual trial. This he half-recognizes, and would first refuse the proffered honour. The Duke insists: Angelo's fall is thus entirely the Duke's responsibility. . . . Angelo, indeed, does not know himself: no one receives so great a shock as he himself when temptation overthrows his virtue. . . . He cannot, however, be acquitted of Pharisaical pride. . . . Now, when he is first faced with the problem of Claudio's guilt of adultery – and commanded, we must presume, by the Duke's sealed orders to execute stern punishment wholesale, for this is the Duke's ostensible purpose – Angelo pursues his course without any sense of wrongdoing. Escalus hints that surely all men must know sexual desire – how then is Angelo's procedure just? . . . Which reflects the Gospel message:

> Ye have heard that it was said by them of old time, Thou shalt not commit adultery:
> But I say unto you, that whosoever looketh on a woman to lust after her hath committed adultery with her already in his heart.
>
> (Matthew, v.27)

Angelo's reply, however, is sound sense:

> 'Tis one thing to be tempted, Escalus,
> Another thing to fall. (II.i.17)

Isabella later uses the same argument as Escalus:

> . . . Go to your bosom;
> Knock there, and ask your heart what it doth know
> That's like my brother's fault: if it confess
> A natural guiltiness, such as is his,
> Let it not sound a thought upon your tongue
> Against my brother's life. (II.ii.136)

We are reminded of Jesus's words to the Scribes and Pharisees concerning the woman 'taken in adultery':

> He that is without sin among you, let him first cast a stone at her.
>
> (John, viii.7)

Angelo is, however, sincere: terribly sincere. He feels no personal responsibility, since he is certain that he does right. . . .

Angelo's arguments are rationally conclusive. A thing irrational breaks them, however: his passion for Isabella. . . . Angelo is now quite adrift: all his old contacts are irrevocably severed. Sexual desire has long been anathema to him, so his warped idealism forbids any healthy love. . . . Since sex has been synonymous with foulness in his mind, this new love, reft from the start of moral sanction in a man who 'scarce confesses that his blood flows,' becomes swiftly a devouring and curbless lust. . . .

Isabella . . . is more saintly than Angelo, and her saintliness goes deeper, is more potent than his. . . . [But] she lacks human feeling. She starts her suits to Angelo poorly enough – she is luke-warm. . . . Lucio has to urge her on continually. We begin to feel that Isabella has no real affection for Claudio; has stifled all human love in the pursuit of sanctity. . . . We are not surprised that she behaves to Claudio, who hints for her sacrifice, like a fiend. . . Is her fall any less than Angelo's? Deeper, I think. With whom is Isabel angry? Not only with her brother. She has feared this choice – terribly. . . . Ever since Angelo's suggestion she has been afraid. Now Claudio has forced the responsibility of choice on her. Her sex inhibitions have been horribly shown her as they are, naked. She has been stung – lanced on a sore spot of her soul. She knows now that it is not all saintliness, she sees her own soul and sees it as something small, frightened, despicable, too frail to dream of such a sacrifice. . . . It is significant that she readily involves Mariana in illicit love: it is always her own, and only her own, chastity that assumes, in her heart, universal importance.

Isabella, however, was no hypocrite, any more than Angelo. She is a spirit of purity, grace, maiden charm: but all these virtues the action of the play turns remorselessly against herself. In a way, it is not her fault. Chastity is hardly a sin – but neither, as the play emphasizes, is it the whole of virtue. And she, like the rest, has to find a new wisdom. Mariana in the last act prays for Angelo's life. Confronted by that warm, potent, forgiving, human love, Isabella herself suddenly shows a softening, a sweet humanity. Asked to intercede, she does so – she, who was at the start slow to intercede for a brother's life, now implores the Duke to save Angelo, her wronger. . . . There is a suggestion that Angelo's strong passion has itself moved her, thawing her ice-cold pride. This is the moment of her trial: the Duke is watching her keenly, to see if she has learnt her lesson – nor does he give her any help, but deliberately puts obstacles in her way. But she stands the test: she bows to a greater love than her own saintliness. Isabella, like Angelo, has progressed far during the play's action: from sanctity to humanity. . . .

So the Duke draws his plan to its appointed end. All, including Barnadine, are forgiven, and left, in the usual sense, unpunished. This is inevitable. The Duke's original leniency has been shown by his successful plot to have been right, not wrong. Though he sees 'corruption boil and bubble' (v.i.316) in Vienna, he has found, too, that man's sainted virtue is a delusion: 'judge not that ye be not judged.' He has seen an Angelo to fall from grace at the first breath of power's temptation, he has seen Isabella's purity scarring, defacing her humanity. He has found more gentleness in 'the steeled gaoler' than in either of these. He has found more natural honesty in Pompey the bawd than in Angelo the ascetic; more humanity in the charity of Mistress Overdone than in Isabella condemning her brother to death with venomed words in order to preserve her own chastity. . . . Therefore, knowing all this, the Duke knows his tolerance to be now a moral imperative: he sees too far into the nature of man to pronounce judgement according to the appearances of human behaviour. But we are told what will become of Vienna. There is, however, a hint, for the Duke is to marry Isabel, and this marriage, like the others, may be understood symbolically. It is to be the marriage of understanding with purity; of tolerance with moral fervour. . . .

. . . The lesson of the play is that of Matthew, v.20:

For I say unto you, That except your righteousness shall exceed the righteousness of the Scribes and Pharisees, ye shall in no case enter into the Kingdom of Heaven.

The play must be read, not as a picture of normal human affairs, but as a parable, like the parables of Jesus. The plot is, in fact, an inversion of one of those parables – that of the Unmerciful Servant (Matthew, xviii); and the universal and level forgiveness at the end, where all alike meet pardon, is one with the forgiveness of the Parable of the Two Debtors (Luke, vii). Much has been said about the difficulties of *Measure for Measure*. But, in truth, no play of Shakespeare shows more thoughtful care, more deliberate purpose, more consummate skill in structural technique, and, finally, more penetrating ethical and psychological insight. None shows a more exquisitely inwoven pattern. And, if ever the thought at first sight seems strange, or the action unreasonable, it will be found to reflect the sublime strangeness and unreason of Jesus' teaching.

Like Wilson Knight, W. W. Lawrence sought to defend *Measure for Measure* from many of the charges that earlier critics had levelled against it. But rather than construe the plot allegorically, Lawrence reminded readers that the Vincentio of the play's action 'is, as it were, a stage Duke, not a real person. In this respect he contrasts strikingly with Isabella and Angelo and Claudio and Lucio, and the low-comedy people.' In *Shakespeare's Problem Comedies* (New York, 1931), Lawrence observed that

In the dramas written before *Measure for Measure*, two agencies stand out prominently as representatives of right and justice in straightening out complications of plot: the State and the Church. The former is represented by the person in supreme lay authority – a Duke in the *Comedy of Errors*, the *Two Gentlemen of Verona*, *Twelfth Night*, the *Midsummer Night's Dream* (Theseus as Duke of Athens), the *Merchant of Venice*, *As You Like It* (the banished Duke); the King of France in *All's Well*. The latter is represented by priest or friar – Friar Laurence in *Romeo and Juliet*, Friar Francis in *Much Ado*, who suggest, respectively, the stratagems by which the Veronese lovers are united, and the honor of Hero vindicated. The law and authority in these pieces is romantic law and authority; it cannot be judged by strict legal or ecclesiastical standards. The quibbles which are the undoing of Shylock are as much a part of popular story as the sleeping potion which sends Juliet to the tomb. Shakespeare used dukes and friars when the peculiar powers and opportunities afforded by their station would help his narrative. He did not bother himself about the strict legality or rationality of their actions. What they suggest or decide has in his plays the binding force of constituted and final authority, and was so understood by his audiences.

The Duke in *Measure for Measure* combines the functions both of State and Church in his person. As Duke, he is the supreme ruler of Vienna, who returns at the end to straighten out the tangles of the action, and dispense justice to all. In his disguise as Friar, he represents the wisdom and adroitness of the Church, in directing courses of action and advising stratagems so that good may come out of evil. But the plots which he sets in motion and the justice which he dispenses are the stuff of story; they cannot be judged as if they were historical occurrences. And the Duke's character cannot be estimated on a rationalistic basis. If he really wished to set matters right between Angelo, Isabella, Mariana, Claudio, and the rest, he had a short and easy way of doing it. He was in full possession of the facts; he could have revealed himself, brought all before the bar of his authority, freed the innocent and punished the guilty in short order, and this would have saved Isabella and Claudio much suffering. Such an arrangement would, however, have been much less effective dramatically than his continued disguise, his suggested ruses, the prolongation of the suspense of the accused, and the false security of the villain. No, he knows what is expected of him as a stage Duke, and makes the most of his part.

For Muriel C. Bradbrook, like W. W. Lawrence, 'The first necessity' in reading *Measure for Measure* was 'to grasp the importance of the Duke'. Writing in the 1941 volume of *The Review of English Studies*, Bradbrook noted that the Duke

belongs to a familiar dramatic type; that of the omnipotent disguised character who directs the intrigue, often hearing strange things of himself by the way. . . . Wilson Knight sees in him a Christlike figure come from a far country to save Vienna: all powerful, all merciful, and perhaps in his marriage to Isabel only ratifying her position as the Bride of the Church. . . .

As the Duke represents unerring Justice, and in his readiness to live as a poor Friar, helping his meanest and most criminal subjects, represents also Humanity as it resides in true authority; so Isabel stands for unerring Truth, and Truth is always merciful. . . .

Angelo stands for the letter of the Law, for a false Authority: he also stands for Seeming or False Semblant. . . .

Claudio and Juliet stand for human nature, original sin; Mariana for *eros* (as distinct from *agape*); Barnardine is contrasted with Claudio to show how much below panic-struck egoism is mere brute insensibility. Juliet, whom Claudio 'wrong'd', is penitent from the first and therefore absolved by the Duke; nor apparently does she ever stand in peril of her life, and she is not given a judgement in the final scene as the others are. In the last scene measure for measure is meted out to all; not, perhaps, their measure according to earthly law – for Barnardine is pardoned – but the measure best devised to save their souls. The main purpose of the scene is to bring Angelo to repentance, and to achieve it against so strong a character terrific pressure has to be brought to bear. The Duke, who is as ruthlessly efficient in his means as he is benevolent in his ends, proceeds to apply the third degree with the skill of a Grand Inquisitor: and to this end he is ready to inflict any temporary suffering on Mariana and Isabel. . . .

In the actions of Angelo, Isabel, and the Duke, the question of Truth and Seeming is stated, and they have thus a double burden of symbolism to carry. Nevertheless, the allegorical nature of *Measure for Measure* does not preclude a human interest in the characters. Though based perhaps on the Moralities, it is not a Morality. Angelo has always been recognized as a superb character study; Isabel and the Duke, though less impressive, are subtly presented. She is possibly the most intelligent of all Shakespeare's women; even poor Claudio recognizes her power in 'reason and discourse'; yet she is young, and pitifully inexperienced. . . .

Measure for Measure remains a problem play, not because it is shallower, more unfinished or more incoherent than Shakespeare's other plays, but because it is stiffened by its doctrinaire and impersonal consideration of ethical values. The dryness, the pain behind the play, seem to depict a world in which external personal relationships are so hopelessly false and unreliable that it is necessary to cut below them to the moral substratum.

Like others who wrote in the 1930s and 1940s about Shakespeare's early seventeenth-century comedies, Elizabeth Marie Pope emphasized the centrality of the Duke. In 'The Renaissance Background of *Measure for Measure*' (*Shakespeare Survey*, 1949), Pope pointed out that

According to Renaissance theory, the authority of all civil rulers is derived from God. Hence, they may be called 'gods', as they are in Psalm lxxxii, 6, because they act as God's substitutes, 'Ruling, Judging, and Punishing in God's stead, and so deserving God's name here on earth,' as Bilson put it in the sermon he preached at King James's coronation. . . . Any Renaissance audience would have taken it for granted that the Duke did indeed 'stand for' God, but only as any good ruler 'stood for' Him; and if he behaved 'like power divine', it was because that was the way a good ruler was expected to conduct himself. . . .

In their capacity as God's substitutes, rulers have four privileges. The first is sanctity of person, especially in the case of an anointed prince. No man may raise his hand against him, or even disparage him in speech or thought. . . . Secondly, the ruler has sovereignty of power: all men must obey him without question, except when his commands directly contradict God's ordinances. Even then, disobedience must be entirely passive, and any retaliation from the authorities endured with patience – although Roman Catholics held that open rebellion was sometimes permissible when the ruler was a heretic. . . .

The third privilege of rulers is the right to enforce the law. In civil matters, the avenging of evil, which God has strictly forbidden to private individuals, is the office and duty of the ruler and his subordinates, to whom the Duke bids Isabella turn when, in her agony at Claudio's supposed death, she momentarily thinks of punishing Angelo herself. . . .

Finally, the ruler has the privilege of using extraordinary means. . . . Hence the Duke in *Measure for Measure* is quite justified in using disguise, applying 'craft against vice' (III.ii.291), and secretly watching Angelo much as King James advises his son in the *Basilicon Doron* [a book James VI of Scotland published in Edinburgh in 1599 and had reissued in London after he became James I of England in 1603] to watch his own subordinates: 'Delight to haunt your Session, and spy carefully their proceedings . . . to take a sharp account of every man in his office'. . . .

But in the eyes of the Renaissance, the Christian prince had not only authority and privileges, but a clearly defined and inescapable set of duties to perform as well. The first is to remember that he is not really God, but man 'dressed in a little brief authority', as Isabella reminds Angelo – mere man, whom his God will in the end call strictly to account, although his subjects may not. . . .

As ever in his great Taskmaster's eye, therefore, the ruler must labour to be what God would have him. To begin with, he must be sincerely religious. . . . Furthermore he must know and be able to govern himself. . . . He should also cultivate all the virtues to the best of his ability, but according to the *Basilicon Doron*, 'make one of them, which is Temperance, Queen of all the rest'. . . . Therefore, when Escalus describes the Duke as 'one that above all other strifes, contended especially to know himself', and 'a gentleman of all temperance' . . . , what may seem rather faint praise to a modern reader would have been regarded as a very high tribute indeed during the Renaissance. Finally, in all he does, the ruler must remember that his life is the pattern for his subjects. . . .

The more practical and specific duties of the ruler are to get a good education, especially in political theory; to love his subjects and be throughly acquainted with them . . . ; to levy no undue taxes, or waste them when collected . . . ; to keep peace with all nations if possible, but to protect his own against foreign injury or aggression; to make his laws clear and plain; to choose wise subordinates, control them carefully, and . . . let them execute any measures so rigorous that the ruler may be suspected of a purely arbitrary use of his power. . . . It should be noted that this is just what the Duke does in *Measure for Measure*. . . .

But the highest and most important of the ruler's specific duties is to see well to the administration of justice. Here more than anywhere else he and his deputies must act consciously as the substitutes of God; . . . 'the Judges raised by [God] to dispense justice in his place, ought always to have the Majesty of him in their minds, and his judgements in imitation.' 'They should think,' adds Henry Smith, in his *Magistrates Scripture*, 'how Christ would judge, before they judge, because God's Law is appointed for their Law' . . . . [In the words of William Perkins' *Treatise on Christian Equity and Moderation*,] Mercy and Justice

are the two pillars, that uphold the throne of the Prince: as you cannot hold mercy, where Justice is banished, so cannot you keep Justice where mercy is exiled: and as mercy without Justice, is foolish pity, so Justice, without Mercy, is cruelty. . . .

[Given these principles, Angelo's] treatment of Claudio [unlike that recommended by Escalus and eventually brought about by the Duke upon his return to power] is from the first inexcusable, even by the strict standards of the Renaissance. For clemency in this particular case would certainly have had 'a good foundation upon reason and equity'; Claudio and Juliet are betrothed; they fully intend to marry;

they are penitent; and the law was drowsy and neglected when they broke it.

By 1950, after a number of commentators had sought to explain away or justify the most disturbing aspects of *Measure for Measure*, E. M. W. Tillyard asserted that they had 'ignored one of the prime facts' of the play, namely that it 'is not of a piece but changes its nature half-way through'. In *Shakespeare's Problem Plays* (London, 1950), Tillyard insisted that

Up to II.i.151, when the Duke enters to interrupt the passionate conversation between Claudio and Isabella on the conflicting claims of his life and her chastity, the play is predominantly poetical, the poetry being, it is true, set off by passages of animated prose. And the poetry is of that kind of which Shakespeare is the great master, the kind that seems extremely close to the business of living, the problem of how to function as a human being. One character after another is pictured in a difficult, a critical, position, and yet one which all of us can imagine ourselves to share; and the poetry answers magnificently to this penetrating sense of human intimacy. Up to the above point the Duke, far from being guide and controller, has been a mere conventional piece of dramatic convenience for creating the setting for the human conflicts. Beyond that he is just an onlooker. And . . . any symbolic potentialities the characters may possess are obscured by the tumult of passions their minds present to us. From the Duke's entry at III.i.151 to the end of the play there is little poetry of any kind and scarcely any of the kind described above. . . . Where in the first half the most intense writing was poetical, in the second half it is comic or at least prosaic. While the elaborate last scene, . . . for all its poetical pretensions, is either a dramatic failure or at best a Pyrrhic victory, it is the comedy of Lucio and the Duke, of Pompey learning the mystery of the executioner from Abhorson, of Barnardine (for Shakespeare somehow contrives to keep his gruesomeness this side of the comic) that makes the second half of the play possible to present on the stage with any success at all. And the vehicle of this comedy is prose, which, excellent through it is, cannot be held consistent with the high poetry of the first half. . . .

Nowhere does the change in the Duke's position show so strikingly as in Isabella. There is no more independent character in Shakespeare than the Isabella of the first half of the play: and independent in two senses. The essence of her disposition is decision and the acute sense of her own independent and inviolate personality. . . . At the beginning of the third act, when she has learnt Angelo's full villainy, her nature is working at the very height of its accustomed freedom. She enters almost choked with fury at Angelo, in the mood for martyrdom and feeling that Claudio's mere life is a trifle before the mighty issues of right and wrong. Her scorn of Claudio's weakness is dramatically definitive and perfect. . . . That is the true Isabella, and whether or not we like that kind of woman is beside the point. But immediately after her speech, at line 152, the Duke takes charge and she proceeds to exchange her native ferocity for the hushed and submissive tones of a well-trained confidential secretary.

If Tillyard reopened the debate over the problematic aspects of *Measure for Measure*, Nevill Coghill soon weighed in with an effort to reaffirm the play's generic identity as a coherently resolved tragicomedy. In 'Comic Form in *Measure for Measure*' (*Shakespeare Survey*, 1955), Coghill said that

Long before there was any inkling that Shakespeare had ever written a 'dark' comedy, *Measure for Measure* had been judged morally shocking, a play horrible in its tragedy, disgusting in its comedy and scandalous in its conclusion. . . .

Since the discovery of a working Shakespeare chronology this view has strengthened, for the play falls squarely in the 'Tragic Period' thereby revealed; it lies deep in what Dowden called 'The Depths'. The turbid sexual anguish, the manifold treacheries, the squalor and injustice of the play found in this fact their explanation. . . .

The argument from chronology, however, can lead by a series of doubtful premises and false syllogisms into many dangerous superstitions; such as that Shakespeare's tragic vision, being concerned with self-torture and waste, is a vision of disillusion and despair; that Art is Self-expression and that therefore a man capable of such a vision must himself be in a condition of disillusion and despair; that such a man will eschew comedy altogether unless he can find in it a further means to vent his edifying blasphemy at the Abyss and die . . . . But if a 'dark' interpretation of *Measure for Measure* is a lawless conjecture, what is the alternative? . . .

[The best answer to this question is to be found in the kind of medieval comedy penned by poets such as Dante, Chaucer, and

Lydgate.] *The Divine Comedy* was its greatest exemplar, and it is to Dante also that we owe a very full exposition of its nature, in his famous letter to Can Grande. . . .

Measure for Measure is in an older and better tradition than any mere morality play; it is, as Wilson Knight has pointed out, in the tradition of the parables of Christ, that is, something fully human, like the narrative of the Prodigal Son. . . .

. . . In *Measure for Measure* the reason [for the Duke's actions on behalf of the Vienna he rules] is the one given in the Sermon on the Mount:

> Let your light so shine before men that they may see your good
> works and glorify your father which is in heaven.

Or, to use the Duke's words:

> Heaven doth with us as we with torches do,
> Not light them for themselves; for if our virtues
> Did not go forth of us, 'twere all alike
> As if we had them not.

Now these words govern the entire action of the play, which pictures the world as a place where all are continually liable to tests, and some to tests increasingly severe, that they may show their virtues. Isabella and Angelo are tested to the core. . . .

Is is of course intellectually possible to twist the story of the Incarnation so as to make it seem as if God the Father and God the Holy Ghost had conspired to slay God the Son. That is what Langland calls 'the drivelling on the dais' and 'gnawing God with the gorge'. In like manner we are drivelling on the dais if we accent what is irrelevant or distort what is apparent in the behaviour of the Duke – if we complain that he pretends to be what he is not, that he lies to Claudio, that he pimps for Mariana, and so on. What is important to notice in the 'bed-trick' (as it has been called) is not what happens to Mariana, but what happens to Angelo. The bed-trick puts him in exactly the same position (with regard to the law which he is charged to administer) as Claudio, whom he has condemned, is in. Both have lain with their contracted wives before marriage; both are equally guilty. That is the whole point, and to glance wryly at the morality of substituting Mariana for Isabella is to refuse proper attention to what Shakespeare is trying to do with the story he found. It is to underline what is accidental and irrelevant instead of what is pertinent and essential, the very core of the situation, long since announced with unconscious but self-condemning irony by Angelo himself:

> When I, that censure him, do so offend,
> Let mine own judgement pattern out my death,
> And nothing come in partial. . . .

[Lucio] is never tempted himself: he is the instrument by which Isabella and Angelo are led into temptation: he is the Duke's adversary and mocker: it is hinted that he has recognized the Duke in the Friar, and he is not afraid of him. It seems almost too obvious what part Lucio plays in the parable of the play. [He is] what Hardy would call the Spirit Ironic or the Spirit Sinister; or Satan, as he is called in that other play of testing, *The Book of Job*. . . . Lucio is not [a demon of the calibre of Milton's Satan], not even that of Lucifer, though the name is suggestive; he is hardly more than a minor fiend, like that fiend in [Chaucer's] *The Friar's Tale*, who claims to be sometimes an instrument of God. . . .

What then happens at the end, when Lucio unmasks the Duke? . . . After calling him a 'bald-pated, lying rascal' and bidding him to show his 'sheep-biting face' he reveals the Duke to the assembly. There is a general movement of stupefaction. For an instant Lucio strikes the pose of a conjuror who has produced a white rabbit out of a black hat, and then he slinks tiptoe away, leaving stage-centre to more important characters, with a line that carries a grimace and raises a laugh:

> This may prove worse than hanging.

And indeed Shakespeare concludes the play in a comic and a forgiving mood; Lucio must of course be kept down, but only by Kate Keep-Down. What matters more is that we are in a swift mood of general amnesty and the uniting of lovers; and the Duke will govern them and lift them up for ever. . . .

If a 'dark' comedy is one in which pessimism or cynicism is uppermost, it has yet to be shown that there is any such thing in Shakespeare. *Measure for Measure* is as easily embraced by the medieval definition of comedy as any other that he wrote, for that definition includes sin as a root-cause of sorrow, as it is also a cause of all Christian joy.

Two years after Coghill's response to Tillyard and other critics of the tone and structure of *Measure for Measure*, Francis Fergusson offered another defence of the play's form. In a chapter on 'Philosophy and Theatre in *Measure for Measure*' in his book *The Human Image in Dramatic Literature* (Garden City, NY, 1957), Fergusson sought to counter the argument that the second half of the play is incompatible with the first.

The Duke starts to intervene when he proposes the bed-trick to Isabella. In Act IV his plans proceed with great speed. The timing is close, and the language is prose, as though Shakespeare by this change of rhythm, this sudden deflation and sobriety in speech, were warning us that playtime is over, the citizens have been given their head long enough, and now we must pay attention to matters of a different kind of seriousness. I find this change of key successful: there is poetic power in the sequence at prison, at night, with the Duke working against time to avert catastrophe and accept his sober responsibility for his flock. But the act is very brief, a modulation from the nascent tragedy of the first three acts to the complex demonstration of Act V. Just before abandoning his role as Friar, the Duke warns us what to expect in the final part of the play: 'By cold gradation and well-balanced form,' he says, 'we shall proceed with Angelo.'

It has often been maintained that Act V is a mere perfunctory windup of the plot, in which Shakespeare himself had no real interest. I am sure that on the contrary it is composed with the utmost care, and in perfect consistency with the basis of the whole play – this quite apart from the question whether one *likes* it or not. It is indeed so beautifully composed that it could almost stand alone. Perhaps we should think of it as a play within a play, presenting the theme of justice and mercy in another story and in another and colder tone. But the new story – that of the Duke's intervention and demonstration – was implicit from the first; and the new cold, intellectual tone may be understood as underneath the more richly poetic manner of the first three acts.

We are invited to watch this last act with a kind of double vision: from the front of the house, and at the same time from the wings, where we can see the actors getting ready to pretend to be what they are not. For, like the Duke, we know what they are; and moreover we have seen the Duke's backstage preparations for the final play. This final public play, unrolling before us and the supposedly ignorant Duke, is in the form of a series of trials. The first begins with Isabella's desperate complaint of Angelo, and ends when her suit is rejected on the basis of the evidence then publicly available: the wild improbability of her story, and Angelo's fine reputation and dignified manner. The second trial starts when the Duke leaves Angelo and Escalus to try Isabella for her supposed lying slander, and it ends when the Duke returns in his Friar disguise as a witness, and is suddenly revealed as the Duke when Lucio pulls off his hood. The third part ends both trials: the Duke, now revealed as both judge and witness, metes out justice to all, but on the assumption which we know to be false, that Claudio is dead. Notice that up to this point the trials and judgments have obeyed the strictest reasoned conception of justice, and the facts insofar as they could be found under the frightened and passionate lies in which they had been hidden. The Duke has been following a Mosaic regularity, and he has also been acting like that image of justice as a woman with bandaged eyes, a pair of scales in one hand and a sword in the other. He had been pretending to rely, not upon his concrete vision, but upon reportable 'facts' and his abstract measuring-machine. But in the final act of this playlet the Duke as it were drops the bandage from his eyes, confesses what he can really see, starting with the fact that Claudio is alive. He then tempers or proportions justice with mercy, abstract reason with his perception of the analogical relationships between real people, in whom truth and error, sin and grace, are mingled in ways which mathematics cannot compute.

I offer this sketch of Act V, not as exhausting its complexities, but to support my view that it is composed with the greatest care and the most self-conscious art. But some of its critics say that it is not poetry, not the proper end of a poetic drama, but only philosophy or abstract allegory. And indeed it is certain that when the Duke establishes an order in accordance with his own wisdom, we have a new relation between the dramatic and philosophic developments of the theme of justice and mercy.

Thus it is possible to read this act as an allegory of the descent of Mercy upon the scene of human judgment. The Duke, like God, comes not to destroy the Law – for he uses it to demonstrate everyone's guilt – but to transcend it. His role throughout the play is like that of Grace, in its various forms, as theologians describe it: he works through the repentant Mariana and Claudio to illuminate their motives and prevent their follies; and here at the end he answers Mariana's prayer after the intercession of Isabella. These relationships are worked out with theological scrupulousness, and I suppose that Shakespeare must have been aware of the possibility of this interpretation.

But at the same time he presents the Duke, not as God or as a mere symbol of a theological concept, but as a real human being; and Act V may be read, therefore, as the end of a *drama*. Mariana's love for Angelo had sharpened her insight: she was able to see through his actual savagery to the bewildered spirit within, which still had the potentialities of good; and the Duke, as Friar, had encouraged her in this strength, charity and understanding. Isabella had a wise *doctrine* from the first, but this doctrine remained helpless and disembodied until she was matured by suffering and appealed to by Mariana. In short, the play has shown how the wisdom of love proceeded from the Duke to the two women, to be finally confirmed by him when they reveal it at the end. Such is the *drama* of the growth of wisdom in Vienna, which finally reverses the tragic course toward anarchy.

For Ernest Schanzer, interpretations such as those tendered by Coghill and Fergusson did not address all the ethical complexities of *Measure for Measure*. In *The Problem Plays of Shakespeare* (London, 1963), Schanzer asserted that 'throughout the play Shakespeare is showing up certain likenesses between [Isabella and Angelo]'. Schanzer argued that the playwright

is manipulating our feelings towards Isabel by alternately engaging and alienating our affections for her, and that he is doing all this mainly to make us question her decision to sacrifice her brother rather than her virginity. He makes us question it without forcing an answer upon us. The majority of critics have, in fact, felt that Isabel could have acted in no other way than she did. . . . There have been others – a minority among critics, but much more numerous, I suspect, among those mute, inglorious Bradleys that constitute the bulk of Shakespeare's readers – who have thought that Cinthio's Epitia and Whetstone's Cassandra [who finally assented to the terms imposed by their equivalents of the corrupt deputy] made the more admirable choice. The manner in which Shakespeare manipulates his material, as well as the evidence of his other plays, suggest to me very strongly that he, too, preferred Cassandra's choice. How he felt towards a legalistic conception of Divine Justice is suggested by his treatment of the churlish priest in *Hamlet*, who refuses Ophelia's body full burial rites because technically her death may come under the heading of suicide. . . . It is the kind of reply which one would like Isabel to have made when Angelo denounces the 'filthy vices' of her brother. Instead we get her 'My brother had but justice, / In that he did the thing for which he died.' By depicting first the inhumanity of Angelo's legalism, followed by numerous parallels between Isabel's and Angelo's characters, and then showing Isabel's legalistic view of Divine Justice, Shakespeare is, it would seem to me, strongly suggesting his own attitude towards her choice. But he leaves it sufficiently unobtrusive to allow the audience to respond to it in an uncertain, divided, or varied manner.

In *The Achievement of 'Measure for Measure'* (Ithaca, NY, 1966), David L. Stevenson wrote in terms quite similar to those employed by Schanzer.

Central to the art of *Measure for Measure* is the fact that it is a deliberately 'uncomfortable' play, one which carefully exploits our own easy, surface response to its substance by forcing us to adjust to a level of apprehension of motives for human actions which lie far deeper than we are usually willing to go. Its way of looking at human sexuality is to show it as always subject to an accustomed discipline by statutory law and orthodox morality. It also shows it as operating within individuals from depths of instinctual feeling only superficially contained by the boundaries of orthodoxy. Isabella's, Angelo's, Claudio's, Lucio's decisions and reactions are dramatized as existing within a world which assumes a certain moral certitude. But the play does not flatter our 'correct' views in sexual matters by keeping us within safe range of such certitude. It does not move us by the obvious. The power of the play comes from its terrifying invitation to us to go beyond certitude. It invites us to recognize both the elemental, instinctual nature of sexual desire and at the same time to recognize that it both mocks, and is mocked by, the private disguises of love and morality which individuals impose on themselves, and which are imposed upon them by society.

More recent comments on the play have continued to focus upon the aspects of it that would seem to defy unambiguous interpretations of its action. Thus, in *Shakespeare, the Dark Comedies to the Last Plays: From Satire to Celebration* (Charlottesville, Va, 1971), R. A. Foakes says that

Like *All's Well, Measure for Measure* is in the end an uncomfortable play because in spite of the marriages that round it off, it forces on us a sense of the gap between belief and act, between what people would be and what they are, or between justice and charity. So, for instance, there is no way of accounting judicially or ethically for the stubborn Barnardine; it is not clear whether the marriage of Angelo to Mariana is more a reward or a punishment to both of them; the Duke's impending marriage to Isabella goes unexplained; and all through virtue gains no notable victories in opposition to licentiousness, but rather loses out in its strictness, while licentiousness carries in it a love of life that wins sympathy and seems generous by contrast. If 'liberty plucks justice by the nose' this tends to prove beneficial in curbing the harshness of the law, and shows how there can indeed be 'a charity in sin', as Angelo and Isabella agree there may, but without seeing the implications of what they are saying. The last act is neat in its contrivance of measure for measure, but the dramatic effect of the play stems from the gap between that neatness and what remains unexplained and unresolved below the surface. Some see mere confusion in this, and not an effect sought by Shakespeare, and some regard the play as limited in its achievement because 'the "incarnation" of ideas, principles, beliefs is not at all points consistent and complete'. A study of the dramatic shaping of the play suggests rather that such a reading is made too plausible by some aspects of what is not basically a drama attempting such consistency. In other words, the weakness of *Measure for Measure* lies not in its failure to maintain the 'incarnation' of beliefs found in Act II and the beginning of Act III, but rather in the overweighting of those scenes. The strong religious feeling here seems to invite too close an involvement with some characters in an action which is generally more concerned with a critical placing of them. The change of key in Act III seems too marked and too abrupt, the revelation of Mariana too easy a way out, and the Duke has too much responsibility as a character here in holding the action together. If Shakespeare had given a serious weight to the action in wholly secular terms, he might have been able to control the play's balance more easily.

In language that echoes Foakes' expression of dissatisfaction with the comedy, Richard P. Wheeler says that 'The range of feeling dramatized in *Measure for Measure* is diminished rather than sustained and controlled as the play moves toward completion. Shakespeare seems not to finish quite so large and powerful a play as the one he starts, but to change the rules – excluding powerful trends of feeling already admitted into the action – so that the play can be finished at all.' Writing in *Shakespeare's Development and the Problem Comedies: Turn and Counterturn* (Berkeley, 1981), Wheeler notes that

> The action of *Measure for Measure* culminates not only in four marriages but in several important acts of forgiveness as well. Both marriage as a social ordering of sexuality and forgiveness as an essential adjustment to transgression are clearly appropriate gestures to end a play that dramatizes deep transgressions within the relations of sexuality and the social order. But the complications that terminate the plot – 'rather intricate than artful' in Dr. Johnson's neat distinction – cannot integrate into the precarious comic conclusion of this play complex developments that lead into it. Gestures of mercy are essential if the ending is to be comic at all. But the mercy granted to Barnardine, Claudio, and Angelo does little to clarify the issues these characters have raised in the play, and the mercy granted to Lucio seems to be a form of punishment. . . . Similarly, the marriages of Angelo to Mariana, Claudio to Juliet, and especially of Vincentio to Isabella do not dramatize a freeing of these characters from conflicted attitudes toward sexuality and marriage developed with great intensity earlier. The marriage of Lucio to Kate Keepdown – a degraded relationship forced to take the stamp of official respectability – comes perilously close to providing an emblem for the entire play. . . .
>
> . . . After Vincentio makes Isabella's relation to Angelo even more complex by noting that the deputy has speeded up Claudio's execution, has essentially murdered her brother before the legally scheduled execution could take place, he drops that matter in order to pardon Barnardine. Then, in nine lines, Vincentio produces a living Claudio, proposes marriage to Isabella, and pardons Angelo. At this moment, all of the relationships that have defined Isabella's experience in the play – to her chosen vocation, to her own sexuality, to Angelo, to her brother, to a Vincentio she has known as a celibate, fatherly priest – are given a final turn that puts them all under great

stress. And Isabella is given nothing to say at all. Vincentio himself simply goes on to the matter of Lucio, parenthetically tucking issues central to the entire play between the absurd pardon of Barnardine and the problematic mercy shown to Lucio.

Or rather, since Vincentio's actions also pose problems regarding his place in the play that the comic design provides no coherent way of addressing, I should say Shakespeare nervously goes on to other matters. The ending of *Measure for Measure* does not 'play out' earlier developments, it plays them down; it looks back to the previous action with an averted, mystifying gaze that has its emblem in Vincentio's anxiety-denying movement from one character and one issue to another in the final scene. The failure of these characters (and these issues) to respond to him – as in Isabella's silence and the silence of Claudio and Angelo – mirrors Shakespeare's inability to find an ending that responds fully to the whole action. The kind of integration of inner impulse with external reality that is established in successful play, and which provides a paradigm for the comic action of *As You Like It*, is not achieved in *Measure for Measure.* . . . Instead of clarifying, either positively or negatively, the relations between individual longings and the social order, or between comic art and experience, Shakespeare seeks unearned reassurance in a comic ending that cannot fully acknowledge previous developments in *Measure for Measure*.

In his theatre-oriented book *Changing Styles in Shakespeare* (London, 1981), Ralph Berry observes that in recent decades

The Problem Plays – the term is still debatable, but I use it as shorthand for *Measure for Measure, Troilus and Cressida, All's Well That Ends Well* – have found their audience. The asperities, the withholding of easy identifications from the audience, the sense of humanity gripped in complex moral predicaments – all this suits our taste well. A refusal to sentimentalize the Problem Plays permits their complexities to be scrutinized in a bleak Northern light. The result now appears as a recognition of their artistic integrity, not as Shakespeare's failure to organize a dramatic experiment. The Problem Plays have 'undergone a revaluation so radical as to amount to a rediscovery'.

The progress of *Measure for Measure* since mid-century, and particularly since 1970, is a guide to the changing values of the era.

The play's litmus quality depends on its final action, the staging of Isabella's response to the Duke's proposal. That is a gesture of climactic significance; it cannot be masked or elided. It defines the import of the entire preceding action. And its meaning has always to be imparted by actors who must ask themselves the only question that matters at the end: Can *this* Isabella accept *this* Duke? If not, why not? There is now no question of a routine or traditional response involving an acceptance – if anything, the practice of the 1970s has established an opposite tradition. . . .

. . . In the 1950s the dominant conception of Vincentio was that of model prince: wise, virtuous, authoritative. . . . 'In the early 1960s professional productions of *Measure for Measure* began, increasingly, to present the Duke as the semiallegorical, God-like figure that some theatrical reviewers had been looking for in the mid-1950s and that literary critics had been discussing since the 1930s.'[1] . . .

That [became] the received view – one might say the Establishment view – of the play. For our purposes here, the contemporary era can be thought of as starting in 1970. . . . The seminal production . . . was John Barton's with the RSC. This can be viewed as extending the line of enquiry observable in David Giles' production at Stratford, Ont. (1969), and also as embodying a general restlessness with Godlike Dukes. In its own right, the production launched a complete theatrical re-examination of the text. The Duke became, not a quasi-religious figure, but an all-too-human, not overly competent functionary: 'In appearance, with his Holbein cap and spectacles, he suggests a university vice-chancellor: a paternal administrator, whose encouraging smiles are always contracting into icy severity.'[2] As for Isabella, a programme-note by Anne Barton supplies the vital perspective: 'Isabella's purity conceals an hysterical fear of sex which scarcely allows her to speak of her brother's fault, and leads directly to her unlovely attack upon him in prison.' And the conclusion leaves Isabella alone on stage, unresponsive to the Duke's overtures, silently resistant. . . .

. . . Isabellas, it seems, always used to accept the Duke's proposal. Nowadays – beginning with Barton's production – they have at least an option.

---

[1] From Jane Williamson, 'The Duke and Isabella on the Modern Stage', in *The Triple Bond*, ed. Joseph G. Price (University Park, Pa.: Pennsylvania State University Press, 1975).
[2] Ibid.

Two primary causes suggest themselves. The first concerns authority. It is a truism that the general esteem in which authority is held –
political, social, institutional – has been declining in the West for some
time now, certainly over the last half-generation. The idea of the
all-wise, omnicompetent, Providential ruler may have reached its
terminus in the reigns of Churchill and de Gaulle, Adenauer and
Eisenhower. . . .

The second cause, equally obvious, is the change in the position of
women. . . . this central theatrical fact dominates the assumptions
relating to Isabella's behaviour in the final scene. In the past, it has
always seemed natural and virtually inevitable for Isabella to accept
the Duke's proposal. And, indeed, there is a formal historical
justification for this: throughout the ages it has been enormously
difficult for women to reject the advances of the Prince himself. . . .
But today a climate of opinion exists in which these assumptions no
longer hold. . . . The primary issue is one of personal integrity.
Isabella's 'more than our brother is our chastity' is a statement that her
entire selfhood is bound up with her chastity. It is not a straightforward matter of morals at all: 'chastity' is the term that sums up *her*
way, *her* choice, and the Duke's brusquely public courtship is
perceived as another kind of assault upon her. Simply, a contemporary actress will not perceive marriage as the automatic close to the play;
and neither will the audience.

In an article entitled 'Providential Improvisation in *Measure for
Measure*' (*PMLA: Publications of the Modern Language Association of America*, 1982), Louise Schleiner presents the view that

the many New Testament references evoke an ironically employed
theological pattern framing the play's central action; that although
the duke attempts to imitate God he is not God but a ruler dissatisfied
with his past government whose efforts to imitate God in justice and
mercy (as rulers were theoretically supposed to do) produce comic
results; that he is a man of tests, a character modeled on the
absentee-master figure in a group of parables from the synoptic
gospels; that his test results prove so discouraging that they force him
to imitate another aspect of the New Testament God as well, the legal
astuteness of the Pauline God, who in the atonement 'found out a
remedy,' a kind of divine lawyer's trick, for guilty man; that the play's
falling in half as discussed by Tillyard results from this planned and

necessary expansion of the Duke's strategy; that his schemes, though imperfect and comical improvisations, aim to bring the characters to their best selves and do not degrade the duke to a mere meddler; and finally that there is a strong earthiness in the play, a forceful dramatization of the power of the drives for food, drink, sex, and comfort – drives that throughout the play challenge the authority of the duke and his deputies. . . .

The duke's decision to delegate his rule and disappear . . . has as its primary model the parables of the synoptic gospels that state or imply that a man planning a journey or absence called in servants and gave them responsibilities. These are the parables of the wicked vineyard tenants (e.g., Matt. xxi.33–43); the wicked steward (e.g., Matt. xxiv.45–51); the traveler and his doorkeeper (Mark xiii.33–37); the master absent at a wedding (Luke xii.35–39); and the talents or pounds (e.g., Luke xix.11–27). A departing ruler or land owner gives responsibility to servants, who will be called to an accounting on his return, for which they are to be constantly ready. The master's destination or motives abroad are of no importance; the servants are to be tested and later rewarded. . . .

Many critics have analyzed the duke's testing of Angelo and Isabella, but we should notice that the duke also tests the minor characters by observing their conduct from his absentee perspective and then determining appropriate judgments. . . . In the Lucan version of the parable [of the talents] the servants include some who have not merely proved 'unprofitable' but have actually spoken against their lord: 'Moreouer those mine enemies, which wolde not that I shulde reigne ouer them, bring hither, and slay them before me' (Luke xix.27). This version may have provided a model for the duke's harsh judgment of Lucio, a death sentence remanded to the comically appropriate marriage to the whore Lucio has slandered in the same breath with the duke. . . .

. . . That the play changes tone in the middle, as Tillyard shows stylistically, is true enough, but the duke, though perhaps not totally consistent, is the testing master from beginning to end. As he says in Act I, Scene iii, he contrives the opening situation to test Angelo, Escalus, and the government he expects of them. . . .

The duke must be present and his role must expand midway in the action, since he must first test and observe, then devise a remedy for the failures, as a teacher seeing the whole class has flunked a test must devise a new pedagogical strategy and new tests. . . .

As imitator of God the duke may seem to have his finest moments in Act V, which the allegorizer sees as judgment day – and so it is, in the play's theological pattern. But here as earlier, the pattern works ironically. Anyone who thinks the play is straightforwardly doctrinal should try to imagine the scene of literal Judgment Day, where the most rebellious and deceitful of the goats can interrupt the proceedings repeatedly with bawdy, self-serving interjections that evoke from God only ineffectual chiding (Lucio's role). Here again, as when the duke casts himself as absentee master and thereby attains the glory of usury, his self-image as imitator of God is humorous. His authority will not be destroyed, but it will be challenged, loudly and appealingly, until the end. . . .

Measure for Measure does not take any stand on the divine right of royal authority, though righteous versus corrupt authority is certainly one of its major themes. What I see as an ironic handling of the 'little God' concept results from a succession of dark moments colored by several brief ironic allusions that were subtle enough to elude King James and his intimates while striking vibrations in the more perceptive of the court audience. For there were many who saw, after only a year and a half of James's rule, that he would fall short of the lofty ideal in 'the king's book' (the monarch's *Basilicon Doron*). His lavish expenditures, his constant escape from matters of state in hunting, his rashness and theatricality in making decisions – typified by the famous gallows scene of condemning then at the last moment pardoning Markham, Grey, and Cobham in December 1603 – such things were already on many tongues and in many letters. Nor could James, any more than could Duke Vincentio, remain unstung by 'base calumniators.' In short, given the controversies of the day, when many were questioning the concept of the ruler as divine image and arm, Shakespeare's audience could not have been impervious to ironic overtures on that point.

Notwithstanding all the ink that has been expended in efforts to demonstrate that *Measure for Measure* is something other than the problem play many of its interpreters have claimed it to be, we can be sure that critics will continue to find fault with it. And what may be the severest attack on the work yet has been levelled by Marcia Riefer in her article ' "Instruments of Some More Mightier Member": The Constriction of Female Power in *Mea-*

sure for Measure' (*Shakespeare Quarterly*, 1984). In Riefer's opinion,

> The debate over Isabella's virtue obscures a more important point, namely that through her one can explore the negative effects of patriarchal attitudes on female characters and on the resolution of comedy itself. In the course of the play, Isabella changes from an articulate, compassionate woman during her first encounter with Angelo (II.ii), to a stunned, angry, defensive woman in her later confrontations with Angelo and with her imprisoned brother (II.iv and III.i), to, finally, a shadow of her former articulate self, on her knees before male authority in Act V. As the last and one of the most problematic of the pre-romance comedies, *Measure for Measure* traces Isabella's gradual loss of autonomy and ultimately demonstrates, among other things, the incompatibility of sexual subjugation with successful comic dramaturgy.
>
> The kind of powerlessness Isabella experiences is an anomaly in Shakespearean comedy. Most of the heroines in whose footsteps Isabella follows have functioned as surrogate dramatist figures who are generally more powerful, in terms of manipulating plot, than the male characters in the same plays. One need only recall the Princess of France and her ladies in *Love's Labour's Lost*, Portia in *The Merchant of Venice*, Mistresses Page and Ford in *The Merry Wives of Windsor*, Beatrice in *Much Ado About Nothing*, Viola in *Twelfth Night*, Helena in *All's Well That Ends Well*, and, of course, Rosalind in *As You Like It*. . . .
>
> It is hardly incidental that in *Measure for Measure* Shakespeare places dramaturgical control almost exclusively in the hands of a male character – Duke Vincentio – who is, in effect, a parody of his more successful, mostly female, predecessors. . . .
>
> . . . Deprived of her potential for leadership, Isabella succumbs to the control of a man she has no choice but to obey – a man whose orders are highly questionable – and as a consequence her character is markedly diminished.
>
> That the Duke's actions are questionable is apparent from the beginning, when he unexpectedly appoints Angelo to rule in his place instead of Escalus, who, as the opening scene establishes, is clearly the logical choice. Throughout the play, the Duke continues to undermine this credibility as a dramatist figure by making decisions strictly

according to his own desires without considering the responses of those he is attempting to manipulate. For instance, his lofty tone in lecturing Claudio on how to make himself 'absolute for death' (III.i.5–41) is far from sensitive to the condemned man's situation. Not surprisingly, his effort fails; within a hundred lines Claudio is begging 'Sweet sister, let me live' (1.132). . . .

Another way in which the Duke perverts the Shakespearean comic paradigm is in his unusual antagonistic relationship to the 'normal action' of comedy, which [Northrop] Frye defines as the struggle of the main characters to overcome obstacles in order to achieve sexual union. The Duke *appears* to be possessed by a comic drive toward union when he proposes the bed-trick (dubious as it is) or when he arranges what Anne Barton refers to as the 'outbreak of that pairing-off disease' in Act V. But his explicit denial that he has anything in common with those sinners and weaklings who allow themselves to be struck by the 'dribbling dart of love' (I.iii.2) – along with his implicit condoning of Angelo's revival of obsolete sexual restrictive policies ('I have on Angelo imposed the office, / Who may, in th' ambush of my name, strike home' [I.iii.40–41]) – sets him apart from earlier comic dramatists, predominantly women, whose desire was to escape, rather than to impose, sexual restriction. . . .

. . . Far from having Vienna's best interest in mind as he claims – and as many critics accept – the Duke is actually setting up Angelo for a fall while protecting himself ('my nature never in the fight / To do in slander' [I.iii.42–43]), and at the same time betraying the public as well, a public whom he admits he has effectively 'bid' to be promiscuous through his permissiveness (ll.36–38). His ultimate intention seems to be setting the stage for his final dramatic saving of the day – a day which would not need saving except for his contrivances in the first place. . . .

The female characters in this play, Mariana and Isabella, are the prime victims of the Duke's disturbing manipulativeness – a significant reversal of the roles women have played in earlier comedies. . . . As Jean E. Howard points out, Barnardine, Lucio, and Angelo, even though punished in the end, do at times 'refuse to be pawns in someone else's tidy playscript': Barnardine refuses to die, Angelo refuses to pardon Claudio, Lucio refuses to shut up. Neither Mariana nor Isabella ever exhibits such defiance. Thus this play creates a disturbing and unusual sense of female powerlessness. . . .

If we examine Isabella's development in this play, we can see how her sense of self is undermined and finally destroyed through her encounters with patriarchal authority, represented emphatically, but not exclusively, by the insensitive Duke. . . .

Our experience of Isabella's being 'thwarted here, there, and everywhere' is reinforced by the intervention of the Duke at [the most] troublesome point in the play. Although his intentions appear honorable at first, in his own way he replicates Angelo's and Claudio's indifference to Isabella's desire to remain true to herself. Like Angelo and Claudio before him, Vincentio sees in Isabella a reflection of his own needs. . . .

This negation of Isabella's essentially self-defined character becomes complete upon the Duke's taking control of the action in Act III. Critics have noted this change variously. Richard Fly, for example, says that Isabella, 'formerly an independent and authentic personality with a voice of her own,' is 'suddenly reduced to little more than a willing adjunct to the Duke's purpose.' . . . Whatever autonomy Isabella possessed in the beginning of the play, whatever 'truth of spirit' she abided by, disintegrates once she agrees to serve in the Duke's plan. As soon as this 'friar' takes over, Isabella becomes an actress whose words are no longer her own. There are no more outbursts. In complying with the role Vincentio has created for her, Isabella becomes his creation in a way that the male characters never do. . . .

The Duke claims, of course, to be acting in Isabella's best interest, just as he has claimed to be acting in the best interests of Vienna. . . . [But] in retrospect, the Duke's promise to comfort Isabella − what Frye calls a 'brutal lie' − appears to be a veiled justification for perpetuating his control over her. . . .

Isabella's last words reveal just how far this imposed role diminishes her character. To those who argue that rather than depriving Isabella of autonomy the Duke is actually releasing her from moral rigidity by arranging for her to plead for Angelo's life, I answer that Isabella's final speech [V.i.437−46], often accepted as representing character growth, in fact represents the opposite. Ostensibly, Isabella is once again displaying her 'prosperous art,' using rhetoric to reveal a new-found capacity for mercy. But the quality of mercy here is strained. . . . Not only the laws of logic, but the concept of justice is twisted here. Isabella claims − as she need not − that her brother's supposed execution was, in fact, just. Her mode of argument is unsettling, not only because she sounds indifferent to Claudio's death, but also because she resorts to specious legalism where one would expect her to appeal to her faith, as she did when pleading for Claudio's salvation in II.ii.75–77. . . .

With the conclusion of her final speech, Isabella is immediately confronted with a series of overwhelming events: a living Claudio appears, the Duke proposes marriage, and Angelo is pardoned. All of Isabella's main assumptions – that Angelo was condemned, that the Duke was a committed celibate, that her brother was dead, and that she herself would remain chaste for life – are challenged, if not negated, in the space of five lines. She remains speechless, a baffled actress who has run out of lines. The gradual loss of her personal voice during the course of the play has become, finally, a literal loss of voice. In this sense, *Measure for Measure* is Isabella's tragedy. Like Lavinia in *Titus Andronicus*, the eloquent Isabella is left with no tongue.

If we see Isabella as a victim of bad playwriting, we can compare her bewilderment at the end of *Measure for Measure* with our own. She has trusted the Duke, as we've trusted our playwright, to pattern events as he has led her to expect events to be patterned – and the Duke, sharing Shakespeare's affinity for surprises in this play, pulls those expectations out from under her. . . . With this play Shakespeare has moved from comedy's romantic pole to its opposite, ironic pole. What he has created in *Measure for Measure* is not a poorly written play, but, to some extent, a model for poor playwriting. . . . By creating in Duke Vincentio a model third-rate playwright – one whose mind-set Jean Howard calls 'confining, inelastic, dangerously reductive,' one who has no qualms about '[draining] the life out of previously vital characters such as Isabella' – Shakespeare calls into question the ethics of his own craft, including the ethics involved in handling characters of the opposite sex. . . .

This play reveals, among other things, the price women pay in order for male supremacy to be maintained. That price for Isabella is, precisely, a mandatory denial of her personal standards. But Isabella's plight is only one element in a larger pattern. As a whole, *Measure for Measure* explores the incompatibility of patriarchal and comic structures. The world of patriarchy, antithetical to the world of comedy throughout Shakespeare's works, comes closest here to overthrowing the comic world. . . .

. . . [But] if Isabella's voice is lost in *Measure for Measure* – to remain mute throughout Shakespeare's tragedies, in which male misfortune and misogyny explode into significantly linked central issues – that voice is rediscovered in the romances, Shakespeare's most mature creations, in which patriarchal and misogynistic values, if present at all, are, as in the early comedies, subverted, and in which the imaginative environment once again allows female characters, like Paulina in *The Winter's Tale*, for example, to exert a powerful, positive force in shaping dramatic action.

SUGGESTIONS FOR FURTHER READING

Many of the works quoted in the preceding survey, or excerpts from those works, can be found in modern collections of criticism. Of particular interest or convenience are the following anthologies:

Bloom, Harold (ed.), *William Shakespeare's 'Measure for Measure'* (Modern Critical Interpretations), New York: Chelsea House, 1987.

Geckle, George L. (ed.), *Twentieth Century Interpretations of 'Measure for Measure'*, Englewood Cliffs, N J: Prentice-Hall, 1970.

Harris, Laurie Lanzen, and Mark W. Scott (eds), *Shakespearean Criticism: Excerpts from the Criticism of William Shakespeare's Plays and Poetry, from the First Published Appraisals to Current Evaluations*, vol. 2, Detroit: Gale Research Co., 1984.

Muir, Kenneth, and Stanley Wells (eds), *Aspects of Shakespeare's 'Problem Plays': Articles Reprinted from 'Shakespeare Survey'*, Cambridge: Cambridge University Press, 1982.

Nagarajan, S. (ed.), *Measure for Measure*, Signet Classics; New York: New American Library, 1985.

Ornstein, Robert (ed.), *Discussions of Shakespeare's Problem Comedies*, Boston: D. C. Heath, 1961.

Stead, C. K. (ed.), *'Measure for Measure': A Casebook*, London: Macmillan, 1971.

Other studies (including modern editions) that include pertinent discussions of *Measure for Measure*:

Adelman, Janet, 'Bed Tricks: On Marriage as the End of Comedy in *All's Well That Ends Well* and *Measure for Measure*', in *Shakespeare's Personality*, ed. Norman N. Holland et al., Berkeley: University of California Press, 1989.

Barton, Anne, Introduction to *Measure for Measure* in The Riverside

Shakespeare, ed. G. Blakemore Evans, Boston: Houghton Mifflin, 1974.

Battenhouse, Roy W., 'Measure for Measure and Christian Doctrine of the Atonmenent', PMLA: Publications of the Modern Language Association of America, 61 (1946), 1029–59.

Bawcutt, Nigel W., Measure for Measure, The Oxford Shakespeare, Oxford: Clarendon Press, 1991.

Bennett, Josephine Waters, 'Measure for Measure' as Royal Entertainment, New York: Columbia University Press, 1966.

Berry, Ralph, On Directing Shakespeare, rev. edn, London: Hamish Hamilton, 1989.

Black, James, 'The Unfolding of Measure for Measure', Shakespeare Survey, 26 (1973), 119–28.

Bowden, William R., 'The Bed Trick, 1603–1642: Its Mechanics, Ethics, and Effects', Shakespeare Studies, 5 (1970), 112–123.

Brown, Carolyn E., 'Erotic Religious Flagellation and Shakespeare's Measure for Measure', English Literary Renaissance, 16 (1986), 139–65.

Chambers, R. W., Man's Unconquerable Mind, London: Jonathan Cape, 1952.

Collins, Michael J., 'Measure for Measure: Comedy in the Rag and Bone Shop', Critical Survey, 1 (1989), 24–32.

Cox, John, D., 'The Medieval Background of Measure for Measure', Modern Philology, 81 (1983), 1–13.

Dawson, Anthony B., 'Measure for Measure, New Historicism, and Theatrical Power', Shakespeare Quarterly, 39 (1988), 328–41.

Dench, Judi, 'Measure for Measure', in Shakespeare in Perspective, ed. Roger Sales, London: Ariel Books, British Broadcasting Corporation, 1982.

Dollimore, Jonathan, 'Transgression and Surveillance in Measure for Measure', in Political Shakespeare, ed. Jonathan Dollimore and Alan Sinfield, Manchester: Manchester University Press, 1985.

Dunkel, Wilbur, 'Law and Equity in Measure for Measure', Shakespeare Quarterly, 13 (1962), 287–97.

Eccles, Mark, Measure for Measure in A New Variorum Edition of Shakespeare, New York: Modern Language Association of America, 1980.

Empson, William, The Structure of Complex Words, London: Chatto & Windus, 1951.

Fly, Richard, *Shakespeare's Mediated World*, Amherst: University of Massachusetts Press, 1976.

Frye, Northrop, *The Myth of Deliverance: Reflections on Shakespeare's Problem Comedies*, Toronto: University of Toronto Press, 1983.

Gibbons, Brian (ed.), *Measure for Measure*, The New Cambridge Shakespeare; Cambridge: Cambridge University Press, 1991.

Gless, Darryl J., *'Measure for Measure,' The Law and the Covenant*, Princeton: Princeton University Press, 1979.

Greenblatt, Stephen, *Shakespearean Negotiations: The Circulation of Social Energy in Renaissance England*, Berkeley: University of California Press, 1988.

Hamilton, Donna B., 'The Duke in *Measure for Measure*: I Find an Apt Remission in Myself', *Shakespeare Studies*, 6 (1972), 175–84.

Hammond, Paul, 'The Argument of *Measure for Measure*', *English Literary Renaissance*, 16 (1986), 496–519.

Harding, Davis P., 'Elizabethan Betrothals and *Measure for Measure*', *Journal of English and Germanic Philology*, 49 (1950), 139–58.

Hawkes, Terence, 'Take Me to Your Leda', *Shakespeare Survey*, 40 (1988), 21–31.

Hawkins, Harriett, 'The Devil's Party': Virtues and Vices in *Measure for Measure*', *Shakespeare Survey*, 31 (1978), 105–13.

—— *Measure for Measure*, Brighton: Harvester Press, 1987.

Hayne, Victoria, 'Performing Social Practice: The Example of *Measure for Measure*', *Shakespeare Quarterly*, 44 (1993), 1–29.

Howard, Jean E., '*Measure for Measure* and the Restraints of Convention', *Essays in Literature* (Western Illinois University), 10, 1983, 149–58.

Hubert, Judd D., 'The Textual Presence of Staging and Acting in *Measure for Measure*', *New Literary History*, 18 (1987), 583–96.

Hunt, Maurice, 'Comfort in Measure for Measure', *Studies in English Literature*, 27 (1987), 213–32.

Hunter, Robert G., *Shakespeare and the Comedy of Forgiveness*, New York: Columbia University Press, 1965.

Hyman, Lawrence W., 'The Unity of *Measure for Measure*', *Modern Language Quarterly*, 36 (1975), 3–20.

Ide, Richard S., 'Shakespeare's Revisionism: Homiletic Tragicomedy and the Ending of *Measure for Measure*', *Shakespeare Studies*, 20 (1988), 104–27.

Kirsch, Arthur C., 'The Integrity of *Measure for Measure*', *Shakespeare Survey*, 28 (1975), 89–105.

Knights, L. C., 'The Ambiguity of *Measure for Measure*', *Scrutiny*, 10 (1942), 223–33.

Lamb, Mary Ellen, 'Shakespeare's Theatrics: Ambivalence Toward Theater in *Measure for Measure*', *Shakespeare Studies*, 20 (1988), 129–46.

Lascelles, Mary, *Shakespeare's 'Measure for Measure'*, London: Athlone Press (University of London), 1953.

Leavis, F. R., 'The Greatness of *Measure for Measure*', *Scrutiny*, 10 (1942), 234–47.

Leech, Clifford, 'The "Meaning" of *Measure for Measure*', *Shakespeare Survey*, 3 (1950), 66–73.

Leggatt, Alexander, 'Substitution in *Measure for Measure*', *Shakespeare Quarterly*, 39 (1988), 342–59.

Lever, J. W. (ed.), *Measure for Measure*, The Arden Shakespeare, London: Methuen, 1965.

Lewis, Cynthia, ' "Dark Deeds Darkly Answered": Duke Vincentio and Judgment in *Measure for Measure*', *Shakespeare Quarterly*, 34 (1983), 271–89.

Macdonald, Ronald, R., '*Measure for Measure*: The Flesh Made Word', *Studies in English Literature*, 30 (1990), 265–82.

Maxwell, J. C., '*Measure for Measure*: The Play and the Themes', *Proceedings of the British Academy*, 60 (1974); London: Oxford University Press, 1975.

Miles, Rosalind, *The Problem of 'Measure for Measure': A Historical Investigation*, London: Vision Press, 1976.

Mortimer, John, '*Measure for Measure*', in *Shakespeare in Perspective*, ed. Roger Sales, London: Ariel Books, British Broadcasting Corporation, 1982.

Nagarajan, S., '*Measure for Measure* and Elizabethan Betrothals', *Shakespeare Quarterly*, 14 (1963), 115–19.

Nevo, Ruth, '*Measure for Measure*: Mirror for Mirror', *Shakespeare Survey*, 40 (1988), 107–22.

Nicholls, Graham, '*Measure for Measure*': Text and Performance, London: Macmillan Education, 1986.

Nuttall, A. D., '*Measure for Measure*: Quid Pro Quo?', *Shakespeare Studies*, 4 (1968), 231–51.

—— '*Measure for Measure*: The Bed-Trick', *Shakespeare Survey*, 28 (1975), 51–66.

Pendleton, Thomas A., 'Shakespeare's "Disguised Duke Play": Middleton, Marston, and the Sources of *Measure for Measure*', in '*Fanned and Winnowed Opinions': Shakespearian Essays Presented to Harold Jenkins*, ed. John W. Mahon, London: Methuen, 1987.

Pinciss, G. M., 'The "Heavenly comforts of despair" and *Measure for Measure*', *Studies in English Literature*, 30 (1990), 303–13.

Rossiter, A. P., '*Angel with Horns' and Other Shakespeare Lectures*, ed. Graham Storey, London: Longmans, Green, 1961.

Schanzer, Ernest, 'The Marriage-Contracts in *Measure for Measure*', *Shakespeare Survey*, 13 (1960), 81–89.

Shell, Marc, *The End of Kinship: 'Measure for Measure', Incest, and the Ideal of Universal Siblinghood*, Stanford: Stanford University Press, 1988.

Siegel, Paul N., '*Measure for Measure*: The Significance of the Title', *Shakespeare Quarterly*, 4 (1953), 317–20.

Simonds, Peggy Munoz, 'Overlooked Sources of the Bed Trick', *Shakespeare Quarterly*, 34 (1983), 433–34.

Skura, Meredith Anne, *The Literary Uses of the Psychoanalytic Process*, New Haven: Yale University Press, 1981.

Stevenson, David L., 'The Role of James I in Shakespeare's *Measure for Measure*', *ELH (English Literary History)*, 26 (1959), 188–208.

Sundelson, David, 'Misogyny and Rule in *Measure for Measure*', *Women's Studies*, 9 (1981), 83–91.

Swann, Charles, 'Lucio: Benefactor or Malefactor?', *Critical Quarterly*, 29 (1987), 55–70.

Tennenhouse, Leonard, 'Representing Power: *Measure for Measure* in its Time', *Genre*, 15 (1982), 139–56.

Thomas, Vivian, *The Moral Universe of Shakespeare's Problem Plays*, London: Croom Helm, 1987.

Watson, Robert N., 'False Immortality in *Measure for Measure*: Comic Means, Tragic Ends', *Shakespeare Quarterly*, 41 (1990), 411–32.

Watts, Cedric, *Measure for Measure*, The Penguin Shakespeare; Harmondsworth: Penguin, 1986.

—— *William Shakespeare: 'Measure for Measure'* (Penguin Masterstudies), Harmondsworth: Penguin, 1986.

Weil, Herbert S., Jr, ' "Your Sense Pursues Not Mine": Changing Images of Two Pairs of Antagonists', in *Images of Shakespeare: Proceedings of the Third Congress of the International Shakespeare Association*,

1986, ed. Werner Habicht and D. J. Palmer, Newark, Del.: University of Delaware Press, 1988.

Wentersdorf, Karl P., 'The Marriage Contracts in *Measure for Measure*: A Reconsideration', *Shakespeare Survey*, 32 (1979), 129–44.

Wharton, T. F., *Measure for Measure* (Critics Debate), Atlantic Highlands, N. J.: Humanities Press International, 1989.

Williamson, Jane, 'The Duke and Isabella on the Modern Stage', in *The Triple Bond*, ed. Joseph G. Price, University Park: Pennsylvania State University Press, 1975.

Winston, Matthew, ' "Craft Against Vice": Morality Play Elements in *Measure for Measure*', *Shakespeare Studies*, 14 (1981), 229–48.

Background and general critical studies and useful reference works:

Abbott, E. A., *A Shakespearian Grammar*, New York: Haskell House, 1972.

Allen, Michael J. B., and Kenneth Muir (eds), *Shakespeare's Plays in Quarto: A Facsimile Edition*, Berkeley: University of California Press, 1981.

Andrews, John F. (ed.), *William Shakespeare: His World, His Work, His Influence*, 3 vols, New York: Scribners, 1985 (articles on 60 topics).

Barroll, Leeds, *Politics, Plague, and Shakespeare's Theater*, Ithaca: Cornell University Press, 1992.

Bentley, G. E., *The Profession of Player in Shakespeare's Time, 1590–1642*, Princeton: Princeton University Press, 1984.

Berry, Ralph, *Shakespeare and Social Class*, Atlantic Highlands, NJ: Humanities Press, 1988.

Blake, Norman, *Shakespeare's Language: An Introduction*, New York: St Martin's Press, 1983.

Bullough, Geoffrey (ed.), *Narrative and Dramatic Sources of Shakespeare*, 8 vols, New York: Columbia University Press, 1957–75 (printed sources, with helpful summaries and comments by the editor).

Calderwood, James L., *Shakespearean Metadrama*, Minneapolis: University of Minnesota Press, 1971.

Campbell, O. J., and Edward G. Quinn (eds), *The Reader's Encyclopedia of Shakespeare*, New York: Crowell, 1966.

Cook, Ann Jennalie, *Making a Match: Courtship in Shakespeare and His Society*, Princeton: Princeton University Press, 1991.

—— *The Privileged Playgoers of Shakespeare's London*: Princeton:

Princeton University Press, 1981 (an argument that theatre audiences at the Globe and other public playhouses were relatively well-to-do).

De Grazia, Margreta, *Shakespeare Verbatim: The Reproduction of Authenticity and the Apparatus of 1790*, Oxford: Clarendon Press, 1991 (interesting material on eighteenth-century editorial practices).

Eastman, Arthur M., *A Short History of Shakespearean Criticism*, New York: Random House, 1968.

Gurr, Andrew, *Playgoing in Shakespeare's London*, Cambridge: Cambridge University Press, 1987 (an argument for changing tastes, and for a more diverse group of audiences than Cook suggests).

—— *The Shakespearean Stage, 1574–1642*, 2nd edn, Cambridge: Cambridge University Press, 1981 (theatres, companies, audiences, and repertories).

Hinman, Charlton (ed.), *The Norton Facsimile: The First Folio of Shakespeare's Plays*, New York: Norton, 1968.

Muir, Kenneth, *The Sources of Shakespeare's Plays*, New Haven: Yale University Press, 1978 (a concise account of how Shakespeare used his sources).

Onions, C. T., *A Shakespeare Glossary*, 2nd edn, London: Oxford University Press, 1953.

Partridge, Eric, *Shakespeare's Bawdy*, London: Routledge & Kegan Paul, 1955 (indispensable guide to Shakespeare's direct and indirect ways of referring to 'indecent' subjects).

Rabkin, Norman, *Shakespeare and the Common Understanding*, New York: Free Press, 1967.

Righter, Anne, *Shakespeare and the Idea of the Play*, London: Chatto & Windus, 1962.

Schoenbaum, S., *Shakespeare: The Globe and the World*, New York: Oxford University Press, 1979.

—— *Shakespeare's Lives*, 2nd edn, Oxford: Oxford University Press, 1992 (readable, informative survey of the many biographers of Shakespeare, including those believing that someone else wrote the works).

—— *William Shakespeare: A Compact Documentary Life*, New York: Oxford University Press, 1977 (presentation of all the biographical documents, with assessments of what they tell us about the playwright).

Spevack, Marvin, *The Harvard Concordance to Shakespeare*, Cambridge, Mass.: Harvard University Press, 1973.

278

Van Doren, Mark, *Shakespeare*, New York: Henry Holt, 1939.
Vickers, Brian (ed.), *Shakespeare: The Critical Heritage, 1623–1801*, 6 vols, London: Routledge & Kegan Paul, 1974–81.
Whitaker, Virgil K., *Shakespeare's Use of Learning*, San Marino, Cal.: Huntington Library, 1963.
Wright, George T., *Shakespeare's Metrical Art*, Berkeley: University of California Press, 1988.

PLOT SUMMARY

I.1   In his palace in Vienna, Vincentio, the Duke of that city makes arrangements for his departure. He leaves the day-to-day government of the city to Escalus, an elder statesman, and appoints Angelo to the rule as Duke in his absence.

I.2   Either at or near Mistress Over-done's inn, Lucio chats with two other gentlemen. Mistress Over-done, a bawd, arrives with news that Claudio, a young gentleman, has been imprisoned. He is to be executed for making his beloved Juliet pregnant. The men leave to check the truth of this. Mistress Over-done's servant, a clown, enters with news of Angelo's edicts.

I.3   Outside the inn, the Provost leads in Claudio and Juliet. Claudio tells Lucio, who has re-entered, that he had promised to marry Juliet. They were not publicly married because they did not have the consent of the trustees of Juliet's dowry. Claudio believes he is being punished – by long unused laws – because Angelo wants to establish his authority as ruler of the city.

     Claudio asks Lucio to tell his sister, Isabella, of his predicament, and to ask her to plead with Angelo on his behalf.

I.4   In a monastery in Vienna, the Duke explains to Friar Thomas that he has made Angelo his deputy so that he can enforce laws that the Duke allowed to lapse. He also wants to see if Angelo is as morally upright as he claims. To find out what is happening in the city, the Duke asks Thomas to disguise him as a friar.

I.5   Lucio finds Isabella in the convent. She is about to begin her novitiate. She agrees to try to persuade Angelo to show mercy to her brother.

II.1   In a courtroom, Angelo, against the advice of Escalus, orders that Claudio be executed the following morning. Elbow, a constable, brings in Froth, a gentleman, and Pompey. Angelo leaves during Elbow's long-winded description of the charge against the men. Escalus sends the defendants away with a warning.

II.2   In an ante-room to the courtroom, Angelo refuses the Provost's request to show mercy to Claudio. He orders that Juliet be taken from the prison to somewhere more suitable for giving birth.

Isabella arrives with Lucio, and tries to persuade Angelo to spare her brother. Eventually moved by her pleas, he asks her to return the next morning for his final decision. When all have left, he admits that he desires Isabella.

II.3 At the prison, the Duke, now disguised as Friar Lodowick, asks the Provost to see the prisoners. He meets Juliet, ashamed and penitent, as she leaves the prison. He goes to visit Claudio.

II.4 At the Duke's palace, Angelo makes an offer to Isabella; he will stop her brother's execution if she will go to bed with him. If she refuses, he will have her brother tortured before he is executed. Isabella refuses and goes to tell her brother what has happened.

III.1 In the prison, Friar Lodowick reconciles Claudio to his forth-coming execution. Isabella arrives and, alone with Claudio, tells her brother of Angelo's offer. Claudio asks her to accept it. Angry with him, she refuses.

Friar Lodowick re-enters, having overheard the conversation. He asks Isabella to wait for him and then tells Claudio that Angelo was only testing Isabella's virtue; Claudio has no real chance of escaping death. The Provost leads Claudio out.

Friar Lodowick then suggests a scheme to Isabella which she accepts. She is to agree to go to Angelo's bed that night. But in her place will go Mariana, a lady who loves Angelo, even though he broke off their engagement when her dowry and her brother were lost at sea. Isabella leaves.

Pompey enters, arrested again by Elbow. Friar Lodowick criticizes his way of life. Lucio enters and refuses to stand bail for Pompey, who is led off to prison. Lucio talks to Lodowick about the Duke's supposed journey, describing the Duke as a lecherous and foolish man.

After Lucio leaves, Escalus enters, accompanied by the Provost with Mistress Over-done. She blames Lucio for her reputation of being a prostitute, and alleges that he has, by another woman, a young son. Escalus sends her to prison and orders Lucio to be fetched.

Escalus and Friar Lodowick talk about Claudio's forthcoming execution. Escalus gives Friar Lodowick his opinion of the Duke, as a temperate man.

IV.2 In a country house, Friar Lodowick meets Mariana and Isabella, as arranged. Isabella tells him that she has arranged to meet Angelo in his vineyard that night. He has her explain their scheme to Mariana, who agrees to her part.

IV.2 In prison the next morning, Pompey becomes Abhorson's, the executioner's, helper. The Provost summons Claudio and shows him the warrant for his execution. When Claudio has left, Friar Lodowick enters and asks the Provost if Claudio is still to be executed. A messenger from Angelo arrives with instructions that the execution of Claudio, and later of Barnardine, must go ahead. Claudio's head is to be delivered to Angelo.

The Provost explains to Lodowick that Barnardine is a dissolute man and has been in prison for nine years. Lodowick asks the Provost to behead Barnardine in Claudio's place, and to keep Claudio concealed for the next four days. To persuade the Provost to trust him, he shows him a document, in the Duke's hand and with his seal, which tells of the Duke's return in two days' time.

IV.3   After they have left, Pompey and Abhorson enter. They rouse Barnardine, and Friar Lodowick re-enters. Barnardine refuses to be executed and returns to his cell. The Provost arrives with news that Ragozine, a pirate who looked like Claudio, has died that morning of a fever. He and Friar Lodowick decide to send his head to Angelo.

The Provost leaves to take Ragozine's head to Angelo. Isabella arrives, and Lodowick tells her that her brother has been executed, but that she should not try to seek any form of justice until the Duke returns on the next day.

Lucio arrives, and commiserates with Isabella, who departs. He leaves with Lodowick, whom he regales with stories of both the Duke's and his own lechery.

IV.4   In the palace, Angelo discusses with Escalus the Duke's command that they meet him at the city gate. There, any who believe they have been unfairly treated are to come and tell the Duke of their complaint, and he will see they are given justice. Left alone, Angelo repents of his seduction of Isabella (as he believes it to be) and his execution of Claudio.

IV.5   In a friar's cell, Vincentio, the Duke, in his own clothes again, tells Friar Peter what he wants done. Varrius, a friend, arrives to talk to the Duke.

IV.6   Near the city gate, Isabella tells Mariana how she has been told to act to the Duke. Friar Peter arrives to take the ladies to see the Duke.

V.1   The Duke arrives at the city gate, where many are waiting, and is greeted by Angelo and Escalus. Isabella, led in by Friar Peter, begs the Duke to punish Angelo for his seduction of her. The Duke, declaring that he does not believe her, has her led away and asks for Friar Lodowick, who instructed her to come to him, to be sent for.

Friar Peter says that Lodowick is ill, and has sent him in his place. He calls forth Mariana to disprove Isabella's story. Mariana tells how she spent the night with Angelo in his garden house. Angelo denies this, and grows impatient at what he says is a plot against him. The Duke has Friar Lodowick sent for, and then leaves Angelo to pursue his investigation of the plot against him. Escalus sends for Isabella.

The Duke re-enters as Friar Lodowick, at the same time as Isabella is led back on. Escalus questions Lodowick, who maintains that Angelo is guilty. Lucio alleges that Lodowick made treasonable comments against the Duke. They try to arrest him, and in the commotion Lucio pulls off the friar's hood, so revealing that Lodowick is the Duke.

Angelo confesses his guilt, and the Duke commands Friar Peter to take him away and marry him to Mariana immediately. To Isabella the Duke then explains that the speed of Claudio's execution upset the plan to save him.

The newly married Angelo and Mariana return with Friar Peter. The Duke orders Angelo be taken away and executed. Mariana begs him to be merciful, and Isabella intercedes on her behalf. The Duke turns to the Provost, and berates him for executing Claudio at an unusually early hour. The Provost replies that he repented of the deed and so saved the lives of two others; Barnardine and a disguised Claudio are led on, along with Juliet. The Duke pardons Barnardine, and, once the Provost has revealed Claudio, pardons Claudio for Isabella's sake. The Duke asks Isabella to be his wife.

He sentences Lucio to be married to any woman who can prove she has had his child. The rest leave to go to his palace.

ACKNOWLEDGEMENTS

The editors and publishers wish to thank the following for permission to use copyright material:

Nevill Coghill Ltd. for material from Neville Coghill, 'Comic Form in *Measure for Measure*', *Shakespeare Survey* 1955);

Modern Language Association of America for material from Louise Schleiner, 'Providential Improvisation in *Measure for Measure*', *PMLA*, 97 (1982), pp.227–36;

Oxford University Press for material from Muriel Bradbook, *The Review of English Studies* (1941);

Routledge for material from Ralph Berry, *Changing Styles in Shakespeare* (1981), Allen & Unwin; G. Wilson Knight, '*Measure for Measure* and the Gospels' in *The Wheel of Fire* (1930), Methuen & Co.; and with The University Press of Virginia for R. A. Foakes, *Shakespeare, the Dark Comedies to the Last Plays: From Satire to Celebration* (1970), Routledge & Kegan Paul;

Random House, University of Toronto Press and Veronica Sankaran on behalf of the author's estate for material from E. M. W. Tillyard, *Shakespeare's Problem Plays* (1950), Chatto & Windus;

Shakespeare Quarterly for material from Marcia Reifer, 'Instruments of Some More Mightier Member': The Constriction of Female Power in *Measure for Measure*, 35, *Shakespeare Quarterly*, 2 (1984);

University of California Press for material from Richard Wheeler, *Shakespeare's Development and the Problem Comedies: Turn and Counter-Turn.* Copyright © 1981 The Regents of the University of California.

Every effort has been made to trace all the copyright holders, but if any have been inadvertently overlooked the publishers will be pleased to make the necessary arrangement at the first opportunity.

THE EVERYMAN SHAKESPEARE
EDITED BY JOHN F. ANDREWS

The Everyman Shakespeare is the most comprehensive, up-to-date paperback edition of the plays and poems, featuring:

- face-to-face text and notes

- a chronology of Shakespeare's life and times

- a rich selection of critical and theatrical responses to the play over the centuries

- foreword by an actor or director describing the play in performance

- up-to-date commentary on the play

£2.99

DRAMA
IN EVERYMAN

A SELECTION

Everyman and Medieval Miracle Plays
EDITED BY A. C. CAWLEY
A selection of the most popular medieval plays **£3.99**

Complete Plays and Poems
CHRISTOPHER MARLOWE
The complete works of this fascinating Elizabethan in one volume
£5.99

Complete Poems and Plays
ROCHESTER
The most sexually explicit – and strikingly modern – writing of the seventeenth century **£6.99**

Restoration Plays
Five comedies and two tragedies representing the best of the Restoration stage **£7.99**

Female Playwrights of the Restoration: Five Comedies
Rediscovered literary treasures in a unique selection **£5.99**

Poems and Plays
OLIVER GOLDSMITH
The most complete edition of Goldsmith available **£4.99**

Plays, Poems and Prose
J. M. SYNGE
The most complete edition of Synge available **£6.99**

Plays, Prose Writings and Poems
OSCAR WILDE
The full force of Wilde's wit in one volume **£4.99**

A Doll's House/The Lady from the Sea/The Wild Duck
HENRIK IBSEN
A popular selection of Ibsen's major plays **£4.99**

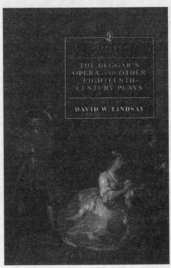

£6.99
